T0374222

REFLECTIONS

WORDS ARE POWERFUL. GOD'S WORD
HAS UNMATCHED POWER. WE DO
WELL TO KNOW AND HEED IT.

CONNIE PINKHAM

WESTBOW
PRESS®
A DIVISION OF THOMAS NELSON
& ZONDERVAN

Copyright © 2017 Connie Pinkham.

All rights reserved. No part of this book may be used or reproduced by any means, graphic, electronic, or mechanical, including photocopying, recording, taping or by any information storage retrieval system without the written permission of the author except in the case of brief quotations embodied in critical articles and reviews.

All scripture quotations, unless otherwise indicated, are taken from the Holy Bible, New International Version®, NIV®. Copyright ©1973, 1978, 1984, 2011 by Biblica, Inc.™ Used by permission of Zondervan. All rights reserved worldwide. www.zondervan. com The "NIV" and "New International Version" are trademarks registered in the United States Patent and Trademark Office by Biblica, Inc.™. All rights reserved.

WestBow Press books may be ordered through booksellers or by contacting:

WestBow Press
A Division of Thomas Nelson & Zondervan
1663 Liberty Drive
Bloomington, IN 47403
www.westbowpress.com
1 (866) 928-1240

Because of the dynamic nature of the Internet, any web addresses or links contained in this book may have changed since publication and may no longer be valid. The views expressed in this work are solely those of the author and do not necessarily reflect the views of the publisher, and the publisher hereby disclaims any responsibility for them.

Any people depicted in stock imagery provided by Thinkstock are models, and such images are being used for illustrative purposes only. Certain stock imagery © Thinkstock.

ISBN: 978-1-9736-0105-0 (sc)
ISBN: 978-1-9736-0106-7 (hc)
ISBN: 978-1-9736-0104-3 (e)

Library of Congress Control Number: 2017913638

Print information available on the last page.

WestBow Press rev. date: 10/02/2017

Reflecting on the power of a single word and the unmatched power of God's Word. May He speak to your heart as He speaks to mine.

EDITING

The book you are reading is a product of journaling my own journey. When I made the decision to publish it, I purchased a digital copy of a blog I had used. From that, I submitted it to a self-publishing company and made what I thought were some improvements to the manuscript format. As it turned out, I made a lot of format problems instead of improvements. For the past few years I have been retyping and trying to learn as I go, removing where I had unknowingly made forced enters, and other technical problems. I am quite sure there are still many errors and certainly, the format doesn't compare with better published material.

As I finally finish up what I set out to do, I marvel again at how over forty writers, over a span of 2000 years, collectively wrote a manuscript that tells one story. The story of the Bible is one story. It is history, but it is HIS-story. The pieces fit so perfectly, the lessons are timeless, the hope eternal.

My manuscript is certainly flawed, but I hope you find some small thing that re-enforces the eternal truth, God is always, and ONLY….good. I know from faith, and I know from experience. May He bless you richly as you seek His Face. And do….DO seek His Face!!

ANSWERS

I don't have them all. What I do have is a source of information. What I do have is an inside scoop to the "Answer Man." "Search the scriptures; they testify of Me" (John 5:39). Sometimes I get answers immediately. Some I'm still waiting on. Sometimes I get a yes, sometimes a clear no. There is nothing special about me; you have the same opportunity to this Answer Man. But following Christ must really be about following Him, seeking His face, not just the blessings of His hand. Oh, don't think I've got this down pat. I'm a work in progress. But I am confident that He will continue His work in me until it is completed (James1:4).

"Turning around, Jesus saw them following and asked, 'What do you want?'" (John 1:38). What is it that you want from Jesus? Do you seek His kingdom or yours? His glory or yours? Be honest with yourself. He knows the truth anyway, but do you?

Lord Jesus, give us sight.

HEAR

I get so tired of sounds. My ears are very sensitive. My mind processes every sound, sometimes yards away from me. I find myself hearing even though I am not listening. Sometimes, I'd like a switch to turn it off. I wish I could hear like that with my spirit and my heart. Jesus often said, "He that hath ears to hear, let him hear." He knows I have ears, but do I have ears "to hear," or have I switched that off? (Seems I have no problem switching off that hearing!) Do I only hear what is comfortable and pleasant? Is my spiritual hearing as sensitive as my ears seem to be sometimes? Or does God have to speak loudly before I pay attention? "And the Lord came and stood and called as at other times ...

'Samuel! ... Samuel!' And Samuel answered, 'Speak: for thy servant heareth'" (1 Sam. 3:10).

"Connie, Connie."

When He speaks, I want to hear—the first time He calls. Don't you?

LOVE

On Valentine's Day, love is in the air, and the banner of love flies high. Restaurants are full of couples and stores are cashing in on the opportunity to sell merchandise designated for your valentine.

"He has taken me to the banquet hall, and his banner over me is love" (Song. 2:4). The entirety of Solomon's book is a romantic love story. It has many rich lessons for us: lessons about our relationships as husband and wife and the love relationship that God has for us, the relationship that God *wants* us to be completely engaged in and committed to. I've been married to my valentine since 1974. He treats me like a lily among thorns (Song 2:2). He makes me feel treasured and beautiful. I am secure knowing his love for me. How great is the love the Father has lavished on me, that I should be called a child of God! And that is what I am! (1 John 3:1 paraphrased).

I am secure in my marriage. My husband puts me as his top priority; nothing outranks me except God Himself. How much more secure I am to be in the love of God. "His banner over me is love" (Song. 2:4). God has stopped at nothing to communicate His love for me. Jesus left the perfection of heaven to step into a body of slowly dying flesh just to communicate the love of God, to dwell among us and to restore our relationship with Him back to the way it was: perfect and complete. "Taste and see ... the Lord is good" (Ps. 34:8). "Whoever is wise, let him heed these things and consider the great love of the Lord" (Ps. 107:43). How I pray you really know Him, know His character and His perfect love for you. He is so good.

RELATIONSHIP

Relationship: that word has popped into conversations from all directions, for days. I've been trying to listen this morning, asking God to help me understand more fully, more deeply. Surely, He is speaking to me about something specific. My husband and I discussed relationship at great length a few nights ago,. It seems God is dealing with him about relationship stuff, too; he woke in the night, this relationship topic heavy on his mind.

My friend and sister in Christ brought it up again, this time in the Sunday school class she leads. She introduced an illustration that was new to me, a triangle depicting three components in our relationship with God: covenant, knowledge, and worship. It keeps coming back to my mind. What does my triangle look like? Balanced on all three sides? Or not?

In our *covenant* with God, we enter into a commitment. He certainly made a costly commitment—the blood covenant of Jesus Christ. I enter this covenant on the merit of Jesus' blood, not my own. I can't speak for you, but I am committed to Him. I fail miserably and often, but the intent from the depths of my heart is to be fully committed to Him in every facet of my being, every moment of my day, every word and action. I'm not happy about everything I find in my heart when I begin to examine it and to examine my commitment. It's a daily choice. I am thankful that God never has the issues that I struggle with. He even helps me overcome my own inability to live up to the commitment I make to Him. He gives me His Spirit as divine Helper and Comforter, which makes me love Him even more and makes me want even more passionately to commit every part of my being in obedience to Him and cooperation with Him.

My *knowledge* is more than some I guess…definitely not a short side of my triangle. I have studied quite a bit and have been a member of a church since, well, I don't remember not being churched! I like to read, and I have read a lot of books—some deeper than others. But most of what I've read is of a spiritual nature. I'm in my seventh year of Bible study fellowship. I have studied the Bible a lot, and I know how to use a lot of available resources, but that's all book knowledge and head knowledge, facts. For many years, I didn't know God. Even though I was thoroughly churched and I knew about God. I was scared to death of Him, really. But I didn't really know Him. I had no intimacy with who He really is; I didn't know His great love for me. Me, the real me. He does love me. And He loves you.

I am learning about *worship,* but I believe my triangle is short on the worship side. That is what I'm waiting to hear from Him about. He's begun to speak to me, little hints so far. Oh, He doesn't need my love, doesn't need my worship. His ego doesn't need bolstering. He knows full well that He is God. I am the one who benefits. Worship brings me into a deeper intimacy with God, and I am safe to go there. And so blessed.

BIRTH

On the day of this writing twenty-seven years ago, it was a birthing day for me. About 7:30 a.m. Kerry and I were deep into that Lamaze breathing stuff. If he missed a breath, so did I, pushing instead! Poor Kerry was hoarse by the time it was all over. I was exhausted. I relive my birthing days every year. I don't know if all mothers do that, but I relive both of mine. I remember what we did the hours before it started and details about the people who were present. I remember that it hurt, but I don't remember the way it felt. I remember the infant son born from my body, nuzzling against me, knowing me, knowing that I was his mother, that I was the source of his nourishment. I remember looking into their little faces, looking deep into their eyes, as they looked for the first time at the grand new world.

Spiritual birth is reality. Just as our physical birth brings us into the world of our parents, spiritual birth ushers us into a spiritual realm, the realm of Jesus Christ and the very kingdom of our Father God. "Flesh gives birth to flesh, but the Spirit gives birth to spirit" (John 3:6). "Flesh and blood cannot inherit the kingdom of God" (1 Cor. 15:50). It doesn't matter how strong you are, how talented you are, how determined you are. You can't be part of what God is involved in and can't be inside the gates of this kingdom without this new birth. I am spiritually reborn, and I know where my nourishment comes from. I labored in the process, not understanding, trying to stay where I was yet grasping the spiritual realm as well. The religious predicament I was confined in offered some sort of security, but a baby can't stay in the confines of the womb; it must be born or die. I am thankful to know the reality of spiritual birth. I'm secure in the love of my Father. He is faithful in His care for me, nourishing me, teaching me, even disciplining me. It's a grand new world, this kingdom of God.

GLORY

Glory: what does that mean? *Webster's Dictionary* says it is brightness and splendor. The word in the original language that is translated *glory* is *doxa*. It means honor, praise, dignity, that which reflects, expresses, or exhibits dignity. "God is not a man" (Num. 23:19). He is not like us, no matter how we try to get Him into the box with us.

He is not in the box of our reality. He made everything we know—everything *in* our reality was simply spoken into existence. "By the word of the Lord were the heavens made, and all the host of them by the breath of His mouth" (Ps. 33:6). From the tiniest of cells to the vastness of the galaxies, "God's invisible qualities, His eternal power and divine nature, are clearly seen, being understood from what has been made, so that men are without excuse" (Rom. 1:20). All we need to do is look around or look into the night sky. There is His glory, clearly seen. He doesn't need me to glorify Him. He has no need. He IS glory, whether I acknowledge it or not. But He wants me to acknowledge Him for Who He is. He wants the best for each of us, He created us! And He didn't create us to watch us suffer. Neither do I have anything to offer Him to make Him bigger and better.

He has gone to such great lengths to communicate Himself to me, to show Himself to me so that I might know Him. He came in flesh in the Person of Jesus Christ to communicate His sacrificial love, that love itself glorified, as Jesus' blood ran down the cross, Him dying instead of me, taking the penalty for what I have done. I continue to try to grasp the depth of His glory. Paul prayed for me, and for you, that we might 'grasp how wide and how long and how high and how deep is the love of Christ, to know this love that surpasses knowledge, that we might be filled to the measure of all the fullness of God.' (Ephesians 3:18) It is ME that needs to glorify Him. I am the one lacking, the one with the sin problem, the one who makes wrong choices and bad decisions. He is God. The Perfect One, The I AM. Glory!!

HUGS

What is a hug? Isn't it just squeezing? It's done with the arms...Wikipedia says it's a demonstration of affection, a form of physical intimacy. Isn't worship like a hug? It is a physical expression. Love without expression...can it even exist?

When we see our children and grandchildren, can we help but express our affection? Our hearts feel as if they will explode if we can't somehow communicate this fullness inside us. God's love for us is expressed by our very existence on this planet, expressed by everything in our reality, given to us as a gift of love, prepared even before He created us. He even went to the great length of stepping off of heaven's throne and into this created realm, knowing death in our stead, in the Person of Jesus Christ.

I can hug a pillow. But there is no expression of anything deep within me in doing so. I can hug a person and it be meaningless. No, the motion of the arms doesn't make it a hug...it's the communication and warmth of heart that makes it a hug.

My grand-daughter sometimes hugs like that...just to appease me but she's really too busy to be bothered about it, she'll squeeze with her arms really quick, and off she goes. The hug I want is the one I didn't ask or beg for, the one freely given, the one she enjoyed as much as I did.

So too, worship is not a physical activity. It is not something that can be touched or even observed. It happens within my attitude, my spirit, my 'heart'. It is more than human emotion, or even the surrender of my personal will. There is a relationship...a reaching out from my heart to the heart of God, and a response!! A response of God's spirit within me, to the Spirit of Himself, "Deep calling to deep..." (Ps. 42:7). It NEEDS to be expressed. It yearns to be received by The One Whom we hug. "Abba, Father...Daddy!! Because you are sons (and daughters), God sent the Spirit of His Son into our hearts, the Spirit Who calls out 'Abba, Father." (Galatians 4:6 personalized by me). His Spirit "testifies with our spirit..." (Romans 8:16).

The purpose of worship is not to somehow ingratiate myself, not only can that not be done, it is not necessary. God loved me when I was yet a sinner (Romans 5:8). I can't provide a service to God, He "needs not to be worshipped with men's hands as though He needs anything" (Acts17:25).

I need not attempt to pay my own debt, which is the curse of death, the death I deserve because of the imperfect condition I find myself in. My expressions of devotion do not change my condition. He does.

How I praise Him today for the depths of His love, and that He allows me these small A-HA!! moments with Him. He is so very good.

OFFENSE

I am offended today. Something was called to my attention that offended me. I felt insulted and immediately angry. So now what?

The thing that offends me has no power over me really...unless I grant it. The question I am faced with is how I will respond. Do I rise to meet it? Challenge it? Maybe I'll just rise up above it, raise the bar even. Maybe I will retaliate, seek revenge. Or do I just bow to it? Ignore it? Turn the other cheek yet again?

There have been many times when I have just simply reacted in situations like this. There are too many times when I do not channel offenses thru my Advocate (1 John 2:1). He is my Defender. He is the One to Whom I should go with everything that offends me. Sometimes I have found that the things that offend me often reveal to me some ugliness that needs to be dealt with. Perhaps that is why He allowed it in the first place. I know that as His child. "The Lord knows those who are His."(2Tim. 2:19) I am sealed, (Eph. 4:30) and nothing comes against me that I can not bear with His aid. "No temptation has seized me except what is common to man. God is faithful, He will not let me be tempted beyond what I can bear, but when I am tempted, He will also provide a way out so that I can stand up under it." (1Cor. 10:13)

I can know no offense that my Lord does not know better. He washed the feet of the very one who would only moments later betray Him. Jesus had every right many times over to lash out in righteous indignation...He was insulted personally time and time again. The only time I recall in scripture where He showed any indignation was over the way His Father's temple was being dishonored....and that incident was of no personal insult, but an insult to His Father.

Yep. I'm insulted. And trying to wait until I understand from Him where to go from here.

BETRAYAL

I have tasted betrayal, I know how hurtful it is. I've even been guilty of it, God forgive me. I could offer excuses, but excuses change absolutely nothing. I've struggled with how Judas betrayed Jesus. Perhaps because I've seen glimpses of myself in him, the selfish agenda, the ambition and preconceived ideas of personal greatness, position that would be gained by riding the coat-tails of Someone he thought would be a warrior king, toppling the Roman government and setting up a grand new Jewish reign. Judas wanted that. Who doesn't want to be successful, and who doesn't have their own definition of just what successful is?

The little band with Jesus carried a 'moneybag' with meager assets designated to help others. Judas was in charge of it, and Judas misused it. "...he was a thief, as keeper of the money bag, he used to help himself to what was put into it.' (John 12:6) How often do I misuse resources? How often do I put my desires above the needs of others?

I don't like the end of this story. Judas changed his mind. He tried to un-do what he had done. "When Judas, who had betrayed Him, saw that Jesus was condemned, he was seized with remorse and returned the thirty silver coins to the chief priests and the elders." (Matt. 27:3)

Oh, if only Judas had just come to Jesus with this...if only he had come clean to the One he turned his back on in betrayal instead of turning to the religious and civil authorities, the priests and elders. Why do we do that same thing? Why can we not learn from this awful story that JESUS is the One to go to with all things?! Our organized governing bodies both religious and civil, cannot remove our guilt...and be not mistaken, we all have guilt, and plenty of it. These entities can't change the course of our lives. Jesus can. We will never be able to un-do what is wrong deep within us. Jesus can. And He longs to be allowed to do so.

I'm comforted in knowing that none of this took Jesus by surprise. He knew the end of the story before the story ever began, before He stepped from the throne of glory into a tiny body of flesh birthed from Mary's womb. He knew Judas' heart when He included Him in the inner circle. And He used even the disobedience, the rejection, and ultimate betrayal to achieve the purposes of God from the very beginning of time.... the bringing about of the possibility of our restored relationship.

Here's what I hope.... I hope that before Judas' last breath, he cried out to God in total belief that Jesus was Who He said He was, even though all of that looked different than Judas had expected and wished for. And I'm thankful that God can and will judge Judas' heart, judging it right...just as He will judge the thief that hung on the cross next to Jesus.

REST

I can't seem to get it sometimes. Oh, I slept last night, I've had two days off, not working today…but still seem to need rest. Why is it I need rest since I've been pretty much inactive for 48 hour? Maybe I'm tired from all the resting I've done! I find myself sighing…over and over. And grunting…. (shudder!!) Whine, whine, whine…. how I detest whiners, and I'm the Queen of Whine sometimes. I've complained to God about it, and seem to get no sympathy. Instead, He seems to be saying:

'ok, let's get past this!' ('how long will you lie there?' Pro. 6:9 'I tell you, get up…' (Mark 2:11)

'Remember my promises!' ('she who dwells in the shelter of the Most High will rest in the shadow of the Almighty.' Ps.91:1)

'I have rest for you, take it!' ('come to Me, all you who are weary…I will give you rest…take My yoke . ' Matt. 11:28, 29)

'you are ok, so enough already…!" ('Go in the strength you have…Am I not sending you? I will be with you…' (Judges 6:14,16)

'keep on keeping' on'. ('Let us not become weary in doing good, for at the proper time we will reap a harvest if we do not give up.' Gal. 6:9)

A primary purpose of The Holy Spirit is to help us remember what God has said. Jesus said He would send the Holy Spirit to ". teach you all things and will remind you of everything I have said to you.' (John 14:26) He can only remind us of what we have heard Him say, and He still speaks thru scripture as recorded in the Bible. But we must on purpose find out what He has said. He doesn't scream it into our lives, forcing us to hear. We must have an ear to hear Him…and a desire to listen. ('He that has ears, let him hear' Matt.11;15)

"The Sovereign Lord has given me an instructed tongue, to know the Word that sustains the weary. He wakens me morning by morning, wakens my ear to listen like one being taught." (Isa. 50:4)

So He has spoken. He has brought to my mind many of the things He has said. Perhaps it wasn't rest I needed after all. Perhaps it was just solitude and an opportunity for Him to speak to some things in my life.

My body is old and tired. It does need rest, God rested (Ge. 2:2). Jesus rested (John 4:6). But Jesus made sure He had time alone with His Father, (Matt.14:23, Mark 6:46, Luke 6:12, Luke 9:28). I have no excuse for keeping a weary mind. Not when He 'will refresh the weary and satisfy the faint.' (Jeremiah 31:25)

DECLARE

I remember my mother and my grandmother often saying 'Well, I declare!'. I probably say it too. How do we get started saying those kinds of things? What did it mean, and does it still mean the same thing, or do we just mindlessly say something that has absolutely no meaning at all to us? Empty words…

There are no empty words. Every word we utter declares something, tells something about us. Jesus said "…men will have to give account…for every careless word they have spoken." (Matt. 12:36) I think maybe I talk too much! Maybe I should think a lot more before I speak. I can't take those words back like I can on this word-process…. can't look them over and decide to delete them or rephrase them in more loving terms. "Eventually there is going to be an inspection. …The inspection will be thorough and rigorous…I won't get by with a thing." (1 Cor. 3:13 The Message) Everything I say and do should be channeled thru the Truth of Jesus Christ. Whew…. that's a tall order! I'm thanking God again for His amazing grace and His patience with me as I grow and learn.

I am not "wise by the standards of this age." but want to be "a fool so that I may become wise" …the "wisdom of this world is foolishness in God's sight." (1 Cor. 3:18,19) "I confess my iniquity, I am troubled by my sin." (Ps. 38:18) I decide afresh that "I will declare Your Name to my brothers, in the congregation I will praise You." (Ps.22:22)

There's a lot of declaring goes on…. even the "heavens declare the glory of God, the skies proclaim the work of His Hands. Day after day they pour forth speech, night after night they display knowledge. There is no speech or language where their voice is not heard. Their voice goes out into all the earth, their words to the ends of the world…" (Ps.19:1-4)

What do you declare today? Better decide…because it WILL be something.

ABOMINATION

I've heard a play on this word, exchanging an O for the A when someone was making known their political views. We don't use the word 'abomination' much today in ordinary conversation. Those of us who are prone to speak 'Christianese' may throw it around a little. The original word of scripture is 'toebah' For any grammar geeks out there, it's the feminine active participle of 'taab' which means to loath, detest, abhor. So basically, abomination is disgusting.

There are a lot of things in scripture that we are told God finds disgusting. Some of them, we quickly agree with Him. "Do not have sexual relations with an animal, it is an abomination" (Lev. 18:22) God said that burning children in the fire to the false god Molech was an abomination to Him. (Deu. 12:31) Our culture seems to be more and more disagreeing with God about this one… "Do not lie with a man as one lies with a woman. That is detestable" (Lev. 18:22) Perhaps we are seeing Romans 1:25-27 coming to pass. "…they changed the truth of God into a lie…. for this cause, God gave them up to vile affections. For even their women did change the natural use into that which is against nature, and likewise, the men, leaving the natural use of the woman, burned in their lust one toward another, men with men working that which is unseemly…'

Don't call me homophobic, God made the rules, not me.

I even found a list. "…. there are six things the Lord hates, seven that are detestable to Him. Haughty eyes, a lying tongue, hands that shed innocent blood, a heart that devises wicked schemes, feet that are quick to rush into evil, a false witness who pours out lies, and a man who stirs up dissension among brothers.' (Pro. 6:16-19)

I felt pretty good about myself until I found this. "Every one that is proud in heart is an abomination to the Lord." (Pro. 16:5) POW !! How's that for knocking you off your little pedestal Connie?!! (My pride is a constant battleground.… I know I'm probably the only one.… right?)

As always, God is good. He disciplines me, chastises me, takes me down a notch when He needs to…and He always encourages me as well. "By mercy and truth, iniquity is purged… and by the fear of the Lord men depart from evil." (Pro.16:6)

I can't know how He needs to change me until I recognize it in myself. What He says…IS. Period. What He says is absolute truth whether I agree or not. And He is merciful in revealing that truth to me rather than watching me sink deeper into whatever thing it is that needs to be purged. Lots of things are disgusting to God. But never so disgusting that He cannot cleanse and make new. We are never so disgusting that He turns His back. "Today, please listen. Don't turn a deaf ear…" (Heb. 3:7,8 The Message)

PROUD

Lots of scripture address the issue of pride, and do so in a negative light. "God opposes the proud but gives grace to the humble." (James 4:6) So are we to have no pride?? I wonder that we don't use the words pride and proud loosely. We equate them with our sense of satisfaction over personal accomplishments, or those of our loved ones. We think of our government, our country, and the armed forces who guard our freedoms...and we sing that we are 'proud to be an American...' We think of self-esteem, taking pains to look our best... personal 'pride'. We consider our advancement in any arena, personal or public, to be something to be 'proud' of.

Perhaps the words 'thankful for' should often be replaced for our use of the words proud. We forget that it is God Who has created everything within the realm of our reality. He gives us the capacity to do any good we do.... we do not accomplish one good thing that does bear His Fingerprints. We can, however, manage on our own to do a lot of damage.... we all suffer from the same eternally fatal disease. Sin. "... all have sinned and fall short of the glory of God." (Romans 3:23)

The word translated 'proud' in James 4:6 is 'huperephanos'. It means to place above, to regard superior. Arrogance comes to my mind. And I've had holy reminders before about what I term 'spiritual arrogance'. God has every right to wear glory feathers in His cap. I do not. It is only by His grace and merciful love that I do not suffer eternal death from this disease of sin we all suffer from, and only then thru Jesus Christ.... not from personal accomplishments or defeating it in and of myself. My symptoms may manifest themselves differently than yours...but we all have the same disease....and we all need saving from it. We need a Savior.

Scripture does not teach us to have no care or regard about all these things we say we take 'pride' in...but it does teach us to remember that 'every good and perfect gift is from above, coming down from the Father of the heavenly lights, who does not change like shifting shadows.' (James 1:17) There are lots of ways to say it…this wrong thing of 'pride'…arrogance and self-conceit, conceit about our own excellence…. anything that contributes to our own importance and exalts our opinion of self or exalts us in the eyes of others. None of this negates the striving for excellence for the glory of God. But let us always be sure, it's for His glory….and not our own.

ALONE

Ever feel alone in the middle of a crowded room? People who have lost their mates struggle with the loneliness that follows. Friends can help, but nothing takes the place of a lost spouse. There's scriptural reasoning for that. "The Lord God said, 'It is not good for the man to be alone. I will make a helper suitable for him.'" (Gen.2:18) Companionship between man and woman was ordained by God. Few there are who, like Paul, are called to remain unmarried. (1 Cor. 7:7-9)

Sometimes, what I feel is not really 'alone', but what the KJV Bible calls 'peculiar'. (I can almost hear you chuckling...quit it!) "Our Savior Jesus Christ...gave Himself for us, that He might redeem us from all iniquity and purify unto Himself a peculiar people, zealous of good works." (Titus 2:13-14)

There you have it...I am peculiar. Sometimes I feel like old Elijah... 'I have been working my heart out for the God of the Angel Armies...and the people...have abandoned your covenant...I'm the only one left...' (quoted from The Message) Elijah was not alone...he whined a little, God listened, and showed him how wrong he was. Read the 19th chapter of 1 Kings for yourself. It will do your heart good.

We are all alone in this way. We alone are responsible for our side of our relationship with God. We do not inherit the faith of our parents like we inherit their blonde hair. We don't inherit our place in the kingdom of God like we inherit their house when they leave this life. Our relationship with God is up to us. He invites us, woos us, gives us so much help in knowing Him thru scripture...yet it's ultimately our choice. His choice is 'yes'! And He even offers to enable us, getting under our burdens with us, helping us to carry them...even carrying them FOR us, teaching us, forgiving us time and time again...cleansing us, re-creating us in His image...perfecting us, showing us His intended purpose for our life, and loving us! He LOVES us. He LOVES you!! Even with all your yuck, He loves you so much. But sometimes we choose a definite 'no thanks'. Then…we are indeed alone.

'. the Father will give you. the Comforter…to be with you forever, the Spirit of Truth…' (John 14:16-17) I will never be alone. I may be lonely, bored, feel out of place, or even outnumbered…but I will never ever be alone…for He is with me.

BUT

It's the perfect word at the beginning of every excuse. "And the word of the Lord came to Jonah… 'Go to the great city of Nineveh and preach against it, because its wickedness has come up before me.'" (Jonah 1:1,2) BUT… 'Jonah ran away from the Lord …' (vs.3) It's a short story, 4 chapters. I encourage you to read it for yourself today.

Israel was the original exclusivist; the nation was commissioned to be the light of the world. Since Abraham, the first father of the nation, their purpose was to 'bless all nations on earth' … 'BECAUSE you have obeyed Me.' (Gen. 22:18) They were to be a 'light for the Gentiles, …to bring My salvation to the ends of the earth.' (Isa. 49:6) I notice that the blessing of all nations comes thru Israel not because of who they are…but simply out of the of their obedient life.

Often, however, they were NOT obedient. Often, they were just proud of their status, the simple fact that God had chosen to work thru them instead of any other people Often they chose not to make any efforts to bring others to the knowledge of God. And I think Jonah was an exclusivist.

Jonah had judged Nineveh, he knew about them. This was the capital city of Assyria, the rising world power, cruel in their methods. They were known for their violence and the multitude of their warriors. Jonah thought it was a good idea to get rid of the whole lot of them, rid the world of the looming threat.

Jonah had already condemned them. He didn't WANT them to repent, he had no desire to see God working on their minds and heart. So, he used their sinfulness as a reason to excuse himself from cooperating with God in ministering His love to them, bringing them to repentance. He used their disobedience to justify his own. I find the circumstances for Jonah's rebellion interesting. We'd often call things like this a 'sign' or a 'confirmation'. Everything just fell into place for Jonah to do what he wanted instead of doing what God had assigned. He went down to the docks of Joppa, a port city of

Judea, and there he found a boat headed just where he wanted to go.... away from where he was…absolute opposite direction in fact. They had a ticket available, he had the money, so off he went. I can just hear the conversation he was having with himself on the way. Maybe he was talking to himself, making bargains… 'if they don't have a ticket, then I guess I am not supposed to go'. 'If God really wants me to do that Nineveh thing, He'll close this door' This must be okay to do…or else it wouldn't have worked out…right?

Like Jonah, I often realize I'm headed in the opposite direction from where God has in mind. He is 'patient…not wanting anyone to perish…. wanting everyone to come to repentance.' (2Peter 3:9) I don't always make the effort to tell others about the love of God. I don't always take the time to encourage them to seek God, repenting and turning away from the lifestyle that will eventually consume and destroy them. I don't always look beyond the moment, looking into the difference the future might hold if only one person chooses God…changing the course of events for future generations.

This nation of people would be the first aggressor upon Israel later in history, carrying them into foreign lands as slaves. If Nineveh had not had this time of repentance, Israel's future might have been even more dreadful. How much worse would the captivity have been, had Nineveh not had this reprieve from their cruel methods? For a few generations, at least, there was a seeking after God and a putting away of the evil that was so prevalent in their society. The captive nation knew the result of that, even if they didn't realize it at the time.

How many Ninevites will we meet in heaven one day because of Jonah's message? Even if it did take an act of God for them to hear it…

GO

Jonah was told to go. He went...eventually.

God told Noah to go. (Gen.6:14 &7:1) Good thing for us he followed the directions!

Abram was told to go. "Leave your country, your people, your father's household..." (Gen.12:1) Later, God told him to "go to the region of Moriah..." (Gen.22:2) That 'go' was tough for both. Leaving everything familiar, and handing over your precious child. here is story after story telling us how God directed the lives of people, how they disobeyed, the consequences they and others suffered from the disobedience. We learn how God is always faithful, 'we know that all things work together for good to them that love God, to them who are the called according to His purpose.' (Rom. 8:28) Even in our disobedience, when we turn again to Him, He takes those awful consequences and brings some benefit to us...growing our faith. Reading and pondering prayerfully over these stories build our own faith. We see how God has worked in ages past. He is still the same God. He still can be trusted. And still, we often stubbornly refuse to obey Him. I have a 'go'. "Jesus said .... 'Go into all the world and preach the good news to all creation.' " (Mark 16:15) I don't preach in Kenya or China or any other foreign land. But I am present by being a financial part of a ministry in other parts of the world, and I invest my prayers for the work there. I 'go' every morning when I crank up my vehicle. I go into my own personal world, and my commission from the Lord is to Re-present Him to all creation. It took a long time for me to come to understand just what that means. To present Christ is the goal of every day, in some small or big way, to present Him to someone He misses from the safety of His fold.

I've learned how much He loves me. And I've learned how much He loves every other person on this orb we call Earth. And unlike us…His love for you does not diminish His love and care for me.

Go……it's a journey. Not a sit still and wait kind of thing….We must get up…. walk it out…it requires action on our part.

Go!! Praise His Name, and worship at the feet of The One Who gave you life

POWER

Ours goes off a lot, especially when it rains. It was off for 13 days in 2000 when we had "The Ice Storm". We miss the power when it goes off. We have learned to depend on it.

You can't miss what you never know, but we all 'know' electricity. All our 'stuff' works by its power. There are more and more ways, every year, to make it useful, helping us in so many ways to get done what needs to be done.... quicker and easier, more efficiently. There are very few people who refuse the electrical power available to them. I can think of only the Amish religious groups who don't use it. Most people think of it as an absolute necessity.

The power of God available to me thru the Holy Spirit is my absolute necessity. (He never goes off by the way....) His power in my life helps me in many ways, and I've learned to depend on Him. I've only begun to realize the power available thru His Presence within me. I know what it is to live without His power. ".... having a form of godliness, but denying the power thereof..." (2 Tim. 3:5)

That was me. I had the form. You would find me in the church building at every service, I followed all the traditions, I suppose I looked pretty good from the outside, at least part of the time anyway. Thank God, because of my heritage, I had knowledge of the truth. (vs.7) I never have led a perfect life, but neither have I been too badly 'led away with divers lusts.'(vs.6) .... (mostly because of fear, but hey... 'fear is the beginning of wisdom' !!) My power, however, was only my willpower...and it went off a LOT!! Not only is the Holy Spirit now the power-source for my life, He is The Holy Reminder. '... the Holy Spirit, Whom the Father will send ... will remind you of everything I have said to you.' (John 14:26)

Please don't miss this...you can't be reminded of what you never heard in the first place. Make it your business to know what He has said. You can't fight the enemy with The Spirit's Sword, if you don't have it.

Jesus Himself fought with 'it is written…'. How arrogant are we to think we can defeat the enemy otherwise? Don't be deceived, we are powerless against the enemy. And he is vicious… he 'prowls around like a roaring lion looking for someone to devour.' (1Peter 5:8)

What God has said to His people down thru the ages…what He has said thru the Person of Jesus Christ…it's recorded. It's available to you. We call it a Bible. It's not just paper and ink…it is communication '…the Word of God, living and active….it will judge the thoughts and attitudes of the heart.' (Heb. 4:12) And from your heart of hearts…if you are truly open to Him, listening for what HE says and not for what you WANT Him to say…He 'will teach you all things…' (John 14:26)

He continues to teach me better listening skills…and how to plug in to The Power ~~!!

VOTE

The day of this writing is an election day. We have the opportunity to have our opinion considered about some issues. It matters. Amidst all the many opinions, yes...just one person's opinion matters.

Jacob had twelve boys. The young Joseph was the golden child, the apple of his father's eye, the child of his most loved wife. Jacob was getting old when this boy Joseph was born, (Gen.37:3) ...he doted on him, perhaps realizing as we parents do, how quickly they grow up. Maybe he looked like his mother... or had a way with a smile. I wonder at what a brat he might have been. His brothers 'could not speak a kind word to him.' (Gen. 37:4) His father gave him a lavish gift of a robe that was not in any way the common garment of the day...(Gen.37:3) ...it had what we'd call a designer label... everyone would recognize it. It would be like sending our children to school with a Louis Vuitton backpack. (Jacob might have been wiser, knowing this was just asking for trouble, and inciting jealousy.) God has a plan for every life, and He had a plan for Joseph's life. I don't think God 'made' the brothers do the bad things they did. That does not fit the Character of my God. But when Joseph's brothers came up with their scheme, true to God's nature, He brought about His purposes despite it, and He even brought blessing out of it. Years later, to his long-lost brothers, "Joseph said, '...you intended to harm me, but God intended it for good to accomplish what is now being done, the saving of many lives.'" (Gen. 50:20) The plan was to be rid of a bratty brother who dreamed dreams of being great...greater than his older siblings. But the voice of one of them had changed the course of events, (Gen. 37:21), saved Joseph's life, and would eventually rescue the entire clan from famine. Judah was in on the plot, but for whatever reason, he 'said to his brother, "What will we gain if we kill our brother and cover up his blood? Come, let's sell him to the Ishmaelites and not lay our hands on him, after all, he is our brother, our own flesh and blood," His brothers agreed.' (Gen. 37: 26,27)

So, it was decided…they wouldn't kill him, or leave him trapped in a pit for the wild beasts to kill. He would be alive…just as a slave in a foreign land, and out of their hair. One voice was heard, and it made a difference. It's an intriguing story. The people involved had no idea of the eternal repercussions.

We too, have no idea of the eternal results of how we use our voice and influence, whether for bad, or for good. Choose and act… prayerfully. It matters.

TERM

Our elected officials serve terms. We put them in office for these designated periods of time, knowing that at the end of that term they will no longer have the authority of the office unless we give it to them again by re-election. I'm glad my stay in heaven won't be a limited term. (1Thes.4:17) I'm thankful my home there will not depend on my job performance but His. It is a matter of '...the blood of Christ, Who through the eternal Spirit offered Himself unblemished to God....' (Heb.9:14) I'm rejoicing about the benefits of this new authority...this King Jesus, who now reigns and rules.

I'm thankful it is not I who pays the penalty of death, the result of the curse of sin...I don't make those sacrifices for sin, over and over and over...as those under the previous covenant were required to do. I'm thankful all of THAT was only for a term!! I'm glad that period of time has now lapsed... a new authority is in place...and this Authority is an Eternal One. (Heb.7:24) Not a term.

I'm thankful my position in His kingdom is not a matter of public opinion, but a matter of God's grace, His love and mercy, and my accepting His sacrificial death in my stead. 'All you who were baptized into Christ have clothed yourselves with Christ, you are all sons of God through faith in Christ Jesus' (Gal.3:27,26) I now have an eternal position. Given, not earned.

I honor and respect Him so very much, but I am not afraid of Him, and I have access to His private chambers at any time. I do not hesitate to approach Him, but instead, I can 'draw near.... with a sincere heart, in full assurance of faith,' and He 'sprinkles my heart to cleanse me from a guilty conscience.' (Heb. 10:22) He's the King. He is the Eternal One. We didn't put Him on the throne. His throne has been perpetual throughout the ages, beyond the concept of our limitations of time. Yet He 'chose to give us birth through the word of truth, that we might be a kind of first fruits of all He created.' His vote is cast. He is for us…but we make the ultimate decision. He does not force His will. How do you choose?

I'm thankful the election is over, the vote has been cast, and my position in the kingdom of God is secure. "He chose us in Him before the creation of the world…. In love, He determined beforehand to adopt us as His sons and daughters through Jesus Christ.' (Eph. 1:4-5 my paraphrase) And I'm His. Not for a term, but for eternity. Hallelujah.

ARSON

I seem to be an occasional arsonist. I've learned some lessons about setting fires, been burned by a few that I've set...still, I seem to forget the lessons, and mindlessly set another fire. '...think about how a small spark can set a big forest on fire.' (James 3:5) I don't play with matches. I have a problem with my mouth. It gets big sometimes, and overactive, spurting out stuff that is better left unsaid. Yes...you've heard this before from me. And yes.... I'm still battling it. I saw myself in a log a few nights ago, my husband put a log on our fire that was not an ordinary log. This log had at one time had a limb attached to the side of it, and the center of the log, all the way to where the little stump of a limb stuck out on the side, was hollow. When he put it on the fire, the flames went crazy. The hollow place created a draft, perfect for fire to really ignite. I have been in situations like that...seeing little glowing embers...and I set my mouth in motion, putting that log on the fire, and just the perfect one to cause a draft ...then the situation turns into a dancing fire. "...wickedness burns like a fire...sets the forest thickets ablaze so that it rolls upward in a column of smoke.' (Isa. 9:18)

The wisdom writer wrote "As charcoal to embers, and as wood to fire, so is a quarrelsome man for kindling strife." (Proverbs 26:21) And this... "without wood, a fire goes out...without gossip a quarrel dies down." (vs. 20)

Seems I have a tendency to be quarrelsome...for I'm guilty of kindling strife on occasion. God forgive me and 'set a guard over my mouth O Lord, keep watch over the door of my lips.' (Ps. 141:3) Whether it's 'big' fire or 'little' fire...or 'big' strife or 'little' strife...it's all the same in the eyes of God. "With the tongue, we praise our Lord and Father, and with it we curse men, who have been made in God's likeness....out of the same mouth come praise and cursing. My brothers, (and sisters), this should not be." (James 3:9,10) I want 'the words of my mouth and the meditation of my heart to be pleasing in Your sight, O Lord, my Rock and my Redeemer.' (Ps. 19:14) They are not always so. If you think I'm writing this for you...I'm not. It's for me.... yet again. Sigh...

But if it spills out on you...talk to God about it. He's heard it before...

STRIFE

It would be interesting to know what you think strife is. It's some pretty bad stuff evidently…it's listed in Gal. 5:20 with idolatry, witchcraft, hatred, and a few other words I need to study and define. But idolatry and witchcraft??…I never want included in that listing!

Paul says 'Let us walk honestly, as in the day…not in rioting and drunkenness, not in chambering and wantonness, not in strife and envying.' (Romans 13:13) Again, I don't know what a couple of those things are really…but I am pretty sure I don't want in that list either. So…what is this thing called strife? My definition before study was: arguments, bickering, dis-harmony etc.

The Greek word translated 'strife' in the Galatians passage is 'eritheia'. Thayer's Greek dictionary defines it like this. 'electioneering or intriguing for office'. God is something' else. After my days of reflecting on 'votes' and 'terms' …then the issue with my mouth…now He brings me to this thing called strife…and up pops this election language again! Maybe that doesn't blow you away..after all, these reflections are about my issues not yours…but it does blow me away, and I just share it with you.

A further word study brings me to phrases like "those who seek only their own" "a motive of self-interest" "scheming for public office or position" "sharpening of feeling of action" I prayerfully examine my heart and find strife there.

Looking out for number one, that would-be ME. Scripture defines it 'strife' when I scheme to keep myself on top shelf. The world's answer to that is "look out for #1, if you don't do it, nobody will." Isn't that what you've been told? Well…this morning, (again)…I've been reminded "This is what the Lord Almighty says: '……whoever touches you touches the apple of My eye'…" (Zec.2:8) It's not my mission to electioneer for office. It is not up to me to stir up the feelings of others in my favor. I am called to RE-present Christ to everyone I relate to. If I am truly Hiis servant, I need not be out electioneering...manipulating public opinion of myself.... trying to keep positioned like I want. His agenda must always come before mine. Trying to keep my agenda and His...? Well......He's not done with me on this topic....

STRIVING...

My definition without study... 'trying really hard'. What think ye?

Yesterday, strife was revealed to me in both positive and negative ways. Now don't misunderstand...I'm not one to stir up a conflict and battle with words. If anything, I'm prone to do the opposite...shut down and shut up. Not a good choice either sometimes, communication is vital in relationships. But there is strife within me, all of it not bad. I think there is a spiritual striving that is vital in the heart of every Christian. The battle against the enemy is ongoing. He is defeated, for Jesus DID die, and DID come out of the tomb alive and DOES live still....and because of that truth, there is no ultimate victory to be had for the enemy of those in Christ. But the skirmishes go on and the enemy can inflict some pain and injury to us while here and in this flesh. He is the cause of much strife.

"In your striving against sin..." (Hebrews 12:4)
So... there IS a striving against it, else we may very well be surrendered TO it

Whether it is sin of any sort, or whether it is the Holy Spirit of God, the decision is mine to make. I am either surrendered to God and His agenda for my life (not my own selfish scheme to position myself like I desire) .... or I am striving against Him in His will for my life and the purposes for which I am created. I want to be co-operating With Him, thru the power of His Holy Spirit, (...not my own willpower and ability to perform). And I want to always be in a spiritual striving against the very real 'spiritual forces of evil' (Eph. 6:12) .... or I'm buying into the lie of the enemy. '...the devil... was a murderer from the beginning...he is a liar and the father of lies.' (John 8:44) '....they......going about to establish their own righteousness, have not submitted themselves unto the righteousness of God.' (Romans 10:3) '...'Seek first the kingdom of God, and His righteousness..'(Matt. 6:33) It's the same story ....choosing. And there will always be times of spiritual strife... thank You Father for Your Help, Your Presence, and Your Power thru Your Holy Spirit. And thank You Lord, that you never give up on me...

VISION

Mine is going. I've never had good eyesight. Began wearing glasses in the 5th grade. Got that surgical procedure a few years ago to improve my distance vision, and it is wonderful!! Then my close-up vision went …sigh…

I remember as a kid, walking home from the post office where my daddy worked, wearing the new glasses that had come in the mail. I marveled at the masses of individual leaves on the trees…. I could SEE them. I could read the signs on the buildings across the street ! This new improved eyesight was amazing! Vision-improved. Last night I saw a person across the room, saw a wave to my direction, thought she looked familiar…but my eyes couldn't confirm that I knew her and that the wave was in fact intended for me. Yep…. it was her. Vision-impaired.

I don't enjoy looking at the news broadcasts or reading the newspapers proclaiming the events that are happening in the world…either locally or globally. Yet what I do learn about current events is that God has foretold it…and it either has already been, it is right now, or the signs of it's coming are there. Vision-selective. 'So, what?' you ask? "… Where is this 'coming' He promised? …everything goes on as it has since the beginning…" (2 Peter 3:4)

Vision. We lose sight of the kingdom calendar and fail to see the activities of God. We buy into the enemy lie that because the eastern sky hasn't burst forth with the return of Jesus, we can assume that neither will we see it any time soon. Whether He had returned before my birth, or if it is after the birth of my great-great-great grandchildren, or even beyond that…He will return, on His schedule…not mine.

My time is limited. My opportunities are bound within the time frame of MY life, not on God's. He knows no limitations of time and space, and I can't fathom what that even means. Vision-non-existent. I choose to believe in faith …from the witness offered in scripture…thru the help and power of

His Holy Spirit. "The Lord gives sight to the blind. He lifts up those who are bowed down..." (Ps. 146:8)

"What do you want me to do for you?" He asked. "Lord," I answer...I want my sight."

(Matt. 20:33 personalized by me)

Father open our eyes and give us vision. 'Nothing in all creation is hidden' from You. 'Everything is uncovered and laid bare before the eyes of Him to Whom we must give account.' (Heb. 4:13) As You did with Saul of Tarsus, remove the scales so that we have a changed life and a clear vision of Your purposes and will for us. (Acts 9)

SHAME

Ever been told 'Shame on you!'?? Guess who I believe started that? Until evil came onto the scene in the garden, when there was no knowledge of evil brought on the Adam and Eve's choice, there was no shame. 'They were both naked .and were not ashamed.' (Gen. 2:25) As I've heard it said, 'it is what it is'...they were just as they were. Then the wrong choice was made and shame began. '...because I was naked, I was afraid and I hid myself.' I love God's reply... 'Who said?' (Genesis 3:10-11 my paraphrase)

Shame was introduced by the realm of evil. It's a dreadful weapon that is used against us still. God had walked with them in the garden, just as they were.... He had never shamed them. Don't let's get shame and remorse, repentance, regret, disappointment, sorrow, or guilt confused. Shame carries with it a desire to hide or cover up. In fact, I believe it is an enemy of repentance. We may have remorse for something, regret it...be sorry about it...be guilty of it.... but hiding or trying to excuse it is only a devil's lie. God knows it anyway. Our hiding only keeps us in our shameful state.

'The Lord God called to the man, 'Where are you?' (Gen. 3:9) He still calls. I believe without a doubt that God knew where Adam was and why he was there. I think God calls us to answer Him so that we must face our circumstance, own our poor choices, and confess them to Him. Only then can He restore us and remove our guilt. 'Wash me and I will be whiter than snow.' (Ps. 51:7)

It's a whole other issue to accept that cleansing. There again the enemy will lie. '...you don't deserve...' 'God won't do that for YOU...' 'you aren't _____ enough' (you fill in the blank with whatever that demon uses against you...smart, pretty, handsome, worthy, brave, good, kind, patient, healthy, strong, or a million other things....) As long as we hide and make excuses...well, de-Nile (denial) ain't just a river... You may be hiding, but you're not hiding from God, and you're hiding WITH what you are ashamed OF. What thing is in that blank? What is it you are hiding with?

FAMILIAR

I find security in 'the same ole' same ole'...I like to move my furniture around, but I don't want to move it to another house. I like my nest. I like the memories attached to it. I like remembering when my grand-daughters and I planted the bulbs that are blooming bright yellow all over my yard this morning. But...some of 'the same ole' stuff sure gets old, the tedious daily tasks that are not 'fun', the stress of days filled with problems to solve, issues to resolve, people to deal with.

As I ready to meet another day, I was seeking God about some of those things, asking Him things like, 'Where do I _____? What does_____? How should I _____ _____? Who will _____?'

'By an act of faith, Abraham said yes to God's call to travel to an unknown place that would become his home. When he left he had no idea where he was going... Abraham did it by keeping his eye on an unseen city with real, eternal foundations...the city designed and built by God.' (Hebrews 11:8.10The Message)

I can only guess at how I'd have reacted to such a call. Something along the lines of; "WHAT?!!" "WHERE?!!" and "WHY?!??" Leaving everything familiar is beyond my grasp of thought. No walking in the dark to the bathroom...no knowing the dry path to walk across the wet yard...not having 'my own bed' to sleep in at night...no favorite place to sit and meditate. I could name hundreds. What would you miss the most? The past is familiar, I've been there. The present is familiar, I am here. The future is far from familiar as yet, but it is secure. I will be safe there. "I have been with you wherever you have gone..." (1Ch. 17:8) " ..surely I am with you always..."(Matt.28:20) God does not ask great things of me....I'm not called to Africa or China. He calls me to the familiar places and familiar things of my 'same ole' life. And even though I am guilty of grumbling about it. I am thankful.

DECIDE

Whether we think about it or not, we make decisions every moment of every day. A lot of them make no big impact...but a lot of the choices we make will change the course of our lives and the lives of others. It is important that we make those choices with our mind in gear and our hearts open to what the Spirit speaks before we decide. My decision to allow the other car to have the parking space might alter that person's attitude just enough to stop them from lashing out in frustration at a poor clerk, or worse, an innocent child. My decision to tough it out in a difficult relationship may end up being a key element in the work that God is doing in that life. My decision to take a firm stand and speak truth when it isn't easy or comfortable may be a necessary element in waking someone up to the absolute truth of God's Word being THE measure of all behavior. How we decide is important, and even more important is the 'how' we follow thru as we act on our decision. 'God wants us to grow up, to know the whole truth and tell it in love...' (Eph. 4:15 The Message) '. conduct yourselves in love' (2John 1:6 The Message)

I am instructed to do ALL that I do... in love. I have found that the hard decisions I make are easier carried out in anger and frustration, or even worse...in judgment. I have a clear revelation of truth in scripture, and I can make decisions accordingly, yet I am not the one to carry out the sentence. '...for man's anger does not bring about the righteous life that God desires.' (James 1:20 NIV)

God sets the standard that I endeavor to live by, and God is the one to issue punishment, not me. Don't let's get punishment and discipline confused...nor the elements of right and wrong, nor love and hate. All of us need discipline, and God, being our Perfect Father, disciplines. Punishment will come, but only to those who refuse Him, His love, and His Son. And even then, not because of hate, but because He gave us our will and honors our choice, and all of us bear consequences of our poor choices. He has gone to such great measure to help us really understand the options before we decide Life or death. Good or evil. '…. choose for yourselves this day whom you will serve…. as for me….I will serve the Lord.' (Joshua 24:15) How very tragic that so many do not know what they are really choosing when the moment comes to decide….

GARDENING

Last year I didn't get the exact kind of seed I wanted to plant in our garden. I waited too long, and the store was all sold out. I've fussed at myself all year, determined that I wouldn't make that mistake this year. We tried to buy them last week. They didn't have them yet. Maybe today... Gardening is a lot of work. The ground must be properly prepared. It can't be too wet, or too dry... it must be tilled, not hard and compacted. The soil must be ready, or else the chances of seed germinating are slim.

Paul speaks in gardening language in 1 Corinthians 3. He talks about the planting and the watering. He uses carpenter language in referring to the preparation time and how important the foundation is. In gardening, the foundation is the soil and its preparation. If you call yourself by the Name of Christ, you're a gardener. You are either tilling soil or packing it down. You're either making a heart softer and preparing it for seed, or you're packing it down, making it harder so that it will reject seed. You may not be a sower, your gifting may not be as an evangelist... (and don't get that confused with a job description that comes with a paycheck). 'Having then gifts differing according to the grace that is given to us, whether prophecy.... or ministry.... or teaching...' (Romans 12:6,7)

Make no mistake, Adam was created a gardener...'The Lord God took the man and put him in the Garden of Even to work it and take care of it. ' (Gen. 2:15) ....and in the New Adam, Jesus Christ, we too are gardeners. The soil of our garden plot is under our feet every moment of our life. 'Go into all the world....and preach...' (Mark 16: 15)

This soil issue is as important as the seed. I can buy the seed store out...throw it on the ground, and see no harvest...no peas on my table. I could plow and till the ground until I drop in my tracks...but if somebody comes behind me with a steam roller, pressing the soil down, the ground will be packed and need yet more attention. I want to be a good gardener. I want always to be making the soil of hearts ready to receive the Seed, whether it is me that sows it or someone else. The Seed will germinate only when the heart is ready.

God forgive us when we pack down soil with our bad attitudes and self-righteousness, hindering the soil of that heart to receive and sprout the Life of God.

FELLOWSHIP

This Sunday will be potluck day. There will be more food than we can possibly eat, and we'll all probably eat more than we should. Our culture seems to build everything around a table full of food. 'Going out to eat' has become entertainment, and even replaced the home cooked meals for some people, opting instead to 'drive thru' and purchase food already prepared.

I wonder that we haven't lost a great deal more than we realize because of our lack of table fellowship these days. My family gathers at the table together at the same time only on very special occasions now, holidays mostly. And even then, it is more about the food than the fellowship. We talk about the food way more than we talk TO each other ABOUT each other.

'They devoted themselves to the apostles' teaching and to the fellowship, to the breaking of bread and to prayer.' (Acts 2:42 NIV) There was about three thousand newly baptized believers in this 'they' of scripture. I don't doubt that jobs and family life continued with business as usual. But I think conversation topics changed, priorities changed and when free time did come…there was fellowship to be had with people who'd had the same experiences and knew the same Jesus. Seems to me they used the simple fact that they HAD to eat as an excuse to spend time together to study and pray. Killing two birds with one stone you might say.

'koinonia' = fellowship in Acts 2. The word in the original language means partnership, literally a participation. It means to commune or communicate. The same word is used in 1 Cor. 10:16 and is translated as communion in the KJV. 'The cup of blessing which we bless, is it not the communion of the blood of Christ? The bread which we break, it is not the communion of the body of Christ?'(the NIV uses the word participation)

Hebrews 13:16 uses the word koinonia also. The KJV translated it communicate. 'But to do good and to communicate, forget not: for with such sacrifices God is well pleased.' The NIV translates it 'to share with others'. Fellowship.... it's about communication.... communing with our spiritual siblings, filling our hearts from the overflowing joy and love of others. It's not about filling our stomachs.

PLANTING

My husband and I don't always agree on how things are best done. We don't agree on planting techniques. I like to plant seeds close to each other. I like the plants to be thick enough to cover the ground and help shade the soil from sunlight...he thinks each plant needs more space so they don't compete for nutrients...he says they need room to grow and bush out. Regardless of whose method is best, both of us have purpose in our planting. We don't go with seed and just toss it out. 'When a farmer plows in order to plant, does he plow without stopping? Does he keep on breaking up the soil and making the field level? When he's made the surface even, doesn't he plant caraway seeds...doesn't he scatter cumin? Doesn't he plant wheat in its proper place? Doesn't he plant barley where it belongs....'

(Isa. 28:24) The 'how' is important. As a disciple of Christ, I am called to tend the garden. Jesus said 'Go into the world.... go everywhere and announce the Message of God's good news to one and all.' (Mark 16:15 The Message)

I don't live in Eden, but I live in God's world, (Mt. 13:38) and there is soil to plow, fields to level, and seed to plant. There is a time to water. Paul planted seed, Apollos watered the fresh young plants. (1 Cor. 3:6) There is a time to remove weeds that threaten to strangle out the life of fruit bearing plants, but the 'how' of that is even another matter. (Matt.13:29) Tending the garden is necessary, and the 'how' is vitally important.

I heard it said once that it is possible to beat somebody up with Jesus. I think there is much truth to that. Our mission is planting a seed successfully, and seeing that seed germinate into new life. I can shove a seed into a hole in hard ground and never see new life. I can toss seeds over sod so rooted with other things that the seed has very little chance of germinating. The technique (attitude), the 'how', ... is important. Don't misunderstand...a seed's germinating is not because of me nor anything I 'do'. God brings new life...not me. "It's not the one who plants or the one who waters who is at the center of this process but God, who makes things grow. Planting and watering are menial servant jobs at the minimum wages. What makes them worth doing is the God we are serving." (1Cor. 3:7-9 The Message)

"We are God's fellow workers…" (1Cor. 3:9) It's time to put on the gloves, get the how…I mean hoe….and get to gardening. The Son is shining!

NEW

One morning I woke to find something new…well, a picture of the something new…. a baby boy.

I knew the process had begun. The waiting has been ongoing…nine months of waiting. The entire family waiting in anticipation for the something new to finally be reality. But in fact, it has been reality for the entire nine months. Preparations were made and a name chosen. Identity. This child was real and greatly loved long before arrival. You may disagree, but I believe (strongly) that life begins the instant the sperm meets the egg, the process set in motion, new life growing until the time comes to leave the nurturing place and enter the world, ready to grow and develop even further, eventually repeating the process of reproducing life.

"For You created my inmost being. You knit me together in my mother's womb." (Ps.139:13)

"this is what the Lord says- He Who made you, Who formed you in the womb, and Who will help you…." (Isa. 44:2)

"Before I formed you in the womb I knew you…before you were born I set you apart…" (Jer. 1:5)

Babies. New life…God's gift. Welcome to our world child…. you are 'fearfully and wonderfully made' (Ps. 139:14)

ASK

I remember when my sons were small, they would point and grunt. In order for them to learn language, I insisted that they speak. I made them say what it was they wanted. I made them ask, and they learned to communicate. I wonder if we don't point and grunt to God. Two times this morning in my reading, I have come to the issue of articulating our desires to God in prayer. Why should it matter if we actually articulate into words, whether spoken, written, or mental? Why go to that extent, when God knows everything already? Why make my child say the word 'water'...when it was obvious to me he was thirsty?

I am convinced that God wants me to tell Him specifically what my issue is. When I name it, I then go on to ask Him to 'fix' it. In my asking, it is ME who learns what the issue really and truly is. ALL of the issue...the deep dark places of it...and sometimes it's not pretty So often when (and IF) I honestly and openly go to God with things, going thru this process. I discover things in my own heart that I didn't realize were there...and should NOT be there. Often, I end up with an entirely different agenda in prayer! Because He instructed me to say what it was I wanted. I learned to communicate TO Him...and in turn, and because of that, I am blessed to have communication WITH Him.

My sons would point to soda. They needed water or milk. I often point to things when in fact, those things are not best. I ask that God use me...then I complain about the difficult situation I'm in, and want an escape. My sons pointed to cookies, and they needed food that would provide nutrients for their growing bodies and sustain longer than a sugar rush. I point to a feel-good place of ministry, and He hands me an assignment that makes me grow faith muscles.

"I cry out loudly to God...I spill out all my complaints before Him, and spell out my troubles in detail..." (Ps. 142:2 The Message)

"Call to Me and I will answer you and tell you great and unsearchable things you do not know." (Jer. 33:3 NIV)

It's not a drive thru window…we don't place our order with God. There's no 'have it your way' slogan. But I can trust Him enough to spill out the entire truth of my heart to Him, revealing it to Him AND to myself…. knowing it is safe to do so. He loves me enough to look at all the ugly with me, and He is mighty enough to make it into something beautiful. I didn't even know some of that stuff was there…even though it was no surprise to Him. Yes indeed…God did know, always knows. But I do not. It is in communication with Him that I learn.

DIET

Everyone is on a diet. You probably are thinking about the 'don't eat anything you really want' diet. . the 'lose weight' kind. Trouble is, a lot of us are on a 'gain weight' diet, or perhaps a 'be unhealthy' diet. If you eat, you are on a diet. Maybe not a specific, conscious, on purpose diet, but you have one. We eat or we don't live long....and sometimes we don't live long because of our eating.

It' a complicated subject, one I am led back to time and time again. My mouth. What I put in it, and what comes out of it.

Jesus said this, 'Don't you know that anything that is swallowed works its way through the intestines and is finally defecated?' (Matt. 15:17 The Message) There is purpose in our eating, and I believe we are to enjoy our meals...Jesus Himself feasted... but the ultimate purpose of food is to fuel the engines of this body we reside in. The nutrients are extracted and the rest is eliminated. It's gross, but that's the truth of it. There is another diet that is critical to our health, the spiritual diet of feeding on God's Word. 'It takes more than bread to stay alive. It takes a steady stream of words from God's Mouth.' (Matt. 4:4 The Message)

What is this 'staying alive' thing in the Matthew 4 passage? Just keeping the motor running? I think not. 'The one who brings a hearty appetite to this eating and drinking has eternal life and will be fit and ready for the final day.... whoever eats this Bread will live always.' (John 6:54,58 The Message)

I have a candy jar on my workstation. People comment on how pretty it is. But when they put their hand in and taste what it holds...they want more. (chocolate easter eggs are gooooood !!) 'Taste and see that the Lord is good...' (Ps. 34:8NIV)

I have tasted...and now I crave Him more and more. It has a much more powerful draw than candy eggs.... I can't sustain a healthy life on candy eggs, but I will have a long life...eternal life. I intentionally feed on The Bread of heaven. He sustains my spirit. He will sustain my life eternally.

'...If anyone eats of this bread, she will live forever....' (John 6:51 NIV personalized by me) Hallelujah.

WRATH

The Bible mentions 'the wrath of God' often. I don't often use the word 'wrath'. When I do, I have in mind uncontrolled anger…. What is wrath in your mind? "He that believeth on the Son has everlasting life, and he that believeth not the Son shall not see life, but the wrath of God abides on him.' (John 3:36 KJV)

After reading that verse, what image do you have of our God? An angry, out-of-control, fit-throwing Deity, lashing out at the very man He created because of their disobeying His directions?

I confess, that was once my image. And it was idolatry, for that is indeed another god…it is not the one and only true God. God has no problem with self-control. In The Person of Jesus Christ, He allowed much ridicule and suffering, even to innocent death on a Roman cross. I would have lost my self-control long before Calvary's hill.

In this passage, the word that is translated 'wrath' is 'orge'. As with all words, it has a wide meaning, some that broadened my view as to what is involved other than anger.

Desire Movement or agitation of the soul

Impulse Indignation Violent passion

I believe with no doubt, that there will be consequences of rejecting God's Son. But it won't be because God is angry and wants revenge. It will be because that has been our choice. Even in our disbelief, God's desire and agitation of His heart is still that we would believe and accept Him in obedient faith. 'The Lord ….is not willing that any should perish, but that all should come to repentance.'(2 Peter 3:9 KJV)

I also believe with no doubt that He will eternally reject those who have rejected Him. And it will be without the life that He offers.... the everlasting life that is ours when we believe on the Son....(believe...another word to consider, 'the devils believe, and tremble' (James 2:19) it must mean more than accepting as fact...)

To enter into the next realm without the life God provides.... that is an option. But I'll choose life. I choose Jesus. I think those who reject Him have no idea what they are choosing...death instead of life. Eternally

MERCY

That is my by-word. Perhaps I should break that habit, after looking closer at the word, I may be using it 'in vain'....

In vain...what is that? A quick word study shows me that it's 'worthless 'or 'useless'. I certain do not want to use the word 'mercy' in such a way that it diminishes the concept of mercy in any way...I don't want mercy to ever be portrayed 'in vain'.

'chanan' is a word that is used 75 times in the Bible. In the King James Version of our Bible, sixteen of those times, it is 'mercy', twelve times it is translated 'merciful' It means to bend or stoop in kindness to an inferior, to favor, to have pity on. Mercy is important...profoundly important.

There are many times when I am faced with situations and circumstances that are beyond my ability to understand. I don't know why young women suffer cancer...or ANYone.... Why do they enjoy renewed health, and suffer yet again? Why do children suffer disease? Why do babies have to suffer and die? Worse still, why do they have to live suffering? Why do people who love and cherish children have inability to have children of their own, while others have child after child only to neglect and ignore them? Why do good people die in tragic accidents, absolutely no fault of their own? Why do spouses decide to reject their vows and turn their backs on commitments? Why do parents reject their own offspring, or even worse...? mistreat and abuse them?

I don't know. And often, I don't know how to even pray about it. I wouldn't know how to give my orders to God even if that were the way to approach Him. But I KNOW that He sees, that He cares, and that He can bring blessing from ALL suffering when we put both the suffering and ourselves in His capable Hand. "...ALL things word for the good of those who love Him, who have been called according to His purpose." (Romans8:28NIV)

".... we do not know what we ought to pray for, but the Spirit Himself intercedes for us with groans that words cannot express. And He who searches our hearts knows the mind of the Spirit, because the Spirit intercedes for the saints in accordance with God's will." (Romans 8:26,27 NIV)

Praise God we who love Him and have been called are not left alone and to our own devices. 'I'm absolutely convinced that nothing...nothing living or dead, angelic or demonic, today or tomorrow, high or low, thinkable or unthinkable...absolutely nothing can get between me and God's love because of the way that Jesus my Master has embraced me.' (Rom. 8:38,39 The Message personalized by me)

Lord God open the floodgates of Your mercy to those who need You so desperately right now.... Hallelujah...

ENTER

Do you pay attention to the arrows that tell you where to enter at the bank drive thru? Ever try to get in another way? Doesn't make drive-thru banking very convenient...

Wal-Mart and some other places now have doors that will open for you from both directions...but a lot of times, you have to pay attention...you can't enter thru the exit door. There is a specific way to come into the building. There is one specific way to enter into The Presence of God. We're blessed in this age to have that privilege...it hasn't always been so. There was a time when only the high priest of that year could enter into that Holy Place, the Place Where He was....and only then after a lengthy set of rituals, rituals rich in meaning for us when we study them...with the knowledge available to us... we can know the 'rest of the story', as Paul Harvey would say.

"No one may enter The Temple of God except the priests and designated Levites. They are permitted in because they have been consecrated...' (2Ch. 23:6 The Message) (That consecration process was something I am SO thankful to not be bound by!!) The consecration process involved way too much to address in this short writing...it involved much time and detail, not to mention the animal sacrifices etc.

To 'consecrate' pictures the actions of making something that is empty of a particular content...no longer so. The reason for consecration was to 'sanctify'...to prepare and purify, to withdraw someone/something from ordinary use, and set them/it apart for a holy work. And it didn't make them/ it so for all time...

There is now a different way to enter...one way. But you don't have to be a certain nationality, or of a certain family line...(as it once was..) There is no need to kill a bull or a goat. (Heb. 9:12) No sprinkling blood on specific places... No need for particular garments. (there was then...) No waiting on a certain day...not a temporary thing that has to be re-done next year.

Jesus fleshed out ALL that this whole thing pictured. He needed no ritual cleansing, He was pure, perfect, and holy. "...we have been made holy through the sacrifice of the Body of Jesus Christ, once for all..." (Heb. 10:10) His sacrificial blood is on the altar of heaven...and He extends the privilege of entrance to the Holiest of Holy Places to us......to me. And you.

I can enter in to that Holy Place. One Way. "Nothing impure will ever enter it...only those whose names are written in the Lamb's book of life." (Rev. 21:27) "I AM the Way, The Truth, and The Life...No one comes to the Father except through Me." (John 14:6)

Praise God for the privilege of coming into His Presence on the merit of Messiah, thank You Lord Jesus...help us to grasp the magnitude of this blessing.

JUDGMENT

Long black robes…the stern face of the person who has the final say.

No…that's the judge. What about judgeMENT? Never mind the WHO of it (God is The Who) ….what about the IT…judgement? Scripture tells the story of how the nation of Israel, who had been called out as a special people for a special purpose, got so settled into their cushy life that judgment fell on them. God had warned… "…when The Lord your God brings you into the land.…..to give you ..houses filled with all kinds of good things you did not provide.…when you eat and are satisfied…be careful that you do not forget the Lord Who brought you out.…do not follow ..the gods of the peoples around you…the Lord commanded us …so that we might always prosper…' (Deut. 6 scattered verses)

God is still the same God. His character has not changed. His mind has not changed. He is still holy and just. And He still metes out judgment in order to accomplish His purposes. He still warns us from the pages of scripture and the circumstances of our life. "My soul yearns for You in the night, in the morning my spirit longs for You. When Your judgments come upon the earth, the people of the world learn righteousness." (Isa. 26:9)

WHEN Your judgments come, not if.…

The Babylonian army came. Life was dramatically changed. They were no longer free, but under tyranny and slavery. They lost their homes, everything they called 'mine' …was no longer.

"Lord, they came to You in their distress…when you disciplined them." (Isa. 26:16) When disaster strikes and tragedy unfolds, we seem always to call Him then. "Oh, God !!" we cry. And because He is The God of perfect Love, He still hears…The judgment comes often BECAUSE of His love. The final judgment will also come. And because He is the perfect Holy God… when time is no more, it will be too late to cry out to Him. People…let's look for His judgment now. Let's see His Hand at work in the world around us. Let's look hard to see His Fingerprints on our life and on our circumstances. He is God. And we are not. He is all powerful. We have only what He gives.

I have no fear for my eternal destiny. But I am fearful of the hardships that may lay ahead for us and for our children's children if we do not return to Him. "IF my people, who are called by My Name..." That is me. And you, if you call yourself a follower of Christ. I don't care about your 'church' label. If you belong to Christ.... we must 'humble ourselves" ...lest He humble us ! We must 'seek His Face'....and stop seeking only His Hand's blessing! We must examine ourselves and not just others.... we must 'turn from OUR wicked ways' ...

"Have mercy upon us, O God..." (Ps. 51:5)

THOUGH

That's a word we use to introduce a new condition, sometimes it connects and combines two. It means nevertheless, even if, even when "...though I walk through...".

Many of us learned to recite the scripture containing these words. As a child, I didn't really grasp the meaning of 'the valley of the shadow of death...' nor understand the concept of the complete helplessness in the face of suffering and death. Death has the final say. Except over Jesus Christ.

Death is something that no other person in this world can help us do. Nobody can do it for me, or for you. Except Jesus Christ. We struggle against cancers and disease. We make dreadful mistakes that cause accidents of horrific consequence. Death's shadow looms over those situations and circumstances, and we are helpless in its presence. Except through Jesus Christ.

Life is uncertain, though we forget that. Every one of us will go thru the experience of our bodies death, though we don't like to think about it, and certainly don't expect it today. "Yea, though I walk through the valley of death, I will fear no evil, for Thou art with me." (Ps. 23:4)

"Oh death, where is your sting? Oh grave, where is your victory? Thanks be to God, which gives us the victory through our Lord Jesus Christ." (1 Cor. 15:55, 57)

"When I walk into the thick of trouble,...with Your Hand...save me." (Ps. 138:7 The Message)

Even when I don't see how, Jesus does. Even if I cannot, Jesus can. Though the weight of sorrow settles in, when the stress of life heaps up...nevertheless,

He is God, and He is my Caregiver, my Friend, My Rescuer, My Comforter…
and He lives. Death has no power over Him. Hallelujah.

"…finish what you started in me, God…Your love is eternal…" (Ps. 138:8
The Message)

"…do not abandon the works of Your Hands…" (Ps. 138:8 NIV)

Many walk the path of death today…may God be so very near, they feel His
Breath.

ARRESTED

They arrested Him last night. It was a long night. Drug before every judge in town.... all of it really illegal. But He never asked for His rights. Imagine the trials of Jesus today, in our courts. There would be such an outcry about violated rights. But don't think our system would have prevented His death. I wonder what methods would be used today to stop Jesus.

Our culture seems to have perfected the political smear tactics. But, that's not a new thing. They did that. They attacked the circumstances of His birth. (John 8:41). When read with some knowledge about the culture, the passage is an accusation that His mother was pregnant when she married Joseph, not a virgin as was claimed. They suggested that Jesus had more than one 'father'. Questioning someone's honesty chips away at the foundation of any relationship. Ask Eve, Satan used that tactic successfully on her in the Garden. He questioned the honesty of God...Eve considered the possibility...and you and I live in the rest of the story.

Perhaps today we would scrutinize His finances, look at His tax returns. They did that too. (Luke 20 and Matthew 17)

Or get a loose woman involved...they did that too. (John 8)

"There is nothing new under the sun..." (Ecc. 1:9) Don't think we're any different than the people who drug Jesus from court to court all night and saw to it that He was nailed to a Roman cross. We are not. But He was different. Hallelujah.... what a Savior.

FINISHED

Finished. Done. Over with. Accomplished. The end. Concluded.

I wonder what a sigh of relief the chief priests and their followers sighed when they saw Jesus sentenced to death. They thought it was finished. Done. Over with. They thought they had accomplished something. They thought this latest bout with a so-called Messiah was concluded. Their positions were no longer threatened. Life would go on as usual. They didn't want their Passover messed up. They wanted Jesus not only quieted, but eliminated. They wanted their traditional and religious holiday to go on as always...all the while with schemes of orchestrating an innocent death. (John 18:28)

Finished. He was dead. He was in the tomb. They thought it was finished.

About the time the lambs were slain on the altar, the Lamb of God spilled His blood on a Roman cross. There were no cries or bleating from this Lamb. He was not drug or carried. He himself, even carried the cross He was to die on. While blood ran from the altar where the lambs were sacrificed, His Blood drenched the timbers of the rugged cross of Calvary.

While the prepared pascal lambs of Passover were laid out on their tables, The Lamb of God lay in a tomb between two angels. (John 20:12)

They feasted on the animals they sacrificed as an atonement for their sin and a reprieve from the curse of death...over and over, year after year. I feast on the Lamb of God...I feast on The Bread of Life. I am not required to sacrifice an animal to atone for my sin. God Himself has done that, once and for all. (Rom. 3:25, Heb. 9:26, Heb.10)

'Through Jesus...I continually offer to God a sacrifice of praise...the fruit of lips that confess His Name....not forgetting to do good and to share with others, for with such sacrifices God is pleased.' (Heb. 13:15-16) He is not dead....'He is risen.' (Luke 24:6)

Hallelujah !!

SADNESS

It is a heaviness of heart we've all felt, brought on by various thing. It needs no introduction, when we are sad, it is evident. It shows itself in our expressions, our body language, our voice...even the words we choose are colored by the sadness of heart. Sadness expresses itself as anger often.... or hopelessness. Circumstances of life deeply affect us, and we process it.... often in unwise and unhealthy ways. Often in cooperation with our enemy instead of with the Holy Spirit of God.

When sadness settles over us, we can listen to the wrong voice and become more defeated, angrier, hopeless, or depressed...or we can listen for the His Whisper and remember His promises. There were some sad faces on the road to Emmaus. (Luke 24) They walked along with it all over their face, obvious to a fellow Traveler.

"What are you discussing...?" the Traveler asked.

"Are you the only one in Jerusalem who hasn't heard...?", they answered.

"What has happened?" the Traveler replied.

"Jesus of Nazareth...He was a prophet, powerful in word and deed before God and all the people !...", they began to tell the Traveler. "...but we had hoped...." (Luke 24:21)

Things hadn't turned out like they had expected. They had the scenario all worked out in their mind...and it didn't turn out that way. So.... the sadness came.

"What things?" Jesus asked. (Luke 24:29) He asked what things brought on the sadness. He is still the same. The sadness we struggle against still concerns Him. Lord Jesus, do not let us be slow to perceive Your Presence with us and in our circumstances. As You did then, on the road to Emmaus, do today…. in the places where we are, the roads we walk on… thru Your Holy Spirit, walk with us and reveal truth to us. As we open our Bible, teach us and enlighten us just as You opened scripture to these travelers on the road to Emmaus.

INFORMATION

How much information to you have? How much is available that you don't have? How much of what you have is accurate?

"What things?", the Traveler asked.

The two traveling on the road to Emmaus had some information about Jesus. He was from Nazareth. He was an inspired speaker, a foreteller of future events. He was powerful in the things He said and did, dynamic. The religious elite had orchestrated His death, a crucifixion. And His body was not in the tomb, it had vanished. I wonder, what do you know about Jesus? What information do you have? Have you even scratched the surface of knowing? .... I haven't. The more I learn, the more I realize how much I do not know and understand. I can hardly wrap my brain around it...God in flesh. (John 1:14)

Jesus said to them, "How foolish you are, and how slow of heart to believe all that the prophets have spoken! Then, beginning with Moses and all the Prophets, He explained to them what was said in all the Scriptures concerning Himself." (Luke 24:25,27)

Moses...that would be the first 5 books of our Bible. THAT is where Jesus started when He decided to explain Himself to these travelers. You see, scripture is ALL about Jesus. From beginning to end, it's about Jesus. From the garden, He has been spoken of and promised. The curse that fell on mankind is only in Him removed. The prophets message was all about Him. The chosen people of God, was all about Him and His Message to the world.

Will you go to Moses and all the Prophets of scripture, open the Bible, and ask Him to show you what is said there concerning Himself? Just like the road to Emmaus, He comes to help us and give us knowledge and understanding when we use what we have already been given. Just as then, there is much more to know about Jesus than the circumstances of His birth and death. So very much more....

POLLEN

There is a green mist in the air. Thankfully, I remembered to start the allergy medicine in time. I've decided not to complain.

I love springtime. I love the budding trees, the fresh growth, the flowers…it always makes me think about Day Three. "Let the earth bring forth grass… herbs… trees…." (Gen.1:11) God had already prepared the place for all this vegetation, He had prepared the earth…light, soil, water. Everything to support plant life was in place, inspected, and approved. Then He spoke and the earth burst forth.

Imagine the earth birthing all plant life for the first time. Imagine how beautiful, how fresh and tender. The colors appearing…on the backdrop of an earth newly divided into dry land and seas. Never again has it been just like that. God said it once. "Let the earth bring forth…." "And it was so." (Gen. 1:11) And it is still so. Just take a look around. He is so good.

HORSES

We don't ride horses like some folks do…but we have had horses for years. We had a horse named Dutch for many years. He became sick with age and finally died.

There are many teachings in scripture using the horse for illustration. "Do not be like the horse…which has no understanding but must be controlled by bit and bridle or they will not come to you." (Ps. 32:9)

Old Dutch was like that. He was hard to catch. Once the bit was in his mouth, he was completely different. And these last few weeks, he has been different. He was old, he probably had cancer, or a failing heart…and he didn't run when approached.

Aren't we so like that? God calls us, and we prance off with our proud tail in the air, blowing back at Him, refusing to answer? When He finally gets His Hand on us, we realize how foolish we were to struggle against Him, that He is kind and gentle, only wanting to groom us and use us for the very purpose we were created. When we are so tired and worn out from our running, when we grow old and weak, sick, needy…we welcome His Presence and His Touch.

I often joke that I am old and tired. But I am not. Neither am I young and ignorant. I have matured, I have experiences, I have training from life and from the Spirit of God working in my life.

Father, help us not to run when You call, but rather to anxiously submit to Your call. Lord, we want to willfully follow, fulfilling the very purposes You have for our life. Help us that we might do that while we are young and strong…not waiting until we exhaust ourselves with running, or when we have become weak and sick. But thank You Father God, that even then you love us and comfort us. Oh God, we want to have no regrets of being disobedient to Your call.

ROW

Did you ever hear someone say 'That's a hard row to hoe."? I remember as a kid hearing older people saying that and I remember thinking they were saying 'road'.... It didn't make a bit of sense to me then. Hoeing is hard period. I avoid it. I bought a garden tiller to do most of that for me. I am thankful for machinery! But the principle behind that old saying is the same even with a garden tiller.

When you start down a row, if it's not straight, it is very difficult. You can't turn around in the middle of a row, you have to go on thru it, even if for some reason, you decide you don't want to. Once you undertake a row, you're committed to finishing it, or destroying it trying to get out of it.

I don't like that truth. I've started down some rows that got very hard to hoe... and really wanted out. "No one who puts his hand to the plow and looks back is fit for service in the kingdom of God." (spoken by Jesus in Luke 9:62)

"So, do not throw away your confidence; it will be richly rewarded. You need to persevere so that when you have done the will of God, you will receive what He has promised... my righteous one will live by faith..." (Hebrews 10:35-36, 38)

That settles it. This row is hard. But He asks me to be completely committed, not halfhearted, and to finish it.

BRACED

My wrists have often had braces on them. I've done such repetitive motion for so many years, there's some wear and tear going on in there, they get tired, weak, and ache They need support and rest, thus, the braces.

I've talked to God about them, thought He might be willing to just zap them. And He has the power…but for now, I believe He just wants me to rest them when I can. So, I got two braces to wear when I'm sleeping or not working at something. The braces keep them from moving much, forcing me to allow those muscles etc. to be still and rest. I thought about Moses and his tired old arms. Moses had these thousands of people who looked to him for leadership in every matter. Moses was the standard bearer. He held the rod that had turned into a snake before Pharaoh, the rod that had been held out over the water as it parted for their escape from Pharaoh's army. The rod that brought the lifesaving water out of the rock in the waterless desert.

Then they got to Rephidim, and the descendants of Esau, the Amalekites attacked them. Once again, all eyes were on Moses. What now? "Choose some of our men and go out to fight the Amalekites. Tomorrow, I will stand on top of the hill with the staff of God in my hands." (Ex. 27:9) So, it was done, the soldiers were chosen and sent, and "Moses, Aaron, and Hur went to the top of the hill. As long as Moses held up his hands, the Israelites were winning, but whenever he lowered his hands, the Amalekites were winning." (vs. 10,11)

Talk about pressure!! Talk about tired arms!! Imagine the heaviness of everything being affected by your behavior, your holding up the standard…. I might have thrown it down and hoped for the best. "When Moses' hands grew tired, they took a stone and put it under him and he sat on it. Aaron and Hur held his hands up, one on one side, one on the other, so that his hands remained steady till sunset." (vs.12)

Moses had the desire, his heart was right, but he needed help in shouldering the responsibility. He needed propping up.... a way to rest even in the midst of doing the work of God.

How might we do that for each other? How might we wrap around each other like this brace on my wrist? Supporting and enabling... even encouraging rest, but without being removed from our own battle station?

Lord, help us to answer in obedience to Your call, and report to our post, ready for battle.

Even the strongest of us grow weary and need the Aarons and Hurs to come alongside us, to enable us to rest, even as we continue to fight and hold our position. And we need Your Holy Spirit, Who is our Strength in every situation. Thank you...You are so good.

PERJURY

Willfully making a false oath. Swearing to something that is false...

There was a time when truth was expected and assumed. People could be taken at their word, to do what they said they would do...whatever they told you was so. Not so much anymore it seems. Perjury could cost you dearly under Jewish law.

"If a malicious witness takes the stand to accuse a man of a crime, the two men involved in the dispute must stand in the Presence of the Lord before the priests and the judges who are in office at the time. The judges must make a thorough investigation, and if the witness proves to be a liar, giving false testimony .... then do to him as he intended to do to the other.... You must purge the evil from among you." (Deut. 19: 16-19)

Wow! You lie to get the other guy...you get what you were setting him up for! Fast forward...Mark 14 "The chief priests...were looking for evidence against Jesus, to put Him to death..." "...some stood up and gave...false testimony against Him...yet their testimony did not agree..." The very ones who held the positions to enforce the laws they lived by, ignored that law. They LOOKED for evidence, it didn't matter how accurate it was. Not only did they not enforce their law, they did not punish the perjurers, they became involved IN the act. "Are you not going to answer?" they asked Jesus. Today, as then, a person on trial is not required to answer questions that would show himself to be guilty.

"Jesus remained silent." and by His very silence, He convicted them of their wrongdoing, convicted them of breaking the law they claimed to uphold. Until...

"the high priest asked Him, 'Are You the Christ, the Son of The Blessed One?'"

"I Am".

Jesus never denied His Father. And they crucified Him for it.

LOOKED

I remember as a child how my daddy could just look at me and I was disciplined. There was no need for words, I knew what he would be saying had he spoken, rather than push him into speaking…I'd comply!

It is said that the eyes are the windows of the soul. It is true that the eyes tell so very much.

"The Lord turned and looked straight at Peter." (Luke 22:61)

Peter was a brave man. He'd lashed out with his sword against armed soldiers, way out numbered… But he'd go down fighting… Except that Jesus called him off and even healed the damage he'd managed to do. (I would like to hear that story from Malchus, the guy whose ear Peter cut off and Jesus healed!) I can only imagine how confused Peter must have been. Jesus had instructed them to take swords. (vs.36) Now he was telling them not to use them. So often, Peter gets remembered for his failures, and I'm glad they are recorded because I identify with him so much. But let's not forget how committed and brave he was. He did use the sword he'd been told to take, however misguided he was. He did get out of the boat and walk on the water, even if he did sink moments later. The rest of the crew sat inside the boat and watched. Peter ran away with the rest of the disciples when Jesus was arrested, but he followed. He saw what was happening. He witnessed it. I'm thankful for that, for I was reading it last night and again moments ago,. He followed, still in the confused mindset of all the events that were happening so fast. How terrifying it must have been, and he was 'sifted like wheat' as he fell into denying that he even knew Jesus much less was he a follower. Then Jesus looked at him.

It makes me want to cry to think how Peter felt then. He'd heard the third call of the night moments before. Then the look….

But how precious our Lord is that he made sure Peter knew that this wasn't a surprise to Him. Jesus made sure that Peter would remember His warning…

Jesus had prayed for Peter. "…Satan has asked to sift you as wheat. But I have prayed for you…that your faith may not fail. And WHEN you have turned back…strengthen your brothers." (vs.32)

How many times Peter must have gone over those last hours and the last conversations.

I hope he never missed the fact that Jesus knew about his failures before he failed. He knew that Peter would turn back even stronger than ever, to strengthen his brothers.

And his sisters….

Thank You Lord for Peter.

TAXES

This is the day. I have to mail that check today.

Taxes aren't a new thing. There are stories of taxation all thru scripture. See if you relate to any of these...

"...We have had to borrow money to pay the king's tax on our fields and vineyards."(Neh.5:4)

"...his successor will send out a tax collector to maintain the royal splendor..." (Daniel11:20)

I can sure relate. The stories that go along with those passages are very interesting, too long and complicated for these short writings. You might check them out. The ruler of the Daniel passage was eliminated, poisoned by one of his employees. I confess that I resent writing those checks. I do NOT resent helping those who cannot help themselves. I do NOT resent contributing to legitimate needs or to supporting efforts to improve our culture.

"...look after orphans and widows in their distress..." (James 1:27)

"...we should continue to remember the poor..." (Gal. 2:10)

(In my humble opinion, more is spent on tearing down our culture than improving it.)

Scripture teaches that we should work together for the common good. Nothing is just about 'Me'. At least it shouldn't be...

"...these...were helping to support them out of their own means." (Luke 8:3)

I don't really like this next verse.... but I want to be obedient......

"Give everyone what you owe him: If you owe taxes, pay taxes... (Rom. 13:7)

I argue with God that I owe them. He reminds me, "Give to Caesar what is Caesar's..." (Matt. 22:21)

Then I complain to Him that it is NOT theirs, why should I be required to give it to them?! That check represents a lot of MY hard work. And again, He reminds me... "Look at the birds, free and unfettered, not tied down to a job description, careless in the care of God. And you count far more to Him than birds." (Matt. 6:26 The Message) He reminds me that I have no need unmet...I have MORE than enough. I wonder that our problems might be far less if everyone adhered to this standard of behavior..." If a man will not work, he shall not eat." (2Th. 3:10) So...off to work I go.

ALONE

I'll be alone this week-end. In a crowd...

I often feel alone. The weight of responsibility, struggles against personal issues, business decisions, financial needs and responsibilities, concerns about family, ...it gets heavy sometimes. Often, the enemy accuses and tries to deceive me...trying to convince me that I am alone...the only one. He is a liar. I am never alone. He tried that on Elijah...had him thinking he was the only one. Then the Lord answered.

"Go out and stand on the mountain in the presence of the Lord, for the Lord is about to pass by." (1 Kings 19:11)

Elijah had been God's mouthpiece. It got him a lot of problems to deal with, especially from Jezebel. She didn't like the message and she was intent on shutting him up. Elijah just got overwhelmed, and did what I often want to do...and have done. Run. Hide. At least he had run to a place that was connected with God...a place where Moses had met with God. Now that he was there, there was "a great and powerful wind......but the Lord was not in the wind. After the wind, there was an earthquake. But the Lord was not in the earthquake." (vs.11)

Ok...He's supposed to be passing by, you'd think it would be a really big thing...but the powerful displays were just shaking ground and blowing wind. No comfort there! "After the earthquake came a fire..." Surely God will communicate thru these appearances of flames...right? "But the Lord was not in the fire." (vs.12)

Sigh... I've looked for God and EXPECTED God to come to my aid in ways like that. Make a grand entrance Lord...come in and rock the house. And He certainly can and has done that. He's there in the powerful miraculous things He does. He's there in the megachurch gatherings, He's there in the big conferences with thousands gathered...He's there in the praise rallies. But it's just hard for me to hear Him in all that noise and activity. So, like Elijah, I'm going off to be alone, and I expect to hear The Whisper…in fact, He's already started this morning, with this reflecting time.

"After the fire came a gentle whisper…When Elijah heard it…. he pulled his cloak over his face and went out…." (vs. 13)

God shows up. Every single time I seek His Face…He shows up.

He is so very good.

REVELATIONS

Not the book in the Bible…that would-be Revelation, no S, not a plural. Only one revelation. However, I have had several revelations over the past few days…

Revelation is the act of disclosing or discovering to others what was before unknown to them. It is the disclosure or communication of truth to men by God Himself, or by His authorized agent.

We have a book in the Bible that contains the Revelation given to John. Yet really, every book of the Bible is revelation. There will always be yet another truth that we have not seen, understood, or applied. It is alive, The Living Word…always fresh and relevant.

There is a Divine Agent who brings the words on the pages to life, giving revelation of the truth there. Jesus said that The Father would send this unseen tutor to teach and instruct us, to be our Holy Reminder… Who will empower us to recall and to apply the truth we are given.

But He'll not force-feed us. He'll not impose His will over ours. "..how much more will your Father in heaven give the Holy Spirit to those who ask Him!" (Luke 11:13)

When I can't get it…when I don't understand what God wants, what scripture says, how to make decisions, where to go from here…I can ask for Help. And He will send Help. But The Holy Spirit of God is not like a pigeon. Pigeons will light on your head, crowd in around you, expecting, searching.

God's Holy Spirit "descended on Jesus in bodily form like a dove…" (Luke 3:22) We know that God does not change. (Num. 23:19, James 1:17, 1 Sam.15:29, Heb. 13:8) His nature and character have never changed and will never change. He is still today, like a dove. So, if you're waiting for Him to crowd in on you like a pigeon, forget it. But if you want His help, ask Him for it. Luke 11:13 tells us to ask. And when you ask…don't put conditions on it. He is trustworthy. There is no need for fear. Father how grateful I am for Your Holy Spirit.

TEMPLE

I have seen pictures of temples, read about temples...but a temple is not ordinary in our culture, so it takes effort to think about it. "You are the temple of God" Paul told the Corinthians, (1 Cor. 3:16)

All those who are disciples of Jesus Christ are temples of God. The Old Testament has many object lessons for us about this temple language. Solomon built a temple that had been long in coming. His Father began the project with the planning and gathering of materials to be used. "Then Solomon began to build the house of the Lord."(2 Chron.3:1)

Every single part of the temple has meaning, but recently, God called my attention to the Most Holy Place, the place where the Presence of God would come. "Solomon built the Most Holy Place....and overlaid the inside with ...fine gold." (vs.8) When I read this, the accuser asked me where the gold was in my heart. (He won't be able to do that always, Rev. 12:10) He got me thinking and searching, sorrowful that there was none that I saw..

Then I found another altar, the Tabernacle that was the first one, the temporary, portable one, the one where God manifested Himself to the wandering Hebrews in the wilderness. The structure was put together in great detail by Divine instructions. There would be sacrifices, and even the manner in which that was done was stipulated. "Make all the utensils.... pots to remove the ashes..." (Ex. 27:3)

Ashes!! Imagine ashes being anywhere around anything overlaid in gold. Disgusting! We have a wood stove, I know about ashes. The killing of animals and dealing with blood...that, I've thought about. Not the ashes though.

And then I realized...I've brought all these needless sacrifices into the altar of my heart, and they are just burned up! Nothing I can 'DO' is of any consequence to remove my guilt. The only sacrifice I need offer is a 'sacrifice of praise, the fruit of lips that confess His Name' (Heb. 13:15)

That doesn't mean I no longer 'DO' good things…'do not forget to do good and to share with others' (vs.16) ..but all those things are to be done in praise of Him and what He has accomplished in me. Else…. they are just burned to ash…creating a black veil that keeps me from seeing the overlay of gold on the altar of my heart…put there by Jesus Christ when He cleansed this temple and made me fit for His Presence.

It is finished. (John 19:30)

"There is no longer any sacrifice for sin." (Heb. 10:18)

'My body is a temple of the holy Spirit…I am not my own, I was bought at a price.

Therefore, I will honor God…" (1Cor. 6:20 personalized by me)

FORCE

Webster says that force is energy that may be exerted, that property which may produce action in another body is force.

I've wanted to force lots of things. I've wanted to force people who have addictions to just STOP. I've wanted to force people who refuse to consider the Message of Christ to just HEAR. I've wanted to force those who cause hurt to others to SEE. I've wanted to force those who won't bear their own personal responsibilities to GROW UP. Can't be done.

Personal choice is just that.... a personal choice. I can only choose for myself.

"But if serving the Lord seems undesirable to you...." (Joshua 24:15) Serving the Lord does seem undesirable at times. Our enemy still deceives us and lies to us. His MO hasn't changed.... (method of operation) In the garden, he caused Eve to question whether doing what God said was really in her best interest. Genesis 3 tells us how that devil questioned what God 'really' said....and why. "...God knows that when you eat.... you will know what He knows...", the serpent hissed. And Eve considered what he said, believed him, and the story continues.

Today, the enemy still will cause us to consider what God has said and why. IF we give him even a moment ...if we stop to consider his lies.... he still wants us to choose to know evil. (...that tree was knowledge of good AND evil... remember?) God always always, always says what He says for a reason. God will never ever force us to comply. Force is certainly within His power. He is the most powerful force that exists. But He has chosen to give us choice. There is and can be...no evil in Him. He longs for us to choose Him. "But if serving the Lord seems undesirable......then choose for yourselves.whom you will serve.."

Who do you serve? What do you serve? What is it that controls your choices?

Father forgive me when I consider the enemy's lies. Forgive me the times I've even for a moment questioned if what You ask of me is good. Help me to see the choices when they come…protect me from deception and enable me to choose You in every situation. "…for me, I choose to serve You."

STRETCH

In the verb form, it is to spread, to be extended without breaking...

There are times I've felt stretched so thin that I would indeed break. I have even had pity parties about it...invited others to the party to pity me, pity with me...and if I got no takers, I'd just go alone to the party.

We are all stretched. Mothers are stretched with responsibilities of the home, cooking, cleaning, homework, laundry, grocery shopping. Men and fathers are stretched to be the bread-winner, shoulder the responsibilities of maintaining the home and rearing children. Stretching in our workplace...whatever your role is, there are times of stretching.

The enemy will present escapes for those times. He is lying about them, but they may seem like a good idea at the time. People turn their backs on spouses, leaving, buying into the lie that there is no stretching in some other relationship. Greener pastures must be mowed as well. Sometimes, even more so ! People turn to alcohol and drugs. Partying or gambling...the list could go on and on. What might you add to it?

"...God will never let you down. He'll never let you be pushed past your limit...He'll always be there to help you come through it." (1Cor. 10:13 The Message)

We have all heard that. It's repeated so often that it sounds like an old cliché. But most of the time I hear it quoted, what I believe is the most important teaching in this verse is overlooked or omitted. "HE provides a way out..." (v.13 NIV)

Never will we be stretched in a way that we cannot bear it with His Help. Never...

This teaches us that when those times come, it is true that we can bear them... WITH HIM, with His help!! Not just alone, but with Him. There IS a limit to our power. There IS a place where we cannot stretch any further. When that time comes, when we feel like we are going to snap...He is there, and He is able. The question always is...do we ask? And when we ask, do we accept His answer and the provisions He makes? Do we follow the instructions He gives us in those times?

I confess, I don't always. Often, I'm so involved in my pity party I am not listening. But He waits til I'm thru whining...after I've stretched to my limit and found out I can go no further. Then I sit and listen...when I've exhausted all other avenues... What an insult to Him.

Father forgive me. Help me to seek YOUR counsel first. Help me to tune my ears to hear YOU. Give me a heart to trust what You say. You are always right. Even when the accuser comes against Your Word, bring to my remembrance that he lies...for You are always right. Always...

SELF-CONTROL

Self-control is a very personal subject. All of us have areas where we lack in controlling our habits, attitudes, and appetites.

Felix did. Paul was in Felix's jail, and Felix considered him an interesting way to spend an afternoon, so he sent for him in order to listen to him again. But Paul's conversation got a bit personal. "Paul continued to insist on right relations with God and His people, about a life of moral discipline and the coming judgment." (Acts 24: 25 The Message)

Paul was talking about living life by God's rulebook. He was getting too personal, you see, Felix had no control of self. He had met a woman he wanted, and took her...even though she was another man's wife. Felix saw no problem with doing whatever he felt like doing and whatever he was big enough to do. I feel sure he felt good about that.... I'm sure he thought he was a big bad guy, very strong and powerful. But he couldn't even master himself.

Today, we are the same. How often we are deceived by the enemy!! Strength is NOT displayed by doing whatever we feel like doing. Strength is displayed in self-control. And the opposite of that....? No control of self-displays a weak and vulnerable area. How will we ever be able to defeat the enemy when we can't defeat our own fleshly impulses? Self-control is in one of those lists in the Bible. "...make every effort to add to your faith goodness, and to goodness, knowledge, and to knowledge, self-control...."(2Peter 1:5)

I think of it as bricks in the wall of my temple. "Do you not know that your body is a temple of the Holy Spirit, Who is in you, Whom you have received from God?" (1 Cor.6:19) God has given a 'measure of faith' (Romans 12:3) The seed of faith must be planted, nurtured, and acted upon...and it grows. (Luke 17:6, 13:19) If it is not...it does not grow, and even perhaps dies. (James 2:14-17)

The brick added to faith is goodness or virtue. The word in the original language is 'arete' and it denotes an attribute of excellence, what in a moral sense gives man his worth, goodness of action. The next brick is knowledge, the participation in becoming aware and comprehending about something. So we have this bit of faith, we build on it by choosing 'good' over wrong/evil, then we make it our business to know what we need to know....and then this thing of self-control. It is foundational. We can have the conviction of faith, we can have the information and knowledge...but if we don't proceed to have the control over personal choices in behavior...the wall never gets any higher. Self-control is not optional. It is absolutely necessary....

FAITH

Growing up, I heard a lot of sermons about the impossibility of being saved by 'faith alone'. Still today, it's a hot topic. The questions of 'works' enters into the equation. It is argued that one can be saved then loose that salvation.... or one might not have in fact BEEN saved in the first place.

The writer of Hebrews defined faith as 'being sure of what we hope for and certain of what we do not see.' (Heb. 11:1) We all live by faith. We believe that when we stand up, we will be anchored to the earth beneath us, even though we can't see the force of gravity. We believe the little gadget we all carry around everywhere we go, will enable us to speak to someone miles away, even though we can't see the digital signal that cellular phones work from.

There is a beginning point in faith. I believe in gravity because I've learned to walk and have never floated off the planet doing so. I believe in cell phones because I've experienced the convenience of owning one, (however, they are much more convenient now than that first bag phone I had !!)

What is the beginning point in faith in God? What is it the hope as far as He is concerned?

My beginning point was fear. I had no love for Him, I had lots of respect for His authority, even though I resented it. I resented it for years,. But I'm thankful for it now. "The fear of the Lord is the beginning of wisdom" (Ps. 111:10, Pro. 1:7, & Pro. 9:10) My fear kept some pretty tight boundaries around me. We call it legalism these days. I no longer live with those fences, but I believe those fences kept me safe, kept me from making mistakes I might have made if I'd had the freedom I now enjoy. Some people don't do well fenced in that way, they break down the fences in rebellion. Thank You, God, fear kept me from doing so.

I'm no longer fearful of Him. The rest of those promises are true too… "…all who follow His precepts have good understanding."(Ps. 111:10) "…fools despise wisdom and discipline."(Pro. 1:7) "..knowledge of the Holy One is understanding." (Pro. 9:10)

God is to be revered and respected, and He is certainly to be feared if not found to be in His Son, Jesus Christ. He IS Who He says He is…and He WILL do what He says He will do.

I have complete faith in that.

JUDGING

You can know a tree by its fruit.

After someone has handed down a verdict about someone else, I've heard 'I'm not judging, I'm just inspecting fruit'. I confess, I'm guilty of using that excuse myself…judging fruit.

But I believe God has shown me the fruit of my own heart in that matter. "…the fruit of The Spirit is love, joy, peace, patience, kindness, goodness, faithfulness, gentleness, and self-control.' (Gal. 5:22-23) I don't see fruit inspecting in that list, nor does that list look like the attitude of my fruit inspecting heart. In fact, it might fit the list of a few verses earlier in that chapter of Galatians! "discord…jealousy…selfish ambition …dissensions …factions…envy" (verses 19-21)

It is true that our character is displayed in the fruit we bear out in our lives. But what kind of fruit is born out of the fruit inspector? When I inspect another person's fruit, what kind of attitude is in my own heart, and do I live up to that standard myself? Do I criticize or condemn them for not having Grade A fruit, when my own fruit is not Grade A? And let's not be deceived… we're not grading apples against apples…. we're grading fruit.

It doesn't matter that 'I' am not guilty in the fruit/thing I'm inspecting in someone else. I may not have that particular rotten apple to deal with in my own life, but I've got some rotten peaches.

The best lessons learned are often those learned out of negative examples. I don't want to be compromising about sin, but neither do I want to be blind to the sin in my own life. When I see rotten fruit in someone else, I want to see it for what it is, but have a heart to encourage and challenge them to a higher standard, not just chunk it out with the trash.

And I want to never, ever have that kind of fruit in my own life.

LIBERTY

We have a statue that we've attached that word to…I wonder if we all share the same definition of what liberty is.

"I shall walk in liberty, for I have sought Thy precepts." (Ps. 119:45)

It seems to me that the more 'freedom' that has been allowed, the more choices people are allowed to take, the worse our culture has become. And it's because when we can choose for ourselves both good AND evil…when we are not seeking to do what is right in God's eyes…we choose poorly. We have chosen much evil in this nation.

I rejoice in the liberty and freedom that I have in Christ. It is no longer because I feel forced to choose His way, for that is not freedom. I have the liberty to choose like the couple in the garden. I can choose good or I can choose evil…and I must choose. God does not insist that I choose His good way. Because I have grown to know Him and love Him, I have come to understand that what He says is always the right way, for my own best interests and the best interests of others. (EVEN when it doesn't LOOK that way!) The choice to follow His good way always brings life, never death. Only by choosing His good way do I find liberty from the permanently established rule that sin=death. "…the law of the Spirit of life in Christ Jesus made me free from the law of sin and of death."(Rom. 8:2)

People who spout off about their freedoms and live their lives making ungodly decisions are not free. They are in the worst kind of bondage. Choices that are not lined up with God's standard bring death. "The wages of sin is death.."(Rom. 6:23) Always.

You can complain about it, hit the dislike button, or throw a fit about your 'rights'…but God is Creator, He gets to pick…what He says IS. Only within the boundaries of Christ is there freedom, for only there is an escape from this curse of sin and death. "If the son shall make you free, you shall be free indeed." (John 8:36) " ...the free gift of God is eternal life in Christ Jesus our Lord."(Romans 6:23)

"For freedom, Christ has set us free..."(Gal. 5:1)

Jesus, The Messiah.... is the good way. My liberty is in my relationship with my Savior. He has removed the curse. And because of that, I am His slave. I will strive to serve Him well.

PERSEVERANCE

Keep on keeping' on. Get back in the saddle. Shake it off. Keep on truckin'. However you phrase it, the message is the same…

Endurance. Persistence. In Greek, the original language of New Testament scripture, it is 'hupomone'. It is a bearing up under, an enduring as to things or circumstances. patience and constancy under suffering in faith and duty. "…prayer is essential in this ongoing warfare. Pray hard and long. Pray for your brothers and sisters. Keep your eyes open. Keep each other's spirits up so that no one falls behind of drops out." (Eph. 6:18 The Message)

I want never to forget the reality of the battle ground on which I stand. There IS a spiritual war going on. There IS a battle of good vs. evil. The enemy is still assaulting God's creation. He is defeated, but until he is cast into the abyss, he continues to deceive and lie. How tiring it gets sometimes. I hear him trying to tell me it's useless. It is NOT.

My God is bigger than any demon. He is bigger than any stronghold. He is mightier than any addiction. He is able to heal any hurt, any painful thing. The only thing that stops Him is our refusal. I wrestle sometimes with the free choice He has given, wishing that in some situations He'd take that free will away and insist on better choices. He would not be holy and perfect were He to do that.…and we would not have a capacity to love, we would be mere robots. So I stand on the battlefield, suited up with the armor of God. (Ephesians 6:13-17)

I have the belt of truth. The enemy's lies will not pierce me.

My heart is shielded with the breastplate of HIS righteousness, not my own.

My feet are fitted with readiness.

I have a shield of faith in the God of creation with which I can extinguish all the flaming arrows of the evil one.

My mind is protected by the helmet of my salvation, the enemy's lies will not enter my mind and cause me to be deceived.

I have the Sword of The Holy Spirit of God, I know what He has said, and I will use the authority that is mine in Jesus Christ to speak that Word to all the demonic forces of the spiritual realm. "Pray for me, that whenever I open my mouth, words may be given me so that I will fearlessly make known the mystery of the gospel...pray that I may declare it fearlessly, as I should." (Eph. 6:19,20)

ENOUGH

What is enough? When is enough, enough? Is there such thing as enough? Who gets to decide?

Webster says that enough is that which is adequate to the wants. A sufficiency. That which is equal to the powers of abilities. I am thankful that God doesn't call enough, enough like I do. He has been so very patient with me for so many years. He has done such work in me, and continues to do so. He didn't throw up His Hands like I am prone to do. "I have had enough, Lord" (Elijah in 1 Kings 19:4)

However, I sometimes seem to hear Him say, as He did to Moses, "That is enough, do not speak to Me anymore about this matter" (Deu. 3:26) When God says something, He means it. When He answers my prayer, He has answered. And I must accept His answer. When I have had enough... that which is equal to my power and ability, He is sufficient. "My grace is sufficient for you, for My power is made perfect in (your) weakness." (2 Cor.12:9) "I can do everything through Him Who gives me strength."(Phil.4:13)

I wonder that perhaps enough is not about a moment in time. Perhaps it isn't about a requirement to be fulfilled. It is about content. "...you have spent enough time in the past doing what pagans do..." (1 Peter 4:3). "You've already put in your time in that God-ignorant way of life, partying night after night, a drunken and profligate life. Now it's time to be done with it for good." (Peter 4:3 The Message)

"You have planted much, but have harvested little. You eat, but never have enough. You drink, but never have your fill. You put on clothes, but are not warm. You earn wages, only to put them in a purse with holes in it." (Hag. 1:6)

"You have made your way around this hill country long enough...." (Deut. 2:3)
"..the Lord your God has blessed you in all the work of your hands...He has watched over your journey...you have not lacked for anything..." (vs.7)

"I know that You can do all things, no plan of Yours can be thwarted."(Job 42:2)

He is Elohim, Mighty Creator God, Jehovah Jireh, the God Who provides, and Yahweh Shammah, the God Who is there....

That is, and will always be.... enough.

CONSECRATE

This is one of those words that is seldom used anymore, unless perhaps in poetry.

We use words like dedicate and devote. Consecration doesn't really make a person place, or thing really holy, (...it is GOD who makes holy), but it declares that person, place, or thing to be set apart, to be especially dedicated and devoted to the service of God. We have ceremonies to dedicate children. In those ceremonies, the parents devote themselves to bringing the child up to know God.

Does all that 'to-do' really matter? Does it change the way the future unfolds? Does it really matter what we 'say' over a person, place, or thing? What good is ceremony? Words spoken...then forgotten....so what? Perhaps in some circles words don't mean much. I regret to say that our culture has lost the sense of value in them. There was a time when a thing spoken could be taken for absolute truth. Vows were said only when they were considered thoroughly and there was intention to keep them.

God spoke to His chosen people, the Israelites, "Consecrate yourselves and be holy, because I Am the Lord your God. Keep My decrees and follow them. I am the Lord, Who makes you holy." (Lev. 20:7-8) It was nothing the people did that made the difference...it was GOD Who made the difference in them. He has spoken to me... " ...you are a chosen people. A royal priesthood, a holy nation, a people belonging to God, that you may declare the praises of Him Who called you out of darkness into His wonderful Light." (1 Peter 2:9) '... from nothing to something, from rejected to accepted.' (vs. 10 The Message)

'Friends, this world is not your home, so don't make yourselves cozy in it. Don't indulge your ego at the expense of your soul. Live your life...so that your actions will refute prejudices...they will be won over to God's side and be there to join in the celebration when He arrives. Make the Master proud of you by being good citizens…It is God's will that by doing good, you might cure the ignorance of the fools who think you're the danger…exercise your freedom by serving God, not by breaking the rules.' (vs. 11-16 The Message)

I am consecrated. My home is consecrated. I work in a place that is consecrated. I live on ground that is consecrated. Some may forget…they may disregard words that spoke vows. They may turn away and go after other gods. determine again today that I will not.

RE-START

Re-start.. Seems like every time I get in the very middle of something on this computer, it has downloaded upgrades and needs to 're-start'.

I've wondered what all that upgrade stuff is about, is it really necessary? Sometimes I liked things better the old way, before the so called improvements. When things work, and fill my needs and requirements, why change it? If it ain't broke…don't fix it! The downloaded upgrades are bad enough, but then I have to stop what I'm doing and let this thing turn itself off and back on.

Then this morning, I was reading over some things I had written a while back, and I realize…there's an upgrade ! New information.

God will never get through with me. (…or you..) There will be regular upgrades. But we can refuse to download them…and we can refuse to install them…and we can refuse to re-start.

The data that is downloaded onto this computer is useless until it is installed into the brain of this machine. And even then, until the machine is turned off and starts up again, the data just sits somewhere inside the technological mind, doing no good, making no difference.

So what kind of downloads are available? Scripture spills over with truths that are current to my situation and circumstance, now and tomorrow, there will be truths that are current for that now. And next month, next year… every 'now' that I walk on this earth, in this body, there will be truths that are current for that 'now'.

Just because you may have read the Bible doesn't mean a thing. The scripture you read for that 'now'…is not necessarily the scripture for this 'now'. Every time I open my Bible, seems as if some phrase or concept will leap off the page and I wonder… 'surely that hasn't been there…how could I have missed this?' The truth contained in scripture is 'living and active. ..it penetrates even to dividing soul and spirit, joints and marrow...it judges the thoughts and attitudes of the heart.' (Heb.4:12) It will never need upgrades, it is complete.

It is US who need upgrades. 'Study to show yourself approved to God....' It is us who need to install them 'correctly handling the word of truth.' (2 Tim. 2:15 KJV, NIV)

I have learned with previous computers that when I don't keep up to date, it causes problems later that take more than the few minutes required to install and re-start. I don't want to live my life like that. I.want to stay current with the God of the universe. So...I'm re-starting this morning. Got an upgrade yesterday, installed it, and I'm operating with new attitudes and motives today. He is ALWAYS current...

BABBLING

I fear I've done a lot of babbling. I wonder how much harm and hurt I have done with some of them. I wonder if I've been in social settings so long that I don't even notice.

Paul said to shun them. He said they would only increase to more ungodliness. (2Tim.2:16) Matthew Henry says in his commentary on this passage that error is very productive. Is that not a horrifying thought?! Error...produces itself. And he goes on to say that error can overthrow faith. God forbid.

The NIV calls it 'godless chatter' and tells us to avoid it. (vs. 16) The Message always drives home the point in street language... 'Stay clear of pious talk, Words are not mere words, you know. If they are not backed by a godly life, they accumulate as poison in the soul.' I sure don't need any poison injected into my soul, especially by my own mouth! So, my babblings are some pretty serious stuff. I determine to examine the words I speak...and the words I write...and ask God to reveal to me how HE sees it. I can justify my words I'm sure...we all can project the guilt onto someone else, justify our actions and words because of someone else's WORSE actions and words. Who gets to decide that? Not me. And not you. It is God who determines, and he sees my heart. And yours.

Let's make a deal...tomorrow, I'm going to begin to monitor my babblings and see if there is any godless chatter going on. With ME. I am sure the devil will point out a LOT of it coming from someone else's mouth. But I'm asking God to reveal to me what I am blinded to in myself. For if it is there... it needs to go.

This may hurt.

MISERABLE

Pity party alert! I am miserable.

It has been years since I've felt this misery. Oh, aches and pains come and go. The occasional virus finds its way into my body and makes me feel icky for a few days. I get down in the dumps about situations. My body gets tired quicker than it used to and I can't keep up the pace I once could. But not like this misery...

Have you ever just considered how powerless we really are? Just stop and think about what can stop us right in our tracks.... shut us down like flipping off the electricity. I am reminded that I am absolutely at the mercy of God and His universe....and the whims of my own choices.

I chose to weed my flowerbeds. And I chose to put that little ivy twig in the pile to be picked up (in my bare arms) and thrown over the ditch out of my yard. I had the knowledge of that evil...(that pretty little green ivy twig only LOOKS pretty). I have the knowledge of the truth...(the little ivy twig is poison).

So...now I am miserable. One touch and I am slowly becoming a mass of whelps that hinder every aspect of my life. I thought about Job. "If only my anguish could be weighed and all my misery be placed on the scales! It would surely outweigh the sand of the seas..."(Job 6:2)

I suppose I'm being a little dramatic, but there's a lesson to be learned here...a lesson far deeper than not handling poison ivy. When I know the danger and warnings about something...pay attention! Don't think 'I can handle this...'. 'I will be really careful' 'Just this once.'

As it is with poison ivy, so it is with all the things God has cautioned us about. '...let us throw off everything that hinders and the sin that so easily entangles us, and let us run with perseverance the race that is marked out for us.' (Heb. 12:1)

I pray often to be easily taught. I haven't had a lesson like this in years….and I doubt I'll soon forget the misery of this itch that I suffer as a result of my own arrogance and poor choices. Who am I to think that I can change the rules of nature? And who am I to think that I am ever safe outside the boundaries of God's will for my life? I can't even handle a little twig of ivy….

GROANING

'anachah'. A moaning or sighing response brought on by physical, spiritual, or mental despair involving both the body and soul.

"I am worn out from groaning, all night long I flood my bed with weeping..." (David in Ps.6:6)

Bless David's heart. This is the same guy who stood with only a slingshot and stones to face a literal giant from an enemy army. I just love how God has given us so many people whose lives we can learn from...people who are the same as me. And you. These characters in the Bible aren't super-heroes. They aren't from another planet endowed with supernatural powers. They just serve a super-natural God...the God I serve. The God you serve. David had a lot on his mind when he wrote this Psalm. And I am so thankful that he was so brutally honest. He pours his heart out, in tears, completely honest with the God whose love he was so secure in. He didn't feel inclined to paint a prettier picture and pretend it was real. He didn't fake it. He didn't deny what he felt. He faced it within himself and took it to God. All the ugly of it...

Paul teaches this in 2 Cor. 10:5. "We demolish arguments and every pretension that sets itself up against the knowledge of God, and we take captive EVERY thought to make it obedient to Christ." (my emphasis)

This thing doesn't happen by accident, this taking captive every thought, (or any thought at all!) I believe it is an 'on purpose' thing. We have to realize FIRST just what our thoughts are, and we can be wrong! "The heart is deceitful above all things and beyond cure. Who can understand it?" (Jer.17:9)

We cannot know and trust our own heart. For we don't know what may lie there, Peter certainly didn't. He, like David, was brave. He proceeded to attack when the soldiers came following Judas, to take Jesus from the garden. Then during the long night ahead, Peter hid like a scared animal and swore he didn't know Jesus. "Then he began to call down curses on himself and he swore to them, 'I don't know the man!!'" (Mt. 26:74)

I wonder how many nights Peter might have groaned all night, weeping in his bed. Regret. Sorrow. Shame. Not many. I don't think so anyway.

"Don't be alarmed...you are looking for Jesus who was crucified. He has risen,...go, tell his disciples....and Peter..." (Mark 16:6,7) "...He appeared to Peter, and then to the Twelve." (1 Cor. 15:5)

That is the Jesus I love.

CAN'T

I've been told many times in years past… 'Can't can't do anything…' (cain't is the way we say it around here…) There's a lot of truth in that. If you decide you can't. You probably cannot. You decide up front, decision is made…

I was reading this morning about Mary Magdalene, Mary the mother of James, and Salome going to anoint the body of Jesus. On their way, they thought about the big stone that would be blocking the entrance. They knew that stones were rolled over tombs. Perhaps they didn't think about that obstacle before setting out that early morning. "…who will roll the stone away from the entrance of the tomb?' (Mark 16:3)

The stone was already gone. NOT to let Jesus out… He later appeared into locked room. No, the stone was gone in order for us to enter. The stone is still gone. If you think you can't enter, you've just decided you 'cain't'. Don't give me the excuses…I don't need them. Tell Him your excuses.

"I just don't have time"
"I can't comprehend"
"I don't understand"
"It is too hard"
Add your own excuse for not entering…what stops you?

That empty tomb is a fact, it testifies to you and me that Jesus did what He said He would do. He IS Who He said He is. He kept His promise to rise from the dead, defeating the ultimate enemy of all mankind. He kept that promise, so we can believe He will keep all the others as well.

Don't decide to not make the trip because you think there's a stone in the way. He will see that there is no stone to block your way. But you must get up and make the trip. If you decide that an obstacle will stop you…. It will. And the enemy will rejoice.

AROMA

Aroma… just a scent, a smell, .a little whiff of a fragrance can stir all sorts of sensations up can't it? I walked into a store yesterday and smelled strawberries. The power of smell is amazing to me. An aroma can't be seen but it can sure invoke some power!! Make me hungry or make me ill. Make me sleepy. or refresh and awaken. Soothing or invigorating. What smells good to me might not smell nice to you. I can't fathom that anyone would not love strawberries…but some people don't.

"We are to God the aroma of Christ among those who are being saved and those who are perishing." (2 Cor. 2:15)

I want to be the aroma of Christ, don't you? But we need to know that that won't smell good to everybody. To those who are perishing, it may have a stench. The message of Christ is life. But to those who refuse it, it is death…. 'for the wages of sin is death…the gift of God is eternal life in Christ Jesus our Lord.' (Rom. 6:23)

"To the one, we are the smell of death: to the other, the fragrance of life. And who is equal to such a task? Unlike so many, we do not peddle the word of God for profit. On the contrary, in Christ we speak before God with sincerity, like men sent from God." (2 Cor.6:16-17)

The message of Christ is the sweetest of any aroma. I can't fathom that anyone would not be drawn to it. But some are not. That does not negate my role…I am to BE the aroma of Christ…in whatever place I am…whatever role I play. It is not what I do., but what He may do through me…not on what I am capable of, but what He is capable of accomplishing through me, in spite of my weaknesses. I can do nothing out of my own merit, but 'I can do everything through Him Who gives me strength' (Phil. 4:13)

I want to smell like Him. And I pray that that scent will be pleasant to everyone around me and make them want Jesus. He is so good.

COMPLICATED

When asked about relationship status, I often see or hear people say 'it's complicated'....

All relationships are complicated. Some more so than others I suppose. It seems to me that the relationships we have that are so very complicated have gotten that way from our own poor choices.

Read the story of Abram and his childless wife. (Gen.16) There was a promise of God. There would be a son. God said so. Yet, it hadn't come to pass yet and Sarai thought perhaps she needed to help God out a bit. So, according to the custom of the day, she sent one of her female servants to her husband. (I can't fathom that...but I read that it was common in the culture of that day.) A child born to this servant would be considered the child of the servant's master .Sarai would finally get what she longed for. Then it began to get complicated. (An understatement, I'm sure !!)

Jealousy. Resentment. Mistrust. Blame. Regret.

I'm prone to think Abram could have nipped this problem in the bud. But he didn't, and after the relationship with the servant girl was established, it could not be un-done. The literal history of the world was changed. Ishmael was born. The Arabs are his descendants.

Complicated? Indeed so. But God is not hindered by our complications. He IS hindered by our refusal to deal with the consequences of our own choices. It is never wise to manipulate circumstances. But when we have done so, the best thing we can do is run TO God, not away from Him. Facing our complications face to face with the God of the universe is the best way to unravel any complicated situation. He has the most amazing way of cutting right through all the complicated messes we make. But we have to make that decision, be brave enough to look at it honestly, with ourselves and with Him....and trust Him enough to act on what He says.

It won't be easy. It won't be fun. But it will always be harder and more painful when we refuse to do so. There is absolutely nothing that is too complicated for God. And the amazing thing is that when we obediently place all of it in His Hands, He brings blessings out of those awful messes ! He is so good.

NECESSITY

Coffee in the morning. Chocolate. A good pillow. Books. Reading glasses. Phone. What would you put on the list?

My husband fusses because I take a bag of books everywhere we go. But I never know when I might have an opportunity to drag one out and read a while. It really depends on the circumstances…but we all have those necessary things, things we think we can't do without. I can't do without books. Especially my Bible. I don't do well without my morning coffee. My friends know I have to have at least a bite of chocolate after I've eaten. I can't read anymore without help from reading glasses. Like most of us these days, my phone is almost always close by. But are any of these things really as necessary as I tend to think? I doubt it.

What is necessary? Really and truly necessary?

Food. Water. Air. Is there anything else that is really necessary?

Jesus said there was one thing. "One thing only is essential…" (Luke 10: 42)

Let's not miss the one necessary thing.

Sit at His Feet today.

HARVEST

I'm looking forward to it already. The tiny little plants are promising. There are a few blooms on some of the plants...yet another promise. The ground was properly prepared, tilled and rid of clumps of grass. Rain came at a perfect time, releasing the fertilizer into the soil and providing the moisture necessary for germination. Seeds were planted and have pushed up thru the soil with amazing speed. The process of life is amazing. There will be a harvest. I want to be prepared and ready.

Pea sheller...check.
Jars and lids...check.
Freezer space...check
Freezer bags...woops...

Even though there is a lot yet to happen before that time, I want to be ready. (better buy more freezer bags!)

Jesus said, "The harvest is plentiful, but the workers are few." (Luke 10:2) What is your role in that? Do you realize you are in the middle of His field? There may be soil ready for a seed to be planted. It may be time to pluck out a weed that threatens to choke out the life of a seedling. There may be a need for watering. There IS a plentiful harvest, whether you think so or not... whether you see it with your eyes or not. Take the time element out, God is not limited by time...the harvest is there. He sees beginning to end, it is you and I that think within time limits.

It's not time to pick peas. But I have, and expect to again.

I may not witness a changed life today. But I have.... Praise God !!... and expect to again.

I dedicate my skills and abilities to Him, (parable of the talents, Mat.25). I am dependent on His 'equipping me for every good work' (2Tim.3:17) I am sent. (Luke 10:3, Mark 16:15)

Now…if I can just find the right row…...

BLESSING

Are you? How do you know? What gives it away that you are, or are not? Can you measure it? How? ....

I thought of what we call 'The Beatitudes' this morning when I wished a friend a happy birthday. I've heard those verses preached so many times... heard the word 'happy' substituted for 'blessed'. Defining it in the negative.... 'not miserable', 'not wretched', 'not deficient' ...or 'not lacking anything'

I've heard people respond to 'How are you?', with a simple statement... 'Blessed'. What does that mean exactly? Do we all have the same criteria for defining what it is to be blessed? 'Makarios' = blessed in the original language of The Beatitudes in Matthew 5. It has to do with having the favor of God. It has little to do with luck or favorable circumstances. (I'm afraid I tend to categorize things as being blessings by the favorable circumstances involved.)

I do know from my experiences with God that He can, He desires to, and He will bring blessing out of even the most difficult of circumstances, if I but place the entire thing into His Hand, trust Him with it completely, and wait. (waiting is really hard for me...) I believe the only thing that truly defines a state of blessedness is the Presence of God within the heart. When His Spirit is within, it doesn't matter the circumstances without. The blessedness manifests itself even in the worst of circumstances.

"When God raised up His Servant, He sent Him first to you to bless you by turning each of you from your wicked ways." (Acts 3:26) The state of my right standing before God, because of the death and resurrected Life of Jesus Christ, is my greatest blessing. He entered into our situation to change it. And because He did, I can be 'happy' even in mourning (vs.4), in persecution (vs.10), or any number of situations, because He 'will never leave me, never will He forsake me." (Heb. 13:5)

So, for anyone who feels wretched or miserable, for those who feel like they have some deficiency, some facet of their life lacking somehow, my Savior has just what you need. Don't fall for the enemy's lie, don't expect blessing to look a certain way. Don't miss it because it seems to contradict. God's way usually does contradict the world's way. Don't court a shadow, follow Jesus Christ. You'll be counting your blessings!

WORK

Warning!! Grouchy alert.…

It is raining as I sit here this morning for my quiet time. How I'd love to just stay here today. My sweet husband and I were wishing for rain yesterday as he helped me put out petunias in my flowerbeds. Our garden needed some fresh moisture too. This morning, the Lord has granted us rain.

We work in this family. My husband works his job, then comes home and works till dark on chores here at home. I work a job, then come home and prepare meals, though now only for the two of us. Our sons work. Then they do other activities. One will fish every spare moment. One will play a guitar with every free second he has. Where did the notion come from that people are not required to provide for themselves? "By the sweat of your brow you will eat your food until you return to the ground, since from it you were taken; for dust, you are and to dust you will return." (Gen. 3:19)

I love the street language of The Message. "Don't you remember the rule we had when we lived with you? "If you don't work, you don't eat." And now we're getting reports that a bunch of lazy good-for-nothings are taking advantage of you. This must not be tolerated. We command them to get to work immediately--no excuses, no arguments--and earn their own keep. Friends, don't slack off in doing your duty. If anyone refuses to obey our clear command written in this letter, don't let him get by with it. Point out such a person and refuse to subsidize his freeloading. Maybe then he'll think twice." (2 Thes.10-14 The Message)

I do have compassion on those who are in need. I know there are situations where people are unable to work. Yet so often, people who are 'unable' to work, are 'able' to do a lot of other things! And simply choosing to be idle is choosing to have an idle mind…and a mind not employed in good, will likely be doing evil. (ever hear that old saying, idleness is the devil's workshop?)

Sigh… Lord, help my grouchiness and unforgiving spirit. I thank You Father that I am able to work. Thank You that I do have a job and a great workplace. Thank You that You have provided for all my needs, given in abundance, not just bare necessities… and thank You that you have even empowered me to help others. And thank You for the rain.

CHANGES

I remember choosing that name for a salon. Now, I often think about the impact of a name, and marvel at how many changes have come to pass. Oh, we changed a lot of hair styles and hair colors. We joke that we all need to change up our hair every now and again. But the changes in the lives of those of us who spent our days there...and the changes that happen in the clients we become so close to...those are the changes that matter.

I am so far from perfect. So very far. But I testify that I am changed. I still struggle against my flesh and against the lies and traps of our enemy. I still make wrong choices, behave in wrong ways. But when I do, I want to feel the prick of The Holy Spirit and hear His reprimand...and I want to respond in obedience. He is always right. Always.

Everything changes. A look in the mirror will confirm that fact. Things droop and slide, grow in strange formations, bulging here and there...hair thins and loses its color. (that is job security for me.) Everything physical changes. Often not for the better. But what about the other part of us? As the wrinkles form on our faces, do we have corresponding wrinkles of soul? Or do we find that spiritual place within us becoming smoother, more at peace, and wiser? God forbid that our spirits should wither like our bodies do !

I sell services that fight against the signs of our aging. My trade involves hiding and camouflaging the evidence of age. But my mission and ministry is to make people aware of the cure for our disease, the remedy for the slow death that we are all experiencing. (...for the moment life was conceived, the process of death is inevitable...)

I want to look as good as I can look, and I want that for you too. But far beyond that, I want you to know the assurance that I know... 'Listen, I tell you a mystery: we will not all sleep, but we will all be changed...' (1 Cor. 15:51) You can be the cutest, most beautiful or most handsome person around. But ' I declare to you, brothers, (and sisters), that flesh and blood cannot inherit the kingdom of God, nor does the perishable inherit the imperishable.' (1 Cor. 15:50)

Changing your hair won't fix what is wrong with all of us. Changing the natural is just a temporary fix. But God can make changes that are permanent. Permanently permanent. And He wants to. But you get to choose. He gives you that right and will not take it from you.

"In the beginning, You laid the foundations of the earth, and the heavens are the work of Your Hands. They will perish, but You remain...Your years will never end. The children of Your servants will live in Your Presence..." (Ps. 102:25-28) He is the only thing that does not change.

WARNINGS

Fever, swelling, headache.…. Flashing red lights, sirens

When our bodies have something amiss, they are designed by The Creator to message us that something is wrong. We ache, run a fever, etc. When we see red lights flashing on the highway, we know there is something to pay attention to in order to avoid danger for ourselves.

We hear the sound of a smoke alarm in our home and we get to our children and crawl out, having been warned that we could die if we stood up. Warnings…

Our oldest son has always had a morbid curiosity about snakes. It's a love/hate relationship. We warned of the danger. He liked to stomp them with the heel of his boot. We warned again. Firmer. He stomped them still. Until the day the fangs stuck in the leather of his boot. I don't think he's stomped another one. He recently told us, (with the hair on his arms standing up), about seeing a cottonmouth water moccasin on the road. Of course, he had to stop and look. The snake had been killed, it's head was missing. Blood was pooled around the headless snake, drying on the hot pavement. Then… the body of the snake moved, slithering itself into an s-shape, writhing. (he shuttered as he told it..)

I've not been able to shake it from my mind, this headless, therefore venomless snake of snakes. 'Cottonmouth' is a name everyone around here knows and fears. They are deadly, and they are aggressive. Most snakes will run from people. Cottonmouths will come for you.

It dawned on me almost as I woke this morning, the parallel of this snake story and the sin in a believer's life. I am saved. I don't deserve it. I cannot be holy and perfect, therefore I could not stand in the Presence of a holy God. I fall short…it's called 'sin'. The death that I DO deserve, the eternal and spiritual death that separates from God,it is paid.…FOR me…BY Jesus Christ. It is finished, settled.

"I will put hatred between you and the women. Your children and her children will be enemies. Her Son will crush your head. And you will crush his heel." (Gen. 3:15 NIrV) The venom is gone. It can't take my life. But there is still danger of sin. It still writhes and can curl itself around in my life. It can ruin my credibility as a witness.

Our enemy strikes over and over. His venom is deadly to those who are not saved from it. His fangs can sink in deep, do tremendous damage, and bring on an eternal death. Don't mess with the snake…don't try to stomp its head… let Jesus do that for you. And then stay away from the writhing body, "… throw off everything that hinders and the sin that so easily entangles, and let us run with perseverance the race marked out for us." (Heb. 12:1)

ADVENTURE

Adventure is to risk, dare, chance…. a bold undertaking, staked upon unforeseen events, of which one has no direction…

When our boys were small and we loaded up in the car to go on a trip, they began asking questions. You know the kind, ' where are we going?'… 'why?'… 'where are we now?'… 'when are we going to be there?' My reply became 'think of it as an adventure.'

Those who know me best know how ridiculous that really is. I am not very adventurous. I like ordinary. Familiar. But God is adventurous. And He has said 'Follow Me.' (some twenty times in the New Testament)

Following Jesus is simple. Yet very demanding. Certainly adventurous. Never was there a bolder undertaking than stepping out of the glory of heaven into the flesh of humanity, knowing the death that loomed there. He has walked this road, lived this life, and 'has been tempted in every way, just as we are, yet without sin.' (Heb. 4:15)

And He says 'Follow Me.'
And I ask 'where are we going'…. and 'why?'….

'Come, follow me, and let the dead bury their own dead.' (Mat. 8:22) He asks me to follow Him above family approval, financial security, or any other condition I might set. He demands complete loyalty. He is first. Period. Nothing is to be placed over a total commitment to Him.

That is tough.

But experience has taught me that when He calls me, He equips me. He secures me. He provides for my needs.

Come on the adventure. Follow Him!!

DEFINING

Defining... Webster says it is determining the limits, describing the properties... to define is to determine or decide...

What is it that defines you? What determines the way you live your life, the way you spend your time? What factors determine the significance of your very existence? Or who/Who?

Can you give a definite answer to that? It gets complicated to think about for me...and has changed somewhat over the years. My desire is that Jesus Christ is the Who that defines my choices. I don't always get it right, but I keep trying, and He keeps helping and forgiving.

When I was a child, my parents were the defining element. There were boundaries, very tight ones. I somewhat resented them at the time, but realize as an adult that there was much security in them. Most of my limits were plainly set and decided for me. As a teenager and young adult, I struggled with defining who I was...it began to be up to me to determine, and it was hard.

I am a wife. When I was a young married woman in a new community, my home-town husband defined me. I got a little frustrated sometimes at being 'Pinkham's wife'.... the badge he wore defined him, and rightly so...but it sure didn't define me. I loved being 'Kerry's wife', but seemed to seldom hear myself to be defined that way. I am defined by my work. I am a hairdresser. When I meet someone in the grocery store, excuses are offered for the bad hair day. (I promise. I'm really not inspecting every head of hair I see. I am NOT the hair police either!!! ...)

When we had children, I became largely defined by them. I am a mother. Their mother. My life was lived out meeting their needs and participating in their activities...making choices for them and trying to help them learn to make good decisions. Now they are grown, one has children of his own. My definition changed... I'm being redefined...I am MiMi.... (it's great, by the way!)

It is a process that will be ever-changing as long as I exist. The roles change, the circumstances of life change, and we grow and change with life as it passes. Moses asked for a definition…he wanted a name…. "Suppose I go to the Israelites and say to them, 'The God of your fathers has sent me to you,' and they ask me, 'What is his name?' then what shall I tell them?" God said to Moses, 'I AM WHO I AM'. This is what you are to say to the Israelites: 'I AM has sent me to you.'" (Ex. 3:13-14)

God says 'I AM'…. and He IS… Eternal and unchanging in power and character. Stable and secure. He has His very Being of Himself…only Himself. Hard to comprehend. He says "I AM". And I say 'Yes, You ARE !!'

But I am ever changing, 'being transformed into His likeness.' (2 Cor. 3:18 NIV) '..our lives gradually becoming brighter and more beautiful as God enters our lives and we become like Him.' (2 Cor. 3:18 The Message) Hallelujah.

DELIVERY

Hospitals have rooms that are specified for deliveries. Stores have big doorways for theirs. Kevin the UPS guy and Jerry the Fed-Ex guy do a lot of our deliveries. I'm expecting some deliveries today at the salon.

In years past, I was delivered of two healthy baby boys. Big ones, I might add, 9 pounders. I was quite ready to be delivered of them too!

Webster defines 'deliver' to free, to release, rescue, save to give or to transfer, put into another's hand or power, pass from one to another. It can also mean to utter or pronounce, to send forth in words. (I guess I'm making a delivery as I type this)

Jesus has 'rescued me from the coming wrath.' (1Th. 1:10) "Giving thanks to the Father...for He has rescued me from the dominion of darkness and brought me into the kingdom of the Son He loves, in Whom I have redemption.' (Col.1:12-14 personalized by me)

He has delivered me in many difficult seasons of life. "...I was under great pressure, far beyond my ability to endure, so that I despaired even of life.... He has delivered me from such deadly peril.... on Him I have set my hope that He will continue to deliver me' (2 Cor.1:9,10 personalized by me)

Why? Simply because He is God, He created me, and He loves me. And He loves you too. He wants to restore us to what we were meant to be before we chose differently, choosing to know evil. (that tree of the knowledge of good and evil...remember? Be careful, they're growing everywhere !! We are wise to stay away from choosing the knowledge of evil...)

That evil is defined for us. It is summarized in Ten Commandments. They were delivered to God's people thru Moses. Now, God's people are delivered from the impossibility of keeping them.... and delivered from the penalty of not doing so. That delivery is called 'grace'. 'Set free from sin...and become slaves to God.' (Rom. 6:22) 'slaves to righteousness." (Rom. 6:18) ' ...not free from God's law, but am under Christ's law' (1Cor. 9:21) ' I am no longer shackled to that domineering mate of sin, and out from under all those oppressive regulations and fine print, I am free to live a new life in the freedom of God.' (Romans 7:6 The Message, personalized by me)

I am delivered. Are you?

MEMORIAL

Memorial : a reminder. To exercise memory, recollect, be mindful of.... remember

There is a holiday week-end we call 'Memorial Day'. I wonder what will be remembered? Last year's bar-b-que? The rain that spoiled the plans one year? The beautiful weather for the big party at the lake? The family reunion? Or what it cost to have those opportunities.?

Let us not fail to remember those who paid that price. And when you remember, jog somebody else's memory so they won't forget either. I can't fathom having lost a child to war. Many a mother will spend the next 3 days remembering, God help them all.

MEMORIAL 2

Memorial…. Webster says "preservation in memory". Once a year, a day is set aside to preserve in memory those who have sacrificed for the cause of freedom. We remember what great cost freedom has. When we remember we realize the value. When we rightly remember, it should cause us to determine ourselves to guard that freedom, to shield ourselves from anything that threatens that freedom. The price of it was lifeblood.

Certain Sundays have been set aside for another memorial day. We call it The Lord's Supper. Jesus said to remember. He said to remember what great cost sin has. When we remember that great cost it should cause us to abstain from it. When we rightly remember, it should cause us to guard ourselves against sin, to be shielded against sin. The cost of sin is lifeblood.

My freedom was paid for by the lifeblood of those who stood in my place. My freedom from sin was paid for by the lifeblood of Jesus Christ, who stood in my place.

Paul wrote some things to the Christians at Corinth about The Lord's Supper. His words are as true today as then, we do well to heed them.

"Let me go over with you again exactly what goes on in the Lord's Supper and why it is so centrally important. I received my instructions from the Master himself and passed them on to you. The Master, Jesus, on the night of his betrayal, took bread. Having given thanks, He broke it and said, "This is My body, broken for you. Do this to remember Me" After supper, He did the same thing with the cup: "This cup is My blood, My new covenant with you. Each time you drink this cup, remember Me." What you must solemnly realize is that every time you eat this bread and every time you drink this cup, you reenact in your words and actions the death of the Master. You will be drawn back to this meal again and again until the Master returns. You must never let familiarity breed contempt. Anyone who eats the bread or drinks the cup of the Master irreverently is like part of the crowd that jeered and spit on Him at His death. Is that the kind of "remembrance" you want to be part of? Examine your motives, test your heart, come to this meal in holy awe. If you give no thought (or worse, don't care) about the broken body of the Master when you eat and drink, you're running the risk of serious consequences. That's why so many of you even now are listless and sick, and others have gone to an early grave." (1 Cor. 11:23-30 from The Message)

MEMORIAL 3

Webster says it is the essential quality of remembering something in the past that has a particular significance. I fear the only memorial most people remember on our Memorial Day holiday is last year's lake adventure, or the menu of last year's cookout. I'm not sure our culture has preserved the tradition of memorials as we should have. I wonder if we realize the importance. Maybe we do, maybe it's just me.

It takes an on purpose discipline to stop the routines of the moment and look back. It is easy to take for granted what cost me nothing personally. My freedom has always been mine. It cost me nothing personally. My life has been sheltered from even the chaos of my police-husband's regular routine. I dont live in it, nor must I deal with it. I have never been hungry, not real hunger. I have never been without comfort. Whether it is warmth, or cool air, I certainly have never felt unsafe. On the official holiday, I find my mind full of scenes from all those war movies my husband loves to watch. Saving Private Ryan, To Hell And Back, Band Of Brothers, Pacific, Black Hawk Down, dozens and dozens more.

I don't like any of them. I can tolerate the older ones, they are less graphic, but the newer ones make it too real. But it is real. To thousands of soldiers, it is all too real.

What a debt I owe for the freedom and peace I enjoy. I owe no greater debt to anyone, except to Jesus Christ who made the ultimate sacrifice that I might live in eternal freedom and enjoy peace with God forever. Hallelujah.

FREEDOM

Freedom costs somebody.

Today is what is called 'Memorial Day' in America. A day to remember the sacrifices that made possible the freedoms we enjoy. Freedom is costly. I haven't paid any of that price. But many did, and do at this very moment. I am so grateful. I do not minimize these blessings. Yet there is another freedom I cherish even more.

"...if the Son sets you free...you will be free indeed." (Jesus, speaking in John 8:36)

I am proud and thankful to be an American, I cherish the freedoms I have enjoyed my entire life, and want them guarded. Yet they can't compare with the freedom given me by my Lord Jesus the Christ. I wonder that we can't really appreciate the freedom of America, we've never known anything else. But I have known the bondage of sin and law-keeping. I know the difference of being set free.

How I pray that I never experience a difference in my freedom as an American.

God help us as ' your people, called by Your Name, to humble ourselves and pray and seek Your face and turn from our wicked ways....then You will hear from heaven and will forgive our sin and will heal our land.' (2 Ch. 7:14 personalized by me)

IDOLATRY

What god do we have? Do you think there aren't any gods… think there is only One God Whom we serve? I wonder….

Molech was a god of the Ammonites in Biblical history. Ammon was the son of Lot, closely related to the Israelites, because Lot was Abraham's nephew. I don't know how it happened, and haven't the time now to research it…but it is true that they worshipped this god called Molech. And the worship practices involved sacrifices. Sacrifices of children.

"Oh, how horrible!!" we say. How could they do that!?

I can't explain where the concept came from that placing a child onto the outstretched arms of a brass figure, to roll back into its belly and a blazing inferno would have a positive outcome…who comes up with that? What a lie to think that would change anything for the better! But look at our culture… look at the lies that people believe concerning the care and nurturing of children…. or even of allowing the life of a child to be birthed and lived.

We discard children to fend for themselves, raise themselves, barely knowing they exist much less 'training the child in the way he should go' (Prov. 22:6) We sit them in front of some electronic device and let it train the child. (usually in the way he should NOT go)

We should purposely be saying "Come, my children, listen to me: I will teach you the fear of the Lord." (Ps. 34:11) I think the practice of abortion is the modern Molech. The outstretched arms where we place the unborn to die so that some god can be appeased. The god of self that doesn't want the responsibility. The god of self that is more concerned with personal guilt and shame than life. The god of self that rejects the idea of sharing personal time, energy, and resources with another person. The god that worships personal image and beauty, and doesn't want it marred, even at the cost of another life.

Oh how horrible indeed.

HEALING

I cut my finger quite often. It heals every time. Sometimes I cut the cape laying around a client. It never heals.... Go figure. Think God has anything to do with that? I do.

I can't make those cells heal...I can help them NOT heal, by not properly taking care of the injury. Or, I can protect them...by cleanliness, even medicine...but I can't make a single cell rejuvenate.

I struggle with issues of healing. Even though I believe that God is El Rapha, the God Who heals, He obviously does not heal every time. People die. Young people die. 'O Lord my God, I called to You for help and You healed me.' (Ps. 30:2) 'Heal me, O Lord, and I will be healed; save me and I will be saved, for You are the One I praise.' (Jer. 17:14)

I wrestle with the fact that many believe, many call on Him, and many still die. Has He said 'no'? If He has, then what is the deciding factor in His answering? There was a time when I was afraid to speak with Him about things like this. I thought of Him as an angry old man who scowled down from His throne and shouted 'because I said so'. (that was a god made in my image...an image that I conjured up from misunderstandings and believing lies of our enemy..)

I respect that He is God. He does not answer to me. Yet, I am secure in His love, secure enough to take every concern to Him and ask Him to help me understand. And when I don't understand, I ask Him to help me accept. Sometimes, there are things beyond my ability to wrap my mind around. (HE is Elohim, Mighty Creator, certainly not me!)

I know that 'by His wounds we are healed' (Isa. 53:5, 1 Peter 2:24) Sometimes, that healing comes thru a miracle. Instantly. Sometimes, the healing comes thru a pill or injection…even a surgery. Sometimes, thru a series of treatments that are difficult. Sometimes, I believe the healing comes from death. Healed eternally.

I am thankful today for the physical health I enjoy. I am even more thankful to be spiritually healed. For just as I can't accomplish the healing of my cut finger, neither can I heal myself of the sin disease we all suffer from. 'By His wounds, I am healed' (Isa. 53:5) Hallelujah.

ANSWERS

Usually we use words to answer. But answers can be communicated with frowns or smiles, even silence.

The old saying 'sticks and stones may break my bones, but words will never hurt me' is an out-right lie of the devil. Words do hurt. Tremendously. There is great power in words, and that power can be wielded in positive ways. To do so is NOT to use stronger words or louder voice. "A gentle answer turns away wrath, but a harsh word stirs up anger." (Proverbs 15:1) The Message puts it like this, 'A gentle response defuses anger, but a sharp tongue kindles a temper-fire'

I've tested it. It is true. But it is difficult to respond with gentle words. The way most of the world thinks, strength is displayed in force. But Jesus showed us thru His life, the characteristics and power of gentleness and humility. Humility is NOT self-degradation. It is knowing the truth about myself, that I am nothing of myself, only valuable because I am created in the image of God, 'So God created man in His own image' (Gen. 1:27) and re-created in the image of His Son. 'I have taken off my old self with its practices and have put on the new self, 'which is being renewed in knowledge in the image of its Creator' (Col. 3:9,10)

Humility is knowing who I am, and who I am NOT. And BEING who I am, and not TRYing to be who I am not. Confused yet?

It is fascinating to study the way Jesus answered people. He had 'the whole world gone after Him!' (John 12:19). which caused much concern in the world of the Pharisees. Great crowds of people gathered around Him wherever He went.... He was 'gentle and humble in heart' (Matt. 11:29) He was the most powerful man to ever impact this world. I want to answer like He answered.

Father, 'create in me a clean heart, renew a right spirit within me'......help me to always answer with gentleness and never with harsh words...make me more like Jesus today.

NUMBERS

Account numbers, confirmation numbers, drivers license and social security numbers, patient number…. What happened to names?

I don't like having to keep up with and remember all the numbers!! I remember when all I had was my name, and everything operated on that. Sigh….. not now.

I sometimes feel like I've lost a bit of my identity, the people I deal with about things don't know my name anymore, they want the stinkin' number, and if you don't have the right numbers….forget it. I can't get an order submitted, I can't get a prescription filled, I can't pay a bill..

God is into numbers too. " …even the very hairs of your head are all numbered…" (words of Jesus in Matt. 10:30)

"The Lord knows those who are His" (2Tim. 2:19) Jesus said, "I know My sheep and My sheep know Me…they listen to My voice: I know them, and they follow Me…" (John 10: 14,27)

"I have called you friends." (John 15:15) Jesus is my friend. He knows my name. He may have a number for the hairs on my head, but I am not a number to Him, He knows my name.

And I am SO thankful!!!

STUMBLING

Have you ever found yourself stumbling around, unable to walk without bumping into something, loosing balance, or even falling down...? God is often a 'stone for stumbling'. (Isa. 8:14)

That is hard to swallow at first. But at further study, it makes perfect sense. When God is not my sanctuary, not placed in the highest place, not calling the shots...then He becomes a stone for my stumbling. He is to be the center of my existence, I am created (by Him) for that to be so.

When I look to possessions or pleasure, or work, or distractions in activities, or power, or whatever else, then I will find myself continuing to stumble over Him! What is created can never fill the place of God in our lives. No person can do that. No relationship other than the relationship with Him can fill that God-shaped hole. When we continue in endeavors to find that satisfaction, we continue to find out that satisfaction is short lived, and we stumble.

We strumble over God.

Of all the people in the world, those of us in these United States should wake up to the truth about physical and material wealth. It is never enough. There is always one more thing. More. Bigger. Better. More expensive. That continuing search is really a stumbling. We are falling right over the God of the universe, the God Who created us and wants to fulfill us in the way He meant for it to be.

I am thankful that He is so long-suffering, that He continues to make attempts to communicate to us how empty our pursuits are. How gracious He is to continue to love us and extend His love and mercy to us. How long will He wait? How far will we fall before we get it? That question is very unsettling to me. Our nation is so much like the situations that Isaiah wrote about.

We are familiar with 2 Ch. 7:14... 'If My people who are called by My Name, will humble themselves....' but what about the verse before it? 'WHEN I shut up the heavens so that there is no rain, or command locusts to devour the land, or send a plague among my people...' What is He shuts up the heavens to us, or causes our land to be devoured, or allows a plague? Or has that happened...or is that happening? The displeasure of our God is something to think about. He continues to make us stumble over Him, but for how long? It seems to me He has let us have what we have insisted upon, and it is eroding and consuming us.

SPITTIN' IMAGE

That's what they say about my sons and their daddy. Looks as if I had nothing to do with it. I assure you that I did.

I woke up this morning with 'image bearer' on my mind. Humanity was created by God to bear His image. "God created man in His own image, in the image of God created He him, male and female created He them." (Gen. 1:27) am intended to bear the image of God. That was His intention. Of course, that got wrenched up and the rest of history has been HIS-story. The story of redeeming and restoring. God still intends for me to bear His image. Oh, how I want to be the spittin' image of my Father! Don't you? Our entire race seems to have lost the knowledge of just who we really are. And we have lost the knowledge of Who our Father is.

Jesus was the spittin' image. Literally. "...the Word became flesh and made His dwelling among us." (John 1:14) John continues to tell us that 'No one has ever seen God....but God.....Who is at the Father's side, has made Him known.' (vs. 18)

I am so often the spittin' image of my father Adam. I make poor choices, pick my way, listen to the voices of others while questioning what God has said. That same enemy influences me that influenced Adam.

But I am 'being transformed into His likeness' (2 Cor. 3:18) And "my life is gradually becoming brighter and more beautiful as God enters my life and I become like Him." (2Cor. 3:18 The Message)

I can't grasp how He will accomplish it, but I believe His promises. "Just as I have born the likeness of the earthly man, so shall I bear the likeness of the Man from heaven....I will be changed...." (1 Cor. 15: 49,51)

He has started His work in me. It is an undertaking that will take my entire lifetime. But the finished work will endure eternity. Hallelujah!

ABBA

In the language of scripture, it is the equivalent of the word daddy. Jesus called God 'daddy'.

"Daddy, everything is possible for You. Take this cup from Me. Yet not what I want, but what You want…" (Mark 14:36 my translation)

I have so often thought about the relationship of father and child, and how our perception of the relationships with our earthly fathers colors our perception of our heavenly Father. I have a good father. I call him 'daddy'. I obeyed him without question. I never feared for my safety, but at the same time, I never questioned the consequences of disobedience.

As an adult with children of my own, I've learned more and more about my daddy. My perceptions of him as a kid growing up were often so wrong. I thought he was too strict, when he was in fact enforcing boundaries that provided safety not just for the moment, but even now, continue to bring me security. I continue to be thankful for those boundaries.

All daddies aren't good. That is a horrible truth. Some just walk away. Some are abusive in devastating ways. I pray especially for those people. There was a period of my life when I thought my daddy was unapproachable. (He never was really.)

There was also a period of my life when I was not confident in approaching God. I assigned to God the image of my daddy. While I was hesitant and afraid to go to daddy with certain things, I was terrified to go to God! ('Let us then approach the throne of grace with confidence, so that we may receive mercy and find grace to help us in our time of need. Heb.4:16 'In Him and through faith in Him we may approach God with freedom and confidence.' Eph. 3:12 Hallelujah.!!)

Let's not make God into the image of our daddy. Whatever fault there is in the relationship, (and there are faults in all human relationships...) let's not forget the tragedy of the garden. Humans all suffer from the disease of sin, we all share the incapacity of achieving perfection, especially in our relationships. Our Daddy in heaven does not mirror our daddy on earth. But we are so very blessed when our daddy here mirrors the Perfect Daddy of heaven.

I thank you Daddy for my daddy here, and for his commitment to You and to the family You entrusted to him. Give him long life and health.

SLEEPING

I remember when sleep was my escape. When I was stressed out about anything at all, I'd get sleepy. I could sleep right thru most anything. When I was sad or mad, sorrowful or worried, I could just close my eyes and turn it off. I've slept thru bad storms, barking dogs. But those days are gone.

I have joked that God wakes me up at night just to have some time alone with Him. I really believe He does that sometimes. Scripture tells us that Jesus slept thru a storm. "Without warning, a furious storm came up on the lake, so that the waves swept over the boat. But Jesus was sleeping." (Matt.8:24)

Do you ever feel like Jesus is sleeping when there's a storm raging in your life? I know the answer to that. The accuser and enemy of our souls would have us believe that Jesus is sleeping and even that He doesn't care about the storm. He is a liar. (Rev. 12:10, John 8:44) "Lord save us!!!" (Matt.8:25) Jesus may have been asleep, the storm may have been frightful, but all was secure. The storm raged, the waves crashed.... but all on the boat with Jesus were safe. Hard for us to feel safe when there's obvious danger. Even harder when circumstances bring harm, destruction, even death. Hard for us to look past the storm. Not hard at all for Jesus. Stay in the boat with Him. When the water is calm, don't get out for a swim. When the storms come, don't bail out to try to escape them. And if you're not in the boat.... get in!! Then when the storms come, the waves crash and beat.... call Him. He is 'Sar Shalom'. The Prince and Keeper of Peace.

PARENTING

Somebody should have warned me it would be so difficult! Somebody should have explained that it's never a done deal. Once a child is born to you, it's a forever thing. It is a relationship that is multi-faceted and ever changing. It is easy when they are little children. Though at the time is seems so difficult, it is so very very important. To a great degree, that early time determines the course of the rest of the relationship, thru the teens and into the adult years.

My parents are both still living as I write this. I wonder at their thoughts about the four of their children. I wonder at the concerns, the frustrations, the joy, the satisfaction. I pray I have not caused them much frustration and heartache. I pray they spent few sleepless nights in concern for me. Children have such an unrealistic idea about parents. I did. Only when I began to face some of the things I was so critical about did I appreciate my parents' parenting. Children have all the answers. Ever notice that? Young adults, they are just as wise as hoot owls! They often think so anyway. I did. Now, the older I get, the more I realize how little I know, and how helpless I am.

I have a lot of regret about my parenting. The enemy would like to continue to use that, but he's a defeated liar, and it's a waste of time to continue to grieve over what is done. 2 Samuel 12 tells a good story about such as that. As long as there is life, there is hope in prayer against even death itself. If we bear guilt, it is right for us to grieve and repent. And it is right that we ACCEPT forgiveness, get up, worship and love God for Who He is, and follow Him past the 'now'. The 'now' may be sad, even heart wrenching...but there comes a time to lay aside the sorrow and hurt...and we must never allow our enemy to influence us to allow the thing to stop us from worshipping God and following after Him. Our failures are against God. Even those failures of parenting. And when we try to 'fix' them ourselves, we butt our heads against a wall if we do not go to Him first, for '...against You, You only, have I sinned...' (Ps. 51:4) "I will restore to you the years that the locust have eaten...." (Joel 2:25) He is God. He can heal and restore ANYthing. Hallelujah!!

NOW

If you are reading these words, you're safe and blessed. You may have a compute before you, eyes that see, a mind that has learned to read, and the opportunity of choice to use these next few minutes as you like Now is all you have. You may not finish this reading. (…if I even get to finish writing down these thoughts!)

What do we do with our 'now'? And do we realize Who/who is responsible for this 'now'? Everything I experience and enjoy in my life is attached to another 'who' and is absolutely because of 'Who'. God has a say-so in everything that touches me, and every choice, every action I take or do not take, has an impact. I must not live my life and make my decisions as if it's only and all about me and this 'now'.

Isaiah 39 tells the story of King Hezekiah. God had caused the sun to retreat backwards several degrees. The Assyrians, prominent world power of the day, worshipped the sun god. The Babylonians were enemies of the Assyrians, and they really liked that Hezekiah's God had power over the sun. They thought it in their interest to befriend Hezekiah and his God. So, they came with gifts. And flattery. Hezekiah accepted not only the gifts, but the flattery. Not only that, he did a little showing off.

"Hezekiah received the envoys gladly and showed them what was in his storehouses…the silver, the gold, the spices, the fine oil, his entire armory and everything found among his treasures. There was nothing in his palace or in all his kingdom that Hezekiah did not show them" (Isa. 39:2)

Do you think there was a little pride going on there? Ever notice how often that of which we become proud is that which is often taken away? Oh, Hezekiah didn't suffer much for it. But the very ones to whom he strutted were the predecessors of the ones who would come and destroy everything he had been so prideful of.

"The time will surely come when everything in your palace, and all that your fathers have stored up, will be carried off to Babylon. ..and some of your own flesh and blood who will be born to you, will be taken away, and they will become eunuchs in the palace of the king of Babylon." It's not just about 'now'. Yes, our choices are important for the immediate, but they have such a profound effect on what days lay ahead. After Isaiah had informed Hezekiah about the real nature of his Babylonian friends, and what they would be capable of in the future, he replied, '.... "The word of the Lord...is good.".... For he thought, 'there will be peace and security in my lifetime.'..."(Isa. 39:8) He was concerned about his 'now'.

I am convicted today that I have enjoyed the peace and security of my lifetime, and horrified that the way we have lived in godless fashion may bring devastation in the days ahead. God help us to repent of our wicked ways, turn back to You, seek Your Face, and humble ourselves completely. Forgive us for living in our 'now' and being blind to the consequences for our sons and daughters. Only You can heal what is so diseased and broken. Help each of us...ME...to be obedient in what You call us to do, help us to live our lives first and foremost for Your purposes...trusting that those purposes are always best for us.

MANIPULATING

To manage or utilize skillfully. To control by artful means to one's own advantage. To change by artful means to serve one's purpose, Manage. Control. Change.

When trusting God is a situational condition and not a complete way of life, I wonder that we are not guilty of trying to manipulate the Creator of the universe. Faith in Him should not be a way out of a difficulty, but rather an in-place covenant relationship that provides comfort, strength, and resolve even as the moment of crisis unfolds.

We want God to meet whatever need we have at the moment. Especially when we haven't been able to fill or meet that need for ourselves. When we try to manipulate our environment and circumstances in order to meet our own needs, with no regard to He Who is Master and Creator, I fear we are guilty of idolatry. We so often put trust in people/things/self, placing them on the throne, with God waiting on the back burner...just in case we can't pull it off. When all else fails, how often do we then begin to bargain with Him? How often do we exhaust every other avenue before throwing ourselves at His Feet? Why is it that we seek after Him when we are faced with situations beyond our ability to manipulate, and don't tip our hat to Him the rest of the time?

Or, maybe I'm the only one guilty. Maybe I'm the only one who forgets that the air I suck into my lungs is there only because of Him. Not to mention the health of the lungs that breathe in that life-sustaining oxygen. Every time I successfully manipulate circumstances in my life to my advantage, I experience only a by-product of His blessed provisions. HE pours HIS life into mine. I create nothing. I dare not take the glory for what goes right and blame God when things go wrong. Even the closer relationship I enjoy with Him is because He has revealed Himself to me Yes, I must choose. Yes, I must obey. Yes, I must commit. But try as I might, I would never know God were He not to reveal Himself TO me. I have not learned how to successfully manipulate God. I am learning how to stop.

JEALOUSY

Suspicious that we do not enjoy the affection or respect of others, or that another is more loved and respected than ourselves.... Ouch.

Seems to me that jealousy and security are mutually exclusive. That security must be in both the relationship with other individuals, and within. I'm secure in my marriage relationship. I have no cause for jealousy, no threat of someone else being more loved than I am. I am loved. I've become secure in my relationship with God. I have come to believe that he really and truly does love me, and that He will do what He says He will do.... grant me the right standing of Christ and an eternal life. I don't need to be jealous in that relationship, because His love for you does not diminish His love for me in the slightest degree. But I realize this morning that I am not innocent. There are areas of my life that are tainted with insecurity and jealousy. Even worse, I fear I may incite a little jealousy in others given the opportunity.

Joseph may have been guilty of such. Gen 37 tells the story. It's worth your time to read it. Joseph was a love child, born to a man of many years. Israel/ Jacob might have been wiser in his doting on the boy. Giving him a brightly colored coat to wear only displayed his favoritism to his other sons. Everyone wore a garment like that, it was used for warmth, to sit on, to bundle things up in, or even as a security for a loan. Robes were plain. Except for the rich and famous. Royalty.

Young Joseph's father gave him the robe of royalty, and young Joseph wore it. Perhaps pridefully, Maybe even to inciting jealousy. Or, maybe Joseph thought everybody loved him like his father did. He was young and unwise to flaunt what he had been given. And even more unwise in sharing his dream about being bowed down to by his big brothers. They took the opportunity to rid themselves of him when a caravan of slave traders came by. This story is full of lessons for us. When I consider the character of each of the individuals involved, I see myself. Are you there?

Father, I confess the jealousy in my heart. Thank You for revealing areas of sin, and Your cleansing from them. Thank You for the help and power You provide, that I may live a victorious life, free from the strong holding power of the sin of jealousy. (Gal.5:20)

FREE

What does it mean to you?

To me it means out of bondage. It is to no longer be compelled or forced.... to be given choice and empowered to use that choice. It is not a release from responsibility, and it is not without boundaries.... but it is an opportunity to fulfill responsibility and the purpose for existing.

"You are free to eat from any tree in the garden, but...." (Gen.2:16)

"Woman, you are set free..." (Luke 13:12) "...the truth will set you free......So if the Son sets you free, you will be free indeed." (John 8:32,36)

"...I have heard their groaning and have come down to set them free." (Acts 7:34)

"...through Christ Jesus, the law of the Spirit of life set me free from the law of sin and death." (Rom.8:2)

Let's not forget where freedom really comes from. As we begin celebrating the Fourth of July and all that it means, let us give Him thanks and all glory for what freedoms we have known in our life time. And let the Body of Christ unite in praying that all Americans who are 'called by His Name, will humble themselves, and pray, and seek His Face, and turn from their wicked way'.... for 'then He will hear from heaven, and will forgive our sin, and will heal our land.' (2Chron. 7:14)

ALLEGIANCE

I've pledged it many times.... 'to the flag of the United States of America, and to the republic for which it stands...one nation under God, indivisible, with liberty and justice for all.

Haven't you done the same? How will we fulfill our pledge? We have promised, and we must take our promises seriously. There are, however, stipulations of our pledge of allegiance...to one nation under God.

In 1 Kings 12 the story is told of Jeroboam. It tells how Jeroboam went about to weaken and break the relationship of the people with God, and to preserve his own position and power. Isn't that familiar? "....Jeroboam thought to himself, '.......if these people go up to offer sacrifices at the temple of the Lord in Jerusalem, they will again give their allegiance to the king of Judah..'... so he said to the people 'It is too much for you to go up to Jerusalem... HERE are your gods, ...'" (selected verses 1 Kings 12) Familiar again. Good ole' Jeroboam, only trying to provide for the people and make their lives easier....by keeping them from worshipping God where and how God had said. Government stepping in....re-drawing the lines....re-describing right and wrong..

I pledge allegiance to the flag of the United States of America, the America that was a republic nation under GOD...not to be divided, not to have liberty or justice removed from anyone's life. That includes mine. I stand with Joshua.... "...Choose you this day whom you will serve....as for me and my house...we will serve the Lord." (Joshua 24:15)

FIREWORKS

We enjoyed a great firework display one Fourth of July. Amazing thing when you really think about it, cardboard boxes and tubes filled with something that somehow explodes in so many different patterns, heights, and colors. We arrived before dark, the fireworks were on floating barges out on water. I sat there looking at it, a large number of boxes, just sitting there. Big deal.

But when it got good and dark, our host pushed the remote that began the series of explosions. We had chosen chairs on the edge of the water, and as the fireworks lit up the sky above us, the smoke began to fill the air, and shreds of paper and ash sprinkled down on us. It was beautiful and awful at the same time.

For the past few weeks, I've struggled to come to better understanding of why tragedy happens. Why out of nowhere, it explodes and rains down shattered fragments of our lives, leaving us to choke on the smoke left behind…embers of what used to be beautiful, now singeing and burning us as the memory of the beauty that was, gives way to the reality and stench of the present. Fireworks are simply raw materials assembled in ways that cause explosions. I've had it explained to me, though I can't restate it. They must be fused, separately or together. There must be a spark. Simply…it's cause and effect. Isn't everything?

God created a world of cause and effect. Everything He created, He created good. (Gen.1) He then issued the memo that informed man of effect. "..do not eat of that tree, because the effect is death….do not choose to know evil, because it brings death." That was the message of Genesis 2. Anything other than God and His goodness, anytime we leave Him out of the mix, the effect is death.

We are created to be in relationship with Him, He is the life-giving, life-sustaining force. Anything outside of that, the effect is death. Immediate or eventual, even eternal. All bad things aren't a result of bad choices. Some are. God does not make all bad things to happen, but certainly He allows all things that do happen. He is God. He has the final say.

God's absolute sovereignty and my own personal free will seem to be contradictions. Only God can remain sovereign in the face of my poor choices and rebellion. His will for my life and my rejection of Him are indeed at odds. How can He be all powerful God, and I still have the power to reject His will? Am I greater than He? (ridiculous.) Sigh...It's a complicated issue, this sovereignty/free-will thing. And it, like our Creator God, is outside the realm of human logic. (...faith to the rescue again...)

This is what I know. When I choose poorly, it is not because He set me up, and not because He didn't give me the information necessary to choose best. He is not incomplete without me, but I will never be complete without Him. Everything He says is spoken out of pure love... (something I am not capable of..) He is not in a box. I am. The box of my reality, that He created to share with me. And sometimes, my box explodes. And when it does, it can be awful and beautiful...sometimes at the same time. You see...I know that my God makes beauty and good come from even the awful and ugl, .if nothing but to empower me thru it, changing, redeeming, and restoring me in spite of it The only question I need ponder is if I have chosen poorly, and if I have, to face it together with Him, learning and growing....thereby avoiding any future adverse circumstances or consequences because of my poor choices. Now...I must move on.

RESCUE

Rescue... 'natsal' It means to snatch away....

Proverbs tells us to "Rescue those being led away to death.... hold back those staggering toward slaughter...." (Pro. 24:11)

There are times I really struggle with this. At times, I have had such strong feelings about the decisions I see someone else making, times when I strongly disagree with the conclusions someone else has come to. It's their choice, their business...right?

There have been situations when I did NOT comment, and have later regretted not being obedient to that nudge to speak to them. Times when I SO wish I had said or done what I had been prompted in my spirit to do but did not.

The accuser (Rev.12:10) often convinces me that I am being nosey, bossy, and that it is none of my business what someone else does. As usual, he takes truth and puts his spin on it, twisting and perverting it. We all do make our own choices. I cannot make yours for you, nor can you make mine. But so, do we all have influence.

"If you say, 'Hey, that's none of my business,' ...will that get you off the hook? Someone is watching you closely, you know.... Someone not impressed with weak excuses." (Proverbs 24:12 The Message)

"My mouth shall speak truth." (Pro.8:7)

"There are things you are to do: Speak the truth to each other, and render true and sound judgment in your courts."(Zec.8:16)

We sang a song in choir class back in high school.... "No Man Is An Island" We have an impact on each other's lives, and when opportunity comes to make a positive impact by speaking truth. I believe scripture teaches that we are held accountable for it if we do not do so. There IS absolute truth. Gray is only achieved by mixing in a little black with pure white. The hardest part is carrying out what I believe, and doing it in a pure spirit of love, communicating that love without it being tainted by the enemy and used for his purposes to cause strife and discord.

JAIL

Webster says it's a place of confinement. We think of it now as a place of punishment. But it is really a 'place'? I believe there are thousands of people walking around free who are in jail cells of bondage. I have experienced bondage.... locked away in a cell of fear and a works centered salvation.

David wrote as if he were in prison. "Set me free from my prison, that I may praise Your Name...." (Ps. 142:7) He wasn't in a jail facility. He was just hiding from Saul. Running and hiding, trying to escape, all of it serving as walls of a prison to David.

I want to be like David, when situations are dangerous and stressful, I want to look to God with praise in my heart and on my lips. It is easy to see the danger, easy to feel the fear, easy to be discouraged. It is easy to hear the accuser's words filling us with doubt and fear. Our enemy wants to keep us in jailhouses, tied up with fear, ineffective to those around us, and away from the Throne of God in prayer and praise.

I'm thankful for the story of the Prodigal Son in Luke 15. This fellow made a series of poor choices. He lived in and for the moment.... chasing a good time. He thought he had found it, for a while at least. Then it all started turned sour. It wasn't fun anymore, only misery, and there was nobody that wanted his company any longer. He didn't have anything to offer them now, so they were gone. He'd left all his family behind, choosing a different life instead of a life with them.

I think the accuser was certainly on the job with this young man. 'Yes...your dad's a great guy, but you've been so bad, he can't restore you! What if he said no? He probably will if you ask him to take you back.'

I feel sure the devil was on duty, filling this young man with guilt and fear. But the young man knew the character of his father. God does not mean for us to live in bondage. But I believe there are times when a jail cell is His blessing. That pig sty was a blessing to that prodigal boy. He had chosen the knowledge of good and evil…another apple off the tree so to speak. He chose wrong, acted in rebellion, yet the knowledge of the character of his father was the means of bringing about restoration. God's last word is always a call for repentance and restoration. Even if it takes being locked up.

…. or slopping hogs.

COVENANT

Webster says it's to enter an agreement, to bind one's self...

In Hebrew, the original language of old testament scripture, the word is 'berith' and it has reference to the custom of cutting or dividing animals in two, and passing between the parts to ratify a covenant. In Greek, the original language of new testament scripture, the corresponding word is 'diatheke'.

There are many examples of covenant in scripture. I fear we have lost the depth of meaning, perhaps the entire concept in some instances, the covenant of marriage in particular.

The covenant of marriage is intended to be sealed, yet how many give away the possibility of that seal to someone to whom they are never married? There is much damage done in doing so and for all concerned.

God can heal and restore even that, but there's a big ol' IF attached to it. We must repent and come to Him with all of it, in obedience and trust, turning away from those wrong choices and actions.

God never ever tells us NOT to do something just to be mean and nasty. When he says 'don't', you can be sure it is because it brings US harm. Our sin doesn't take anything away from God, it doesn't diminish His character nor deplete His power. But our hurting hurts Him. THAT is what He wants to prevent. Simply because of His perfect love for us. "Just as He Who called you is holy, so be holy is all you do..." (1 Peter 1:15)

Like it or not, agree or disagree, obey or rebel, God sets the standards for morality. We are wise to believe that fact. And we are blessed when we know

Him well enough, knowing His character and His love and intentions, that we can follow His directions without rebellion.

We are wise to have learned from the garden scene NOT to try to find out for ourselves if what He says is really true. What He says IS. It has always been that way…and will always be.

SUDDENLY

Unexpected. Ever had a 'suddenly' moment? The TV program is interrupted with a news flash? The doctor says, 'it's a tumor'. The phone rings, the news is bad. Someone nearby collapses. He/She says 'I want out'.

Suddenly moments when suddenly your perspective and your world is changed. Suddenly, security is gone, and we are faced with what was in fact true all along…there is no security. We are incapable of securing anything. "While people are saying, 'Peace and safety,' destruction will come on them suddenly…" (1 Thes. 5:3) "If he comes suddenly…do not let him find you sleeping…" (Mark 13:36).

Don't wait until your suddenly moment to think about Him. Don't wait until a suddenly moment to pray, to consider what He has said to us, what He has done for us.

"…. I know the plans I have for you… plans to prosper you and not to harm you, plans to give you hope and a future. You will seek me and find me when you seek me with all your heart. I will be found by you," declares the LORD…" (Jer. 29:11-14)

TRAGEDY

It comes. No invitation. No respecter of person. And we ask why...

The age-old question. Why?

Faith in God nor obedience to Him shuts out afflictions and death. My heart hurts. Tragedy strikes, friends die, children die, those who survive suffer. As much as I grieve, I realize that it pales in comparison to the ones who have been left behind. I can only pray that I never get any closer to tragedy than this day. I do not want to be like Job's friends, who had all the answers and all the reasons why the bad things that happened to Job had befallen him.

I do not know why God has allowed this tragedy. I do not believe the God I serve caused these awful things to happen. Yet, I know He is all powerful, and could have stopped it. Why He chose not to do so, I can't imagine. At the same time, I wonder in what ways He did act during the tragedy. Who did He comfort and calm as the flood waters swept? Who did He speak to? In what way will He minister to families in the days, weeks, and even years to come? What good will He work out of all this misery and grief? Of one thing I have absolutely no doubt. He was there.

I know is He is God. And I am not. I hope, were tragedy to strike much closer to me, that I would say with Job 'Though He slay me, yet will I hope in Him.' (Job 13:15)

SUDDENLY 2

I don't like suddenly. I like slow and easy. Expected, not surprised.

I like ordinary. I find comfort in routine.

I'm finding new meaning to one of my favorite verses. "I will extend peace to her like a river..." (Isa. 66:12) I think of it every time I am near water.

Water has always brought me such a feeling of peacefulness. I have seen stagnant water. Dead fish were everywhere. I found no peace there.

I have heard about the devastation from a flash flood. People I love are gone... suddenly. There is no peace there for sure.

I've sat and looked at water for hours on end over the years. He has spoken to my heart so many times during those moments. Sustaining my life. Cleansing me. Healing me. Refreshing me. Exciting me. Calming me. Soothing me. Providing for me. Nourishing me. On and on goes the list,

But then the circumstances of nature and life bring a cold hard reality. Water can kill.. Suddenly.

Our Father provides many blessings here. My mind cannot stretch to understand when and why it seems as if those blessings are withheld and circumstances often feel like curses. I don't understand why one is taken and another left. There is a negative side to every physical aspect of this realm. There is no absolute security except in the eternal realm. I am thankful to Him for that truth. I find my peace and security in Him, and commit myself afresh this morning to His care, whatever my future may hold.

"Alongside Babylon's rivers we sat on the banks we cried and cried, remembering... Alongside the quaking aspen trees we stacked our un-played harps... Oh, how could we ever sing God's song in this wasteland" (Ps. 137:1,2,4 The Message)

I will never again sit by water and not remember.

Father, as the waves of grief pound, "Restore the joy of Your salvation and grant a willing spirit, to sustain." (Ps. 51:12)

BEAUTY

What makes something beautiful? Is it a permanent condition?

I've been to Albert's Pike many times. I considered it beautiful. I haven't seen it since the flood except in pictures, but it's not so beautiful now. The rocks and trees are still there. There is still water in the river. All the things that defined it as beautiful to me are still there. What changed? Nothing really... everything just got re-arranged. Including people and all their belongings. God thought up beauty in the first place. It reflects His character. But to be beautiful there must be harmony, balance, symmetry, perfect rhythm... Like Him.

I can't achieve that on my own. How grateful I am that He has made provision for my failure. "He is my refuge and strength, an ever-present help in trouble. I will not fear, though the earth give way and the mountains fall into the heart of the sea, though its waters roar and foam and the mountains quake with their surging. There IS a river whose streams make glad the city of God, the holy place where the Most High dwells.

God is within her, she will not fall. God will help her at break of day.... Be still, and know that I am God. The Lord Almighty is with us..." (selected verses from Ps. 46)

Father, as families bury their dead, remembering the horror of this flood, and grieving over the precious ones who are snatched away, I beg You to make Yourself known thru these circumstances. Lord, I ask that You bring not only comfort and healing, but new and deeper dependence on You. Protect them from lies of the enemy, make them to see truth, never doubting or questioning Your love. 'Hear O Lord, and be merciful, O Lord, be their help, turn their wailing into dancing, remove their sackcloth and clothe them with joy...' (Ps. 30:10,11)

DIFFICULT

Easier to define in the negative...what difficult it NOT.

It's NOT easy. NOT compliant. NOT accommodating. NOT yielding.

Life seems to get more and more difficult. The longer our stay here, the further reaching our relationships become, the more entangled we are with each other. It is difficult at times, but I wouldn't have it any other way would you?

I'm glad I hurt when others hurt. I do not want to have a heart that is not touched by others pain. I am so grateful to the Divine Helper. If there was no Hope past this realm and all it holds, how and why do we go on in the midst of difficulty? If there was no Help, would anyone be able to rise above the difficult times?

"Is anything too hard for the Lord" (Gen. 18:14) No!! Hallelujah. I'm so thankful, because I don't go thru a day when I'm not faced with circumstances that are too hard to 'me'. I have witnessed and experienced the fulfillment of the promise.... "My grace is sufficient for you, for my power is made perfect in weakness." (2 Cor. 12:9)

At our weakest point and greatest need, His power in our lives is stronger than ever. We are limited, He is not. Our Father does not intend for us to be weak and ineffective. But when we are, when circumstances of life knock the wind out of our sails and disable us, He can be depended on, never to fail. Grace is there in proportion to need. I don't have the grace at this moment to face a tragedy... But I am certain that if tragedy were to strike, there would be abundant grace to see me thru.

I have no doubt that abundant grace is available to those who do face tragedy right now. I pray each one finds The Source and clings to Him as they 'walk thru the valley of the shadow of death'. (Ps. 23:4)

TODAY

Now. At present. Not future. Not past.... "..encourage one another daily, as long as it is called Today, so that none of you may be hardened by sin's deceitfulness." (Heb. 3:13)

This verse has always haunted me. 'Today'. That's all we have. No promise for tomorrow, yesterday is certainly gone...and even today may be short-lived.

I don't profess to know all things, my mind struggles to wrap itself around concepts like this. My life is so defined by time. I can't understand how it will be, to be free of those limitations. I can't grasp that God is not in this time box with me, He is not limited by anything, even time.

The only limits God has, are the ones I choose to set. He allows me that freedom, and will never take that choice from me. Even when I make bad ones...and the part about sin being deceitful and the danger of it hardening my heart.... what's that all about?

New meaning on yet another of my 'today's.

Sin has no pride, is not put off by circumstances....in fact, cashes in on each opportunity. When we are at our lowest, 'like a roaring lion' it creeps in to devour. (1Peter 5:8) We need God's strength and protection even more during those times...we need encouragement from our spiritual siblings to help us keep our eyes on Jesus and not our situation. We need to live 'today' while fully expecting the promises of His tomorrow, trusting Him without reservation with our future. (we certainly can't secure it...) If we do not have Him, we push our way thru the difficulties of this life, depending on self, and callous ourselves against the pain of living, and living in this place can be so painful. It is a dire mistake to try to stop that pain. If we choose to slowly protect ourselves from that pain, we wake up one day having slowly calloused ourselves over, so that we no longer hurt…but we are just as insensitive to God as we are to the hurt that comes from living in this world.

"If we can only keep our grip on the sure thing we started out with, we're in this with Christ for the long haul. These words keep ringing in our ears: Today, please listen; don't turn a deaf ear…" (Heb. 3:14,15 The Message)

NOW 2

Time is not new...but it is important. Now is all we have. Live fully in it. Not in the past. Not waiting for that perfect time yet to come. Now.

"Teach us to number our days aright, that we may gain a heart of wisdom." (Ps. 90:12) Oh Lord, help us to be wise in our 'now'.

Grief...yes, I've tasted it, but have never had to drink the cup that has been to the lips of so many. Again today, some drink of it. I have no help...nothing to offer...no way to take it away. I think again of Job's story, .."If only my anguish could be weighed and all my misery be placed on the scales...it would surely outweigh the sand of the seas.."(Job 6:2) I cannot imagine the heaviness of the sorrow some bear at this moment. I can only offer myself to God and ask Him to use me in some small way to bring His comfort. He is the only answer.

"In my distress I called to the Lord. I cried to my God for help From His temple He heard my voice. My cry came before Him, into His ears. (Ps.18:6) I purpose to live in my 'now'. It is all I have. And I purpose to live it as God leads. He has brought me to this place, He will lead me forward from here.

LOST

Lost. Destroyed. Wasted. Employed to no good purpose. Mislaid. Cannot be found. Forgotten.

This past week has brought many losses. Much was destroyed. Many things were wasted and made unusable, no longer suitable for any good purpose. Belongings can't be found.

But the loss will not be forgotten. Ever.

Those who mourn their lost loved ones begin to count…marking the passing of time.

Jesus' purpose in coming was 'to seek and save what was lost.' (Luke 19:10)

He is the One to turn to with our loss. 'Salvation has come…'(vs.9)
He is Savior.
He is Redeemer.

Lord help the brokenness. Bring spiritual wholeness, a capacity to accept and continue…and an assurance that this is not the end of the story.

WHY

We look for reasons. We want to explain...

"...who sinned.... causing him to be born blind?" (Jesus' disciples concerning a blind man in John 9:2)

"...I have observed, those who plow evil and those who sow trouble... reap it."(Job's friend Eliphaz in Job 4:8)

The age-old question...why do bad things happen to good people? "No one is good, except God alone." (Jesus Christ in Mark 10:18)

I suppose perhaps the question should be why not? While scripture clearly teaches that we reap what we sow, it is also clear that we don't always get what we deserve.

Paul didn't deserve to be an apostle. (1 Cor. 15:9)

The centurion didn't deserve having his servant restored to health. (Matt. 8:8)

The prodigal son didn't deserve to be restored into the family. (Luke 15:21)

Jacob didn't deserve protection from Esau. (Gen. 32:10)

....and I have done nothing to deserve the privileged life I have enjoyed. Why was I born into a church-going Bible-believing family? Why was I born an American and not an Ethiopian? Why have I not had some dreaded disease? Why do I not have a physical disability? There is no answer. Certainly, the reasons are not of my own doing.

What IS of my doing is the choices I have made. I can prevent some bad things from coming into my life sometimes, simply by choosing to be obedient and NOT choosing the participate in evil. (...it's that same principle of choosing evil, picking and eating the fruit from that awful tree...)

But just because I do not, doesn't guarantee a trouble-free life....Just ask Job.

STORMS 1

I've ridden out a few pretty scary ones. I've put my kids under the bed and in the closet. I've put other people's children in a bathtub and covered them with pillows. I've ministered to people who left everything behind and were at other people's mercy for food, clothing, and shelter. Tornados. Hurricanes. We can know about these kinds of storms. We can be warned and take steps to prepare. If we are wise....

There are other storms in life that come without warning. The doctor says 'it's cancer'. The officer says 'there's been an accident'. A spouse says 'I'm leaving'. Nothing we can manage prepares for that kind of storm. But like all storms of life, they blow in, damaging everything in proximity. Ripping shelter, dislodging foundation, taking what was 'ours'. When the storm comes, and goes, those who remain take stock of what is left behind. Decisions are made, pieces are picked up, broken pieces inspected and repaired or discarded.

We are wise to prepare for storms. We are wise to have a strong relationship with The One Who is Master over every storm. For THAT is the only real way to prepare for storms....

"When the storm has swept by, the wicked are gone, but the righteous stand firm forever." (Prov. 10:25)

STORMS 2

Thirty minutes ago, it was hailing. The rain was pouring down, thunder was booming, lighting flashing…power flickered off and on, interrupting the routine of my morning.

Now, the sun is shining, the sky is a bright blue, the birds are singing… The storm is past. There is a song I like to sing, "I will praise You in this storm…" Life has so many storms. My will is to praise Him… even in the middle of those storms. But it's hard. My will often crumbles when life's storms come. It's hard to hear that still small voice over thunder. It's scary when it's dark and threatening….and I am unsure of what He is doing to calm the storm… or if He will…. or even if He is close by.

I choose to believe, yet often pray like the father in Mark 9:24. "I do believe… help me overcome my unbelief!" I know what He has said, over and over… "Never will I leave you." (Heb.13:5) "Be strong and courageous. Do not be afraid of terrified …for the Lord your God goes with you, He will never leave you or forsake you" (Dt. 31:6) "The Lord Himself goes before you.."(Dt. 31:8) "No one will be able to stand up against you…I will never leave you or forsake you.."(Joshua 1:5)

The power for my survival is HIS power, provided to me thru The Holy Spirit. That power never flickers, it never has an outage or shortage…but sometimes I'm prone to yank the plug, disconnecting myself. It is never Him who deserts me, "..The Father will give you another Comforter, that He may abide with you forever…" (Jesus, in John 14:16) I continue to be tutored, learning that just because I don't understand, or 'see' His Hand at work…just because I don't recognize His activity, just because I don't see what I expect to see… never ever means that He isn't at work.

I continue to submit myself to Him, learning more absolute trust of Him, and committing myself time and time again to be obedient to what He says. He is always right…I've learned that by experience, some of them very painful.

When it seems like the storm looms so threateningly close, and I don't sense Him, I continue to choose...gritting my teeth sometimes...that He is God, and He is faithful to His promises to me. Even when I'm scared to death of the storm...His love for me is beyond measure.

The storm will pass. And even if it leaves a path of destruction, I am safe.

For I am His.

SECURITY

Webster says it is protected from danger. How secure are you?

Do you pay for one of those security systems for your home so that when you are in danger, help will come to the rescue? Do you have an arsenal ready to meet intruders? Do you have securities? Stocks and bonds. Equities and options. Certificates. Mutual funds. Money in the bank? Do you have a dead bolt on your door that would keep out the uninvited? Just what is it that you put on the list of things that make you secure?

Perhaps it is government…. the law of the land…laws that forbid anyone or anything to steal your secure status. Perhaps it is medicine, physicians and surgeons so that if/when sickness or injury comes, there should be a pill, treatment, or surgery to prevent your secure health from being compromised or lost.

Whatever it is you put on your list. It's a lie. There IS no security other than the eternal security in Jesus Christ.

Laws won't do it; the Ten Commandments are a witness to that fact.

Government won't do it. It is impossible to legislate right behavior. There is a presence of evil in our world. "…for what the law was powerless to do in that it was weakened by the sinful nature, God did by sending His Own Son…" (Rom. 8:3)

Money won't do it. The value changes, it is unstable and unreliable. And what is it really except paper or chunks of metal? Who decides what it's value is? "Since you trust in your deeds and your riches, you too will be taken…." (Jer. 48:7) "though your riches increase, do not set your heart on them."(Ps. 62:10)

Guns and armies won't do it. Battles and wars have been taking lives the entire history of our race, and still we struggle to be secure. "Woe to those…who rely on horses, who trust in the multitude of their chariots and in the great strength of their horsemen, but do not look to the Holy One of Israel, or seek help from the Lord." (Isa. 31:1)

"My hope is certain. My hope is something for my soul to hold on to. My hope is strong and secure. My hope goes all the way into the Most Holy Room behind the curtain. That is where Jesus has gone. He went there to open the way ahead of me…" (Heb.6:19 NIrV personalized by me)

I am forever secure. Hallelujah.

BOTTOM 1

Bottom…. Ever hit rock bottom? Or see someone else heading there?

I suppose all of us have. And certainly, all of us who are parents want to prevent our children from ever going there. But sometimes, it's unavoidable. Sometimes, it may even be the best thing to do…. let them hit rock bottom. I think they call it 'tough love' these days.

The prodigal of Luke 15 hit rock bottom. "And when he came to himself…." (Luke 15:17)

(After he found himself on rock bottom, there was a big A-HA! "….so maybe dear old Dad was right about some things…")

It is difficult to see someone suffering the consequences of their own poor choices. But what joy to see them 'come to their senses' (Luke 15:17 NIV), turn around, and begin a new and better path.

Pity it takes some of us so much longer than others to 'begin to think clearly again'. (Luke 15:17 NIrV)

BOTTOM 2

Ever hit rock bottom? Or see someone else heading there? I suppose all of us have.

All of us who are parents want to prevent our children from ever going there, but sometimes, it's unavoidable. Sometimes, it may even be the best thing to do…. let them hit rock bottom. (I think they call it 'tough love' these days.)

The prodigal of Luke 15 hit rock bottom. "And when he came to himself…." (Luke 15:17) After he found himself on rock bottom, there was a big A-HA! ("….so maybe dear old Dad was right about some things…")

It is difficult to see someone suffering the consequences of their own poor choices. But what joy to see them 'come to their senses' (Luke 15:17 NIV), turn around, and begin a new and better path.

Pity it takes some of us so much longer than others to 'begin to think clearly again'. (Luke 15:17 NIrV)

PITS

Sometimes I just slide off into one....

Sometimes I fall into a pit by accident, tripping or stumbling over something, finding myself at the bottom of the pit. often it is ignorant blindness... "If a blind man leads a blind man, they will both fall into a pit." (Luke 6:39 my interpretation) Sometimes I get shoved in.... somebody wants me there. "... without cause they dug a pit for me..." (Psa. 35:7)

I guess sometimes I jump in. Sometimes, like all of us humans, I just make the wrong choice and dive right in. "She who digs a hole and scoops it out falls into the pit she has made." (Psa. 7:15 personalized by me) I've dug lots of pits out of fear...as if I could dig a place that would hide me, save me somehow. Digging with a shovel named fear. Big lie... No pit is a safe place.

The pits I dig are dug by different shovels...often shovels of exhaustion. When I get overtired, seems I look up and find I've slid off into that pit again.... shovel in hand, digging furiously as if there is relief down deeper. Another big lie...

Exhaustion for me is usually mental rather than strictly physical. Why does it take so much energy to think, feel, and listen? (.... watch out with those blonde jokes...).

Some of the pits I've been in are other people's diggings, and I've mistakenly thought I could get them out of their pit, so I climbed down there with them, only to find myself stranded in THEIR pit. And pits are pits.... whether I dig them or you do...not a good place to be, and nobody's company adds much to the atmosphere.

Nobody can rescue us from the pits...not really. Somebody else may pull you up a little, you may see a little light, you may be relieved of that slime at the bottom...but there's really no way out of a pit except from the Divine Rescuer.

He may call us to encourage and help someone, but nobody stays out of pits unless He delivers. "I will free......from the waterless pit..." (Zec. 9:11)

"I called on Your Name...... from the depths of the pit. You heard my plea.... You came near when I called You, and You said, "Do not fear." (Lam. 3:55,56)

"To the roots of the mountains I sank down.... but You brought my life up from the pit, O Lord my God." (Jonah 2:6)

Life itself is the pits...it simply ends in death unless He breaths His Spirit into us, and with It, eternal Life with Him. There'll be no shovels in heaven...

ROCKS

My friend Barbara caught a couple on her windshield yesterday. It has happened to me. You too, probably. A little tiny pebble, powered by some unseen force, flying thru the air, striking a heavy shatterproof glass windshield…and there's a break. Unless the repair guy can stop it, it will run little fingers across the entire windshield.

The information and instructions we find in scripture are like that. A verse can fly off the pages, hit us right in the face, and crack the wall of defenses we've built around us. That wall… (and yes, you've got at least one)…is called a stronghold in scripture. ("For the weapons of our warfare are not weapons of the world…. they have divine power to demolish strongholds." 2Cor. 10:4)

You and I put up windshields. The natural, fleshly, carnal way of human beings since the incident in The Garden is to keep the Wind of God away from us. Just like Adam and Eve, we think we can hide. Then one of those verses is quoted… in print, or spoken aloud by someone…and POW!! Cracks in the windshield. The thing is…we'd be so much better off to stay away from that guy that wants to stop the effects of it. He is not repairing…and he is not our friend. He is the enemy. ("…your enemy the devil prowls around like a roaring lion looking for someone to devour." 1 Peter 5:8)

His purpose is to "steal, kill, and destroy…" John 10:10

He is a liar. Invented it, in fact. ("…the devil…is a liar and the father of lies." John 8:44)

Satan's mission is to separate us from God. He accomplished that by influencing the wrong decisions made in The Garden. Ever since that happened, God has been at work to restore us. And those nuggets of scripture that fly into your face…well, those are the Words of our God!! He wants to crack thru the strongholds of sin. Don't repair those!!…don't stop His Word from spreading across your heart and changing your entire being!! You do not need protection from His Spirit. Let His Word take out that entire shield, open yourself up to Him completely. You will love the wind of His Love blowing on your face.

He speaks. But the choice is yours. He won't over-ride your decision about your windshield. Will you listen? …. or keep the shield up, stop all His attempts to break thru…and miss out on experiencing the Wind of His Spirit?

"He sends His Word and melts them…He stirs up His breezes, and the waters flow. He has revealed His Word…. Praise the Lord." (Psalm 147:18,20)

Father, today…throw some good rocks. Make some good clean breaks in the barriers that have been erected in our lives. Help us to trust You enough to allow, even ask You, to remove the shields that keep You distanced from us. And blow into us, Your breath of life.

HOARDING

Have you ever seen a place that's stacked and piled up with all kinds of 'stuff'? There is a TV show about it now. 'Hoarders' it's called. I've seen this up close and personal....

I remember the rooms being normal, chairs to sit in, tables to eat off of, floor space for children to play games on. Then over a period of years, all of it becomes consumed and overtaken with 'stuff'. Then the stuff begins to collect layers and layers of dust. (you just can't clean piles of 'stuff') Family may try to approach the problem, but after attempts are rejected with reprimands about interfering in personal choice....the hoarding person is allowed to live as they please. Personal choice, free will....

God allows us that as well.

People's lives also get consumed and overtaken with what the Bible calls 'sin'. Where does it begin? How does someone ever become a murderer? a drug addict? Wrong choices. Sin. God doesn't like our choices, but they are ours. He will not over- rule them. Human-kind chose knowledge in the Garden. Knowledge of both good and evil. ('of the tree of the knowledge of good and evil, do not eat...or you will die.' Gen.2:17)

"Since the creation of the world, God's invisible qualities have been clearly seen...men are without excuse...they neither glorified Him as God or gave thanks to Him, their thinking became futile and their hearts darkened... therefore God gave them over to the desire of their hearts...to sexual impurity...worshipping and serving created things rather than the Creator... He gave them over to shameful lusts. Even their women exchanged natural relations for unnatural ones...men also abandoned natural relations with women ...committing indecent acts with other men...they did not think it worthwhile to retain the knowledge of god, so He gave them over to a depraved mind, to do what ought not to be done...they know god's righteous decree that those who do these things deserve death, they continue to do them and even approve of those who practice them." (Romans 1:20)

Sexual sin is just one of a number of areas I could list that begins with one wrong choice. We then begin to know the evil of it…and it brings death into our lives. One wrong choice begins the process…unless we allow God to intervene and rescue us from wrong paths. ('Guard my life and rescue me, let me not be put to shame, for I take refuge in You.' Ps.25:20)

Hoarding and turning your home into a trash pile is a process. A life consumed and completely surrendered to sin began somewhere…it was a process. Hoarding can be undone…family can come in and carry all that stuff away and clean house. ('Rescue me from the mire. Do not let me sink..' Ps. 69:14)

God will allow you to hoard sin in your life. The longer you hoard it, the worse it will get. Call on Him today to come carry all that stuff away and clean house. Like the hoarders…it will be painful to let go of some of that nasty stuff you've become involved in. But it's never too late for Him. He is God. He is more than able.

STUMBLE

Stumble…not a desirable thing to do, but we've all done it. Stubbed a toe and stumbled, or for absolutely no reason…just stumble. Then, embarrassed, look to see if anyone saw it! In the language the Bible was written in, 'hamartano'=miss the mark. We miss the mark of our step and down we go.

Our mother has some difficulty moving around, bad knees…and we are concerned about her stumbling. A stumble could result in a fall, and worse. So…we are removing obstacles. I spent part of a day with my sister, cleaning and removing 'stuff' from our parents' home. What looks like trash to me, looks like a treasure to our mother because of the memory it stirs. She was surrounded by things that witnessed about something pleasant.

We chose the best things. Some of them were ok…colored pages or handmade crafts, gifts from children. Half burned candles. Trinkets from all sorts of places, souvenirs. Framed pictures of children who HAVE children now. Some of the things were better. Figurines of birds and glass candlesticks. Then the best…things that belonged to my mother's mother, photos of her grown children and her grandchildren, a small chest for jewelry that was a gift from my daddy (she has had it ever since I can remember).

Sometimes we have to strip off some 'good' things just so we can see the best things. Sometimes we must rid ourselves of 'ok' stuff…just so we don't stumble. Life is like that. There are some things we'd be better off to let go of., or at least get off the shelf.

Some friends who aren't as committed to the Lord.

Wrong friends who will get us off course.

All sorts of activities that crowd in and consume too much of our lifetime.

Maybe even too much religious activity. Good stuff…but so much of it that we miss hearing God's Voice, we forfeit that quiet time sitting at His Feet.… and we stumble.

'..preserve sound judgment and discernment…they will be life for you… then you will go on your way in safety, and your foot will not stumble…' (Pro. 3:21-23)

God will give discernment. He will help us to choose the best. Trouble is, we often don't ask Him to show us the best choices, we choose the ok stuff and miss out on so much. We cling to those ok things, and forfeit moving forward with God in adventuring into the best things He has waiting for us. We stand still and collect dust with all this 'ok' stuff…and never see the treasures He wants to give us. And often end up stumbling on the clutter.

We all stumble. "..for all have sinned (harmartano)…and come short of the glory of God' (Romans 3:23) None of us walk thru this life without stumbling and sinning…because we are not God. Jesus was the only One who lived a life without sin. He personified the glory of God. In skin. 'In the beginning was the Word….and the Word was God….and the Word was made flesh and dwelt among us' John 1:1,14 You can stay with the ok stuff. You can collect dust on it. Maybe you won't stumble…. maybe. Or you can run with God and ask Him to show you the better stuff, and He'll give you the best!

'…we are surrounded by such a great cloud of witnesses, let us throw off everything that hinders and the sin that so easily entangles, and let us run with perseverance the race marked out for us.' Heb. 12:1

BOTTOM

Ever hit rock bottom? Or see someone else heading there?

I suppose all of us have. Certainly, all of us who are parents want to prevent our children from ever going there. But sometimes, it's unavoidable. Sometimes, it may even be the best thing to do…. let them hit rock bottom. I think they call it 'tough love' these days.

The prodigal of Luke 15 hit rock bottom. "And when he came to himself…." (Luke 15:17) After he found himself on rock bottom, there was a big A-HA! "….so maybe dear old Dad was right about some things…" It is difficult to see someone suffering the consequences of their own poor choices. But what joy to see them 'come to their senses' (Luke 15:17 NIV), turn around, and begin a new and better path.

Pity it takes some so much longer than others to 'begin to think clearly again'. (Luke 15:17 NIrV) close to someone else's splashing. (Thanks to "The Shack" for the imagery of life's pool)

RECOVER

There's not a single one of us that doesn't need to. We all suffer from the same fatal disease. The horrible truth is that if we lose the battle with this disease, the death is eternal. There is One Cure. One. It's not a pill. Not a diet. Not a set of exercises. It's not a lifestyle. It's a Person. His Name is Jesus. We are wise to cling to Him.

There is a lot to a name. Especially His Name. In our culture, we've lost the concept of the meaning of names. Pity. There were twins born to Isaac and Rebekah in Genesis 25. One of the twin boys came forth from the birth canal hanging onto his brother's foot. They named that baby Jacob. It means 'heel holder'. That baby was born hanging on. His name would always bring that to mind. And hang on he did. His life story examples both good and bad aspects of that part of his personality.

Jacob was an ambitious deceiver. He grabbed hold of life and got all he could get. Sometimes underhanded. Eventually, he'd made a pretty bad situation for himself, and was trying to find the way out. That's when he had an encounter with a messenger from heaven.

"..and Jacob was left alone. And there, he wrestled....' (Genesis 32:24)

God had allowed Jacob his choices and methods. Then when Jacob used up all his resources, all his ideas and schemes...when he needed help in preserving his life and the lives of his family, he had a meeting with God. "...and Jacob called the name of the place Peniel: for I have seen God face to face, and my life is preserved." (Genesis 32:30)

Peniel. Facing God. Hallelujah. May we keep our faces turned to Him.

WORD

What is a word but a vehicle of communication? God has given His Word, and it is the absolute. The list of ten were once referred to as 'The Ten Words'. It's a pretty remarkable set of ten words. Shalts and shalt nots. Ten words that would solve every problem of mankind if we would just follow them. (can't be done, unfortunately...sin has entered the equation...)

My writing today is being done on a 'word' processor. It enables me to write and rewrite at will, corrects my spelling, all sorts of helping devices, most of which I'm unaware of or don't know how to utilize. They are still available... even if I'm ignorant of them, even if I choose not to use them.

Communication has changed immensely in my lifetime. Once, I would have worn out two erasers on a writing like this, wasting much more paper than the one page it ends up on. All in an attempt to capture my thoughts, articulate them, and get them into 'words'. My thoughts are just mine until they are processed into 'words'. Then, you can share them, agree or disagree.... like or dislike....be benefited, unimpressed, or even offended. In the same way, God's Word is not much use to me unless it is available to me and relative to my life.

God's 'Word' is recorded... in the documents contained in our Bible. There are lots of translations that use languages from The King's English, to the street language of today. What He has said is readily available in dozens of formats. It is available in words that I am able to fully understand and apply. His 'Word' was communicated in an even greater way...in the Person of Jesus Christ. "In the beginning was the Word......and the Word was made flesh and dwelt among us..." (John 1:1-2)

Today, I speak words into cell phones, over Skype to the other side of the planet...I write words into machines that put them out into cyberspace for anyone to read. I can write them, publish them, broadcast them...I'm still fairly free to stand up and speak them. God has spoken in lots of ways. He certainly didn't have to. He is God. He gets the final say. But His desire is that we hear and understand Him. He has gone to great lengths to make Himself available and approachable. He has shown us His character, His love…the good intentions He has for us. Time and time again in scripture, we see how He relates to mankind, whom He has created to be in relationship with. None of it because we deserved another chance…all of it because He will do whatever it takes to reach out to us, anything required to restore and redeem…. everything. Even to the death. The only thing God will not do is take away our choice, or change the rules of what is right and wrong, good and evil. He has not nor will He ever change the absolutes of Himself. What He says…IS…and will never change. Right, as He has dictated will never change. Likewise, wrong will always be wrong.

While He is unchanging, we are not. Our culture changes, our methods change…and our enemy sees to it that he uses every change to our disadvantage and disaster. Make no mistake, he has no pride or shame. There is no honor in his methods. From walking in the cool of the day, leading by pillars of fire, writing with His Finger on tablets of stone….to leaving heaven and moving into a barn…. God has done so very much to communicate and relate to us. He hasn't required me to carry around a stone tablet, hasn't required me to learn to read and understand Greek or Hebrew… My methods of hearing what He has said don't matter to Him. It just matters that I listen.

KNOW-YE-NOTS

Know-ye-nots… negative of knowing…

There are lots of things I don't know. It is quite impossible to know everything…lots of the things I DO know, I wish I did NOT. And…there are a lot of things I SHOULD know and NEED to know that I do not know. Jesus knew about know-ye-nots. He taught that there were many things we should be concerned about knowing. We begin with the elementary.

"Don't you understand (know-ye-not) this parable?" …but He says we must not stop there… "How then will you understand any parable?" (Mark 4:13) The parable in this passage stresses to us the importance of understanding basic truth and building on it. There is absolute truth. It is imperative to accept that fact, submit, and seek it. Scripture has many know-ye-nots that we should be sure we benefit from.

"Know ye not that friendship of the world is enmity with God?" (James 4:4)

"Examine yourselves…do you not realize (know-ye-not) that Christ Jesus is in you unless, of course, you fail the test?" (2Cor. 13:5)

"Know-ye-not that they which run in a race run all, but one receiveth the prize? So, run, that ye may obtain." (1 Cor. 9:24)

"Know ye not that he which is joined to an harlot is one body?…flee fornicication…Know ye not that your body is the temple of the Holy Ghost which is in you, which ye have of

God, and ye are not your own? For ye are ought with a price…" (1Cor. 6:16, 18,19,20)

"Know ye not that the unrighteous shall not inherit the kingdom of God? (1Cor. 6:9)

"Know ye not that a little leaven leaveneth the whole lump?" (1Cor. 5:6)

"Know ye not that to whom ye yield yourselves servants to obey, his servants ye are…" (Rom.6:16)

"Know ye not that so many of us as were baptized into Jesus Christ were baptized into His death?" (Rom. 6:3)

Ignorance causes a lot of damage. "God overlooks it as long as you don't know any better…but that time is past. The unknown is now known, and He's calling for a radical life change. He has set a day when the entire human race will be judged and everything set right." (Acts 17:30,31 The

Message)

Ignorance is no excuse. Not anymore. Especially when Truth is so readily available and easily accessed. It is simply a choice. Know what God has said.

Or know-ye-not.

NOTS

Nots…. Or knots. Either, or both?

I remember a particular sermon from years ago, the preacher was one of those hell fire and brimstone kinda guys. He'd often turn absolutely red in the face standing in the pulpit, delivering his message to us. This sermon was entitled "The Nots In The Devil's Tale". It was all about how putting the little three letter word 'not' into a sentence was a way the devil worked his treachery.

There must have been some truth to the sermon, the sermon title stuck with me all these years. Certainly, it made an impact…truth always does. Unfortunately, lies can as well. I don't remember what any of the 'nots' were. But I can think of some now. The first was in the Garden. God had said not to eat of the Tree of Knowledge of Good and Evil or they would die. Satan added a not. "…ye shall not surely die'. (Gen.3:4) One Knot in his tail…lots of knots in all human life thereafter.

I also think of Jesus' words in John 14:6. "I am the way. I am the truth. I am the life. No man comes to the Father but by me." The enemy would have us believe that Jesus is not the only way. That 'not' could bring eternal separation from God. Jesus IS the only way. The devil's 'not' doesn't change truth. Jesus also said "I am the Light of the world." (John 8:12) The devil says 'not'…he lies and says that there are other sources of light.

"He will punish those who do not know God and do not obey the gospel of our Lord Jesus. They will be punished with everlasting destruction and shut out from the presence of the Lord and from the majesty of His power…" (2Thes. 1:8) A 'not' in that scripture is deadly. God will punish. Simply being cut off from His Presence is beyond horrible.

I serve the 'God Most High, Creator of heaven and earth'(Gen. 14:19). He is the God of love (1 John 4:8), mercy (Eph. 2:4), and grace (1Peter 5:10). I love Him because He first loved me (1 John 4:19) I can't put a 'not' in one truth of scripture and leave the 'nots' out in others. If He is the God of love...He is also the God of judgment. (Ps. 50:6, Ecc. 3:17)

The preacher who shouted this sermon seemed miserable to me. I felt that misery myself for years. But I have gotten the 'nots' out of the places they don't belong, and put them where they do belong.

My God is not mean and nasty. He does not wait, anticipating when He might punish me for messing up. But at the same time, He means what He says... and it's always in my best interest to believe Him and do as He has said...

...Because HE WILL do as He says. There is definitely no 'not' there....

FEAR

The word appears 400 times in the King James Translation, 258 times in the New International Version. We are told to fear God, yet time and time again scripture says 'fear not.' So which is it?

I struggled with the issue of fear for a very long time. Still I can't wrap my mind completely around the concept at times. But we have a Helper Who aids our understanding. "...if you accept my words and store up my commands within you, turning your ear to wisdom and applying your heart to understanding, and if you call out for insight and cry aloud for understanding, and if you look for it as for silver and search for it as for hidden treasure...THEN you will understand the fear of the Lord and find the knowledge of God." (emphasis mine, Proverbs 2:1-5)

Understanding fear is possible. Scripture has lots to say about it. What it is, what it is not. It is 'to hate evil, pride arrogance, and the evil ways...' (Prov. 8:13)

It is 'a fountain of life'. (Prov. 14:27)

It is '...required of thee...to fear the Lord and walk in all His ways...' (Deut. 10:12)

Many other times scripture tells us about 'fear'. The Hebrew word 'yare' is a verb and is translated some 330 times as 'fear'. But it's meaning can be both being afraid, or being reverent and respectful. There is a huge difference in the two.

As I look for answers and understanding, I take great comfort in these words...

"...Fear not...for I know that you seek Jesus..." (Mat.28:5)
"...God is my salvation. I will trust and not be afraid..." (Isa.12:2)
"In God, I have put my trust. I will not be afraid." (Ps. 56:11)

Hallelujah

PASTOR

Pastor… A job? A gift? Sometimes both? Sometimes not?

The word pastor was not in the vocabulary of my particular religious heritage. We had 'preachers'. Sometimes the preacher was also an 'elder'. The elders made the decisions for the congregation at that place. Other religious groups allow each person who has their name written on the document of the church roll to have a 'vote'. Everybody has an official say-so.

I find that word only used nine times in the KJV. Eight of those times is in the book of Jeremiah. One time, it is used in Ephesians 4:11 "And he gave some, apostles, and some, prophets: and some, evangelists: and some, pastors and teachers."

"He gave…" Sounds like a gift to me. And surely there must be a difference in a pastor, a teacher, and an evangelist…else they wouldn't all be listed.?

The following verse states a purpose, "for the perfecting of the saints, for the work of the ministry, for the edifying of the Body of Christ." (Eph. 4:12)

I looked into the word 'shepherd'… (Read this with a little humor please.…) "The hired hand is not the shepherd.…" John 10:12

I've been pastored, I've been taught, and I've been preached to. In my opinion, there is a huge difference. Sometimes it was by the hired hand…often not. I realize I have some radical views sometimes…especially when it comes to organized religion. I heard it said once that it was possible to organize the organism right out of the church.

The Body of Christ is alive. But it is often not well. I fear we have 'paid' someone to do so many things for so long that we've organized a monster that is often hard to feed. Because of my religious past, I rely very little on preachers or pastors. They are just as human as I am, perhaps more educated or more experienced, but they have no more access to God than I do. Jesus intercedes for them just like He does for me. When they are exercising a God-given gift appropriately, I have been blessed, nurtured, admonished, and encouraged. When they were exercising the description of the job, I've been hurt, shamed, angered, and humiliated.

That's my baggage. I am sure you have your own...and we probably both need to unpack it, take it all out, look it over good, and ask the Lord to give it a good scrubbing.

"Whiter than snow..." (Ps. 51:7)

LIVE

We want to live, not the alternative. We have expectations about its duration. . We have a place to live. What is it to really 'live'? Is it to just exist? Breathe and have a heart beat? Is it to push the limits, be adventurous, even rebelling against what is expected or right? Have a 'good time'?

I'm reminded of that thing about what's between the dash. You remember… that dash that connects your date of birth and date of death on your tombstone…. I need to think about that dash today, because I'm in it. But the question is, what am I living for? Am I living simply because I haven't died yet? Am I living to work and spend? Or living to work so I can save and count it? Am I living for the next thrill? The next fix of my own brand of addiction?

Sigh…

Thank You Lord that I have died already. "Who His own self, bare our sins in His own body on the tree, that we, being dead to sins, should live unto righteousness: by whose stripes ye were healed." (1 Peter 2:24)

And thank You even more that I live. Jesus died so 'that I might die to sins…. and LIVE for righteousness…' (same passage, personalized by me)

I have ceased to exist as far as sin is concerned. My existence is for the righteousness. "Since Jesus went through everything I'm going through and more, I must learn to think like Him. Think of my sufferings as a weaning from that old sinful habit of always expecting to get my own way. Then I'll be able to live out my days free to pursue what God wants instead of being tyrannized by what I want." (1 Peter 4:1,2 The Message, personalized by me)

Thank You Jesus !!

CHANGES

Changes… Looks like some big ones are headed our way. We thought it was a great name for a hair salon. I have said dozens of times, 'Change is good!'. Now, changes in my life…. that's another matter! We tend to cling to the familiar around here, do the same things over and over, go to the same places, eat the same thing… There is security in the familiar.

"There is a time for everything, and a season for every activity under heaven…" (Ecc.3:1) Perhaps it's the birthday coming up, "There is a time to be born, and a time to die." (v.2a) I'm counting them off pretty fast these days. Perhaps it's that life hasn't unfolded as I expected. My children have full successful lives, just not what I expected. "There is a time to plant, and a time to uproot… there is a time to embrace, and a time to refrain…" (v. 2b, 5b)

Whatever it is, the changes that may come are challenging. But "I know that everything God does will endure forever. Nothing can be added to it, and nothing taken from it…"(v. 14)

I have influenced decisions in the past, and regretted it. (…….there's that time of refraining I was not obedient in…..)

My only influence should be before the throne of God in prayer for His perfect will to be done. My roles have changed several times…and will change again. Who will I be next? Where will this path wind up? What lies in my future, and the future of my family? I do not know. I cannot fathom what God has done from beginning to end…' (v.11b)

But I know The One Who does know. "He has made everything beautiful in its time." (v.11a) And ' I am convinced that neither death nor life, neither angels nor demons, neither the present nor the future, nor any powers, neither height nor depth, nor anything else in all creation, will be able to separate us from the love of God that is in Christ Jesus our Lord.' (Rom. 8:38,39)

That includes all the way between Texas and New Jersey….

SCHOOL

End of summer means it is almost time to start…. then again, is it ever really over? We have buildings especially built for schooling. We have a calendar where the first and last official day are set, with special days in between set aside. But schooling should never really end. We should always be in the process of learning, especially from our mistakes.

God will never waste the tiniest bit of pain, IF we go to Him with it honestly, admit our failures and mistakes, and allow Him to use it. He can and WILL bring blessing out of every difficulty, if we only allow and accept.

"Show me how you work, God. School me in Your ways. Take me by the hand, lead me down the path of truth…" (Ps. 25:4,5a The Message) The lesson to learn though, is that there is indeed truth…A path of truth. That path is NOT an eight-lane highway with a mix-master going in all directions. No, it's a single path. And guess what? God marked the path.

"We don't have to rely on the world's guesses and opinions. We didn't learn this by reading books or going to school. We learned it from God, who taught us person-to person through Jesus, and we are passing it on to you in the same firsthand, personal way." (1 Cor. 2:13 The Message) Those are the words of the apostle Paul. If he didn't rely on guesses and opinions, how can I? No…the Truth came in the Person of Jesus Christ, and it will never change. No matter what they teach in any school. He "didn't receive it through the traditions, and he wasn't taught it in some school…He got it straight from God…" (Gal. 1:12 The Message) So can I. Simply by opening scripture, and relying on the promises and power of the Holy Spirit "Whom the Father will send in Jesus Name" (John 14:26) He will open them up to me.

Don't know how? "God delights in genuine prayers." (Pro. 15:8) Ask HIM!! Sunday school won't automatically do it. Neither will 'church services'. Both will be empty and lifeless without the Spirit breathing His Life into us. "It's a school of hard knocks for those who leave God's path, a dead-end street for those who hate God's rules." (Pro. 15:10 The Message) I

f you don't like the rules, you just don't understand the 'why' behind the rule. I promise, even when we don't understand, there is always a reason behind what God says, and it's always to our advantage. He is ALWAYS right. And He ALWAYS wants the best for us.

So…is school out? Think you're smart enough? Have you decided to stop learning? Have you refused to learn from where you have been and what you have experienced? Or have you decided you're just not smart enough to learn anything else? Is it too hard, or too much trouble? (…maybe a bit lazy?) Please get this…. really, really get this…. "Listen to good advice if you want to live well…. An undisciplined, self-willed life is puny; an obedient, God-willed life is spacious. Fear of God is a school in skilled living…first you learn humility, then you experience glory." (Pro. 15:31-33 The Message)

It may seem like an awful choice, the enemy will do his best to make you believe that….but following God is the only way to truly live. If you haven't experienced it, you have no idea what you are missing.

WITHDRAWAL

Withdrawal: the act of taking something away, taking away something which a person is addicted to thereby causing discomfort or pain.

My friend Kathy said she missed me and was having withdrawals. When I had not written in several days she gave me some very exaggerated flattery, but it was nice to hear. It is good to be missed.

Missed. Tthe word can mean fail to be present for something, omit or leave out. Looks like we will soon miss my oldest son and his family. We will certainly have withdrawals, as they live just next door.

Our son has a career move that calls them to New Jersey. We are very proud of his accomplishments, and excited about this opportunity. Yet we will all suffer withdrawals as we adjust. I've never been to New Jersey, but I'm sure it exists. I'm even more sure that God is sovereign in New Jersey just as He is sovereign in Texas. He is big enough and powerful enough to care for my family even there. I wonder if Abraham's mother was alive when God instructed him to leave his homeland and go to a faraway place? Wonder how his family reacted when he said he was moving?

"Leave your country, your people...and go...I will bless you...So Abraham left..." (Genesis 12: 1,2,4) I've prayed often for my children. This was not what I had in mind. But God has proven Himself faithful to me. As doors swing wide open in New Jersey, and doors here remain closed, I trust my God. "God's love is ever and always eternally present to all who fear Him, making everything right for them and their children as they follow His covenant ways and remember to do whatever He said." (Ps. 103:17,18 The Message) Now I continue to pray... that God is now preparing the way before them, preparing the Body of Christ to enfold them as they find the church that will meet their spiritual needs, that He will guide them to the home He has for them there, bless them with friendships, and that this job will indeed be a blessing in every way. I ask that He is so close they will feel His Breath, every step, every moment....and give us all His peace.

BOXES

They come in many varieties. I have some plain cardboard. I have others of plastic. I have some pretty wooden ones, others that have pictures on them. They're all boxes though.

The purpose it to be a container. I have one in my vehicle that I bought just because it was so pretty. Haven't decided what to do with it yet, so it's still in the backseat.

It came in very handy one day. I took our oldest grand-daughter to purchase a Bible to commemorate her baptism a couple weeks ago. She's distraught about the upcoming move from Texas to New Jersey, and was asking a lot of questions.

The questions took a turn in the direction of God, heaven, and life after death...you know, all those questions you can't really find a pat answer for.

Where is heaven? I'd rather live here...
Will we be able to walk around and talk? I want to be with you...
Will we know each other? I don't want to be by myself...
Is God nice? He sounds mean on that video at your house...

The questions kept coming and got even harder. I was forced to say that I just didn't know, but I knew that it would be perfect. Then I remembered that pretty box in the backseat...

Think of it like this, I told her. Every single thing that is a reality to me, or even to the most brilliant and knowledgeable person to ever live...all of that reality, is in that box. Every person. Every thing. Every star in the universe. Everything that exists that we can possibly have knowledge about now or in the future, is in that box.

In that box is all we can know….and we are confined to it.

God is not confined to that box. He MADE the box and everything in it. Unlike us, He can be in the box WITH us, and He can also be outside the box.

He is omnipresent. We are not.
We are finite. He is infinite.

The only things we can understand have to be the things inside the box. To help us understand any concept that is NOT in the box, God uses something IN the box to help us, He uses word pictures. "Streets of gold" "Whiter than snow" "The Lord roars"

How can He communicate to us any other way than thru what we 'know'… thru what is in fact a reality to us? When He is telling us something that is absolutely NOT yet reality to us, we must choose to believe and trust Him. We call that faith. It is a hard concept.

Then she asked me if the devil was real.

sigh……… :)

DREAD

Dread: Apprehension of evil or danger. Uneasiness or alarm excited because of expected pain, loss, or other evil.

I dread days when. I am overbooked. There will be no time for fun conversation, no time for breaks. Maybe no lunch or even potty breaks. Yep...I dread it. But I'm sure thankful for my job and for my clientele. Very thankful.

"What have I to dread, what have I to fear, leaning on the everlasting Arm" It took me several minutes to recall that line, it is a very old hymn. I am reminded that on difficult days, it is most important to be leaning on that Arm and not leaning on myself. Today will be full, but 'If the Lord delights in my way, He makes my steps firm' (Ps. 37:23 personalized by me)

There are lots of things on my mind that I dread with all the changes looming in our lives. I am not afraid. I do trust Him. Dread is different from fear, it is not sudden but it is more continued. So, I am admonished to put that dread also into His Arms and trust. I am told that if I'm not careful with this matter, I may become 'a dread to my friends, those who see me on the streets may flee from me.' (Ps. 31:11 personalized by me)

Even the best of friends can become tired of the voicing of my dread!!

TRANSLATIONS

There are dozens of different ones, yet some people think that the King James is the only reliable one. It might even be the one Jesus used... (That was a joke.)

The only scripture Jesus used was what we call the Old Testament, and it was written in Hebrew....and on scrolls. I love the King James. I don't use it anymore. I'm not good at memorizing and quoting, but what little I can quote verbatim is from the King James, it was what we used when I was a child. A lot of what I read and heard might as well have been Hebrew. I have never spoken "The King's English", and I didn't understand a lot of what King James's translated Bible said. Sometimes, what might otherwise be very familiar words, is very profound said differently. Same message, same content, same application...different words...and POW!! You get this big A-HA!!

Here was one of mine:

. "...I tried keeping rules and working my head off the please God, and it didn't work. So, I quit being a 'law man' so that I could be God's man. Christ's life showed me how, and enabled me to do it. I identified myself completely with Him. Indeed, I have been crucified with Christ. My ego is no longer central. It is no longer important that I appear righteous before you.... or have your good opinion...and I am not longer driven to impress God. Christ lives in me. The life you see me living...is not 'mine'...but it is lived by faith in the son of God, Who loved me and gave Himself for me. I am not going to go back on that. Is it not clear to you that to go back to that old rule-keeping, peer-pleasing religion would be an abandonment of everything personal and free in my relationship with God? I refuse to do that, to repudiate God's grace. If a living relationship with God could come by rule keeping, then Christ died unnecessarily."

Wow.... (That is in Galatians 2 for you KJV folks that might want to check.)

PLANS

Plans...there are plenty today. God has always had a plan, ."..to prosper you and not to harm you, plans to give you hope and a future,"(Jer.29:11) We can follow His plan, or "continue with our own plan, each of us following the stubbornness of his evil heart."(Jer.18:12) Our plans end in eternal death without Him. The fear of the Lord leads to life. (Pro.19:23)...eternal life.... even after the last heartbeat...Hallelujah

GRIEF

...I've tasted it, but have never had to drink the cup that has been to the lips of so many dear friends. Again today, a dear friend drinks. I have no help... nothing to offer...no way to take it away. I read again Job's story, ."If only my anguish could be weighed and all my misery be placed on the scales...it would surely outweigh the sand of the seas.."(Job 6:2) I cannot imagine the heaviness of her sorrow. I can only offer myself to God and ask Him to use me in some small way to bring His comfort. He is the only answer. "In my distress, I called to the Lord. I cried to my God for help From His temple He heard my voice. My cry came before Him, into His ears. (Ps.18:6)

SEPARATION

"If you loved me, you would be glad that I am going to the Father..."
(John 14:28)

In children, we have labeled it 'separation anxiety'. Children most often cry when their parents leave them. Had I walked and talked with Jesus, I have no doubt I would have had separation anxiety too. The disciples did not find it easy to hear when Jesus was preparing them for what was about to happen. But they needed to hear it, and He needed to say it. The purpose of His life was not to just live it out. His purpose was far greater. In fact, the end of His life was the very reason He was born.

We are never anxious to be separated from those we love and rely on, yet the time comes when we are all separated from each other. Death comes if nothing else. Today, people I love are faced with coming separation. I pray that God will remind each one who struggles with the anxiousness of the moment.

".... you do not belong to the world, but I have chosen you out of the world."
(John 15:19)

"Precious in the sight of the LORD is the death of his saints.: (Psalm 116:15)

We may be apart from each other for some period of time... a very short time in the eternal scope of things, but we can be confident that we are never really separated. Not when it is the very love of God that binds us together with Him. Hallelujah.

FAKE

I have some things that are not 'real'. Lots of costume jewelry, some imitation furs, lots of cut glass, fake diamonds, fake mink, fake crystal. It doesn't matter to me that they are imitation. They are just as pretty. I am pickier about some things. I don't like fake leather. If you know me very well, you know I'm an original bag-lady. I like handbags, and I want 'real'. Don't give me some fake leather, I know the difference.

I heard a challenge via a radio message that caused me to pause and consider my taste in authenticity. I had just been shopping for a handbag I thought I wanted...till I felt of it and found it to be made of something called pvc. (I think that must be plastic...)

I didn't buy what I thought I wanted because it wasn't 'real' I like leather. Real leather. Soft leather. Certainly, not plastic.

The radio speaker challenged me about the authenticity of something else. My professed faith. He said it is easy to fake religious convictions. Just learn the language, wear the clothes, and go to the right places. You'll blend right in. I want authentic leather in my handbags. I want to be authentic in the professions I make.

Lord, help me walk the talk, because if you don't, I'm sure to be faking it. Help me, Father, to "do my best, fill my mind and help me to meditate on things true, noble, reputable, authentic, compelling, gracious--the best, not the worst; the beautiful, not the ugly; things to praise, not things to curse. Help me put into practice what I have learned..." (Philippians 4:8- The Message)

UNCLEAR

I don't like the unclear. I like it plain as day. I don't like surprises, I like knowing what is ahead, what to expect…and I like understanding the who, what, when, where, and why of it. I've studied the eleventh chapter of Hebrews recently, and again looked at the portraits hanging in the 'hall of faith' we are shown there. "By faith Abraham, when God tested him, offered Isaac as a sacrifice. He who had received the promises was about to sacrifice his one and only son, even though God had said to him, "It is through Isaac that your offspring will be reckoned." Abraham reasoned that God could raise the dead, and figuratively speaking, he did receive Isaac back from death." (Hebrews 11:17-19)

There is a song I like to sing that calls on this event. The lyrics are: "'There he stood upon that hill, Abraham with knife in hand, was poised to kill. But God, in all Your sovereignty, had bigger plans, and just in time, You brought a lamb. Cause You were there, You were there, in the midst of the unclear. You were there, you were there….always. You were there when obedience seemed to not make sense. You were there. You were always there."

I find it incredible that Abraham intended to obey at such great length. Killing a son who was promised, the son who would supposedly be the beginning of a great lineage. Multitudes of heirs to be born in the future. It just didn't make sense. Abraham figured God would just over-rule a dead Isaac, and make him alive again. God could certainly do that…HAS done that.

The lyrics of that song haunt me and accuse me. In the midst of the unclear, am I obedient? When obedience doesn't make sense, do I obey anyway? Will my picture ever hang in a hall of faith? I hope I don't have to be tested to find out……

CHOOSING

There is an Indiana Jones movie line that is repeated often around our house. "He chose poorly..." The greedy villain in the movie was choosing which vessel might be the holy grail and looked over the wooden cup, choosing instead a very ornate solid gold one. He chose poorly.

I thought about that while studying the characters of the "Hall of Faith" of Hebrews 11. Moses chose well. " By faith, Moses, when grown, refused the privileges of the Egyptian royal house. He chose a hard life with God's people rather than an opportunistic soft life of sin..." (Hebrews 11:24-25 The Message) I

t sure didn't look like a good choice. I'm quite sure it made absolutely no sense to the woman who had taken him from the river to the king's palace and raised him as a prince of Egypt. I bet she had a fit, and I bet the royal family was quite insulted. But Moses chose to seek God.

Lord, help me that I not choose poorly. Help me to see the opportunities to sin for what they are, help me to see past the pleasure of that moment, and choose to seek You with an undivided heart.

I'm sure Moses has no regrets about his choices. I want to have no regrets about mine....

DISAGREEMENTS

Why is it easier to disagree in anger? Why can we not just agree to disagree and move on? It seems to me that anger is often a tool in the enemy's hand, a genuine emotion that is twisted and used against us. I wish I could say I never enter there. I wish every conflict I face could be dealt with without anger being a factor. But, I'm not there....

It is not true that conflict can always be avoided. It is not required of us to be a doormat to someone who disagrees with us, but conflict can be worked out. God can and will continue to work out His will.

"Barnabas wanted to take John, also called Mark, with them, but Paul did not think it wise to take him, because he had deserted them in Pamphylia and had not continued with them in the work. They had such a sharp disagreement that they parted company."(Acts 15:37-39)

There is a lot of applicable lessons in this situation recorded in scripture. Disagreements happen even in the most spiritual of us. We are all in an imperfect state, there was only One Who had no faultiness in His Personality. We may disagree and disagree passionately, but we must not disagree on the purpose before us, and that is to re-present Jesus Christ to anyone we can influence.

You may do that differently than I do. And God is ok with that...It's His work anyway, remember?

RESULTS

I like to see results quickly, or else I usually get discouraged. Something I struggle with is walking in obedient faith. Faith is not being sure of what we see. It is not hoping intensely for what we hope for, not wishful thinking, or even positive thinking. It is "being sure of what we hope for. It is being certain of what we do not see." (Hebrews 11:1)

Reading in Acts about Paul and his companions beginning a second trip to find people who might listen and respond to the message of Jesus the Christ, "......we traveled to Philippi, a Roman colony. It is an important city in that part of Macedonia. We stayed there several days." (Acts 16:12) Several days. What can be accomplished in a mere 'several days'?

When this little band of mission minded, sold-out-to-Jesus, born-again sons of God traveled to Philippi and stayed a few days, a lot was accomplished. Paul ministered there and some years later wrote a letter to those same people. That letter is the book of Philippians in our Bible. That letter has brought me more encouragement than I can recall....these being just a few.

"...He who began a good work in you will carry it on to completion."(1:6)

"...this is my (Paul's) prayer: that your love may abound more and more in knowledge and depth of insight, so that you may be able to discern what is best..."(1:9-10)

"Each of you should look not only to your own interests, but also to the interests of others. Your attitude should be the same as that of Christ Jesus" (2:4,5)

"...continue to work out your salvation with fear and trembling, for it is God who works in you to will and to act according to his good purpose." (2:12,13)

"I consider everything a loss compared to the surpassing greatness of knowing Christ Jesus my Lord." (3:8)

"I want to know Christ and the power of his resurrection, not that I have already obtained all this, or have already been made perfect, but I press on to take hold of that for which Christ Jesus took hold of me, forgetting what is behind and straining toward what is ahead, I press on toward the goal"(3:10,12,14)

".... our citizenship is in heaven...He will transform our lowly bodies so that they will be like his glorious body." (3:20,21)

"Rejoice! Let your gentleness be evident to all. The Lord is near. Do not be anxious about anything, but by prayer .... present your requests to God. And the peace of God, which transcends all understanding, will guard your hearts and your minds in Christ Jesus. whatever is true, whatever is noble, whatever is right, whatever is pure, whatever is lovely, whatever is admirable —if anything is excellent or praiseworthy—think about such things. Whatever you have learned or received or heard from me, or seen in me— put it into practice. and the God of peace will be with you. (4:4-9)

Thank you my brother Paul, for going to Phillipi and staying for 'several days'. For getting acquainted with those people to whom you later wrote this letter. I can't tell you have many times I've read it and been encouraged by your words...by knowing that even you struggled, by hearing how you dealt with difficulty, from your admonishments to rejoice, to pray, to think on excellent things...

You could never have known the results...you certainly didn't see them.

USUALLY

We humans tend to have patterns of behavior. Habits are made easily, both good habits and bad habits. We have lots of encouragement from our enemy to make the bad ones. Making good habits is encouraged by the God Who loves us, but He doesn't force us. It has always been our choice, and the operating procedure of the enemy hasn't changed. He tempts, lies, deceives, and encourages poor choices. What do other people expect of you? What is your 'usually'?

Last week I didn't have my iPod playing the music I like. People asked about it. They said, "it is 'usually' playing". I wasn't at church last week, this week people asked why, "You're usually here…" they said. My husband asked if I was taking a nap after we had lunch Sunday, "You usually do." He said.

Yes, I exhibit many definite patterns of behavior. Certainly, not all good. (…I'll not reflect on those here…)

In studying the events of Paul's travel, I was struck with his 'usual'. "….as he usually did…" (Acts 17:2 The Message) "…Paul went into the synagogue, and on three Sabbath days he reasoned with them from the Scriptures, explaining and proving that the Christ had to suffer and rise from the dead."(Acts 17:2-3 NIV)

Paul's main objective was to inform every person he could influence about Who Jesus is, that Jesus was not dead but alive, and what that meant to them personally. He always had an audience at the local church house. He might not be welcomed for long, they might reject his message and throw him out, or throw him in jail, but he went. And he told them truth. That's what he usually did.

What do I usually do? Do I look for opportunities to talk about who Jesus is? Or is my 'usually' something far different? Lord, help me to never miss an opportunity to relate to someone else the awesome truth of Who You are and what You have made possible for us.

IMITATE

My sons have fun with imitating people. They have been especially known for imitations by telephone conversations. (...stirred up quite a ruckus on occasion before they 'fessed up to the person on the other end of the line...)

I know that I am the subject of imitation sometimes. In the summer, when it is swimming pool time, a simple movement of the hands in a certain way brings a response of laughter. Everyone knows who is being imitated. Me.

Lots of money is made by comedians who imitate famous people. Lots of hurt feelings come from unkind imitations of others. Being imitated is sometimes done out of humor. Sometimes, it's out of ridicule. Sometimes it is the highest form of flattery.

"You became imitators of us and of the Lord..."(1 Thessalonians 1:6) Paul wrote a lot of follow up letters. He had been with the people of this city, taught them the truth about Jesus Christ, and educated them on the salvation that was not possible for all people. It is incredible to me that Paul stayed humble. He could have been very prideful about all the imitators of his gospel message. He could easily have been tempted into taking credit. Satan tempted Jesus in that way, I feel sure he wouldn't hesitate to tempt Paul in that way. What these new believers imitated was merely Paul's own imitation of Jesus Christ.

I pray that any person I can influence to Christ, will fully understand, that they are to imitate only Jesus Christ in me. There will be opportunity to see shortcomings. Certainly, there will be things I would never want imitated. How I pray to be a good example, a good role model, and that they will be pointed past me to Him. He is the absolute only good in me.

FLATTERY

Webster says "commendation bestowed for the purpose of gaining favor and influence, or to accomplish some purpose." Flattery is used a lot for self-interest. People flatter others to push forward their own agenda, gain favor, be benefited.

Flattering words are always easy to hear. The flattering words might have shreds of truth in them, but there are phony. They are self-serving, far different than a simple compliment, and it covers up a person's real intentions. I'd never thought this much about flattery, never considered its root, nor its purpose. I've experienced flattery, and have recognized it as being manipulative. It is difficult for me to take a simple compliment, so flattery has always been quite distasteful. While I don't enjoy a harsh delivery of truth, neither do I enjoy or want to be buttered up.

"We are not trying to please men but God, who tests our hearts. You know we never used flattery, nor did we put on a mask to cover up greed—God is our witness. We were not looking for praise from men, not from you or anyone else..." (1 Thessalonians. 2:4-6)

In writing to his spiritual family in Thessalonica, Paul assured them he had no ulterior motive in his ministry to them. It was always about God and his love in providing salvation. He didn't do anything to make it easier to hear. He didn't hold out the need for repentance and a change of heart, change of attitude, and changes of behavior. And, he didn't flatter them by needing their praise. When someone else is so important to me that I need their approval regardless of whether it lines up with God's will, .I flatter them. And I insult God.

Paul didn't go there. I wonder how often I do. How about you? Do you use words of praise to bring some benefit to yourself? Do you need someone to think highly of you so much that you make compromises? Like me, have you been guilty of attempting to make the truth easier to hear? More easily acceptable?

TEMPLE

I've never seen a building called a temple, but I have studied a lot about the worship conducted in the temple of God in scripture. The temple was very costly to construct. It was damaged by enemy forces, and restored, but was completely destroyed in 70 A.D. Some people think it will be rebuilt, some don't. It's according to your interpretation of end-time events. One thing that is certain, I am a temple. Now.

"…Do you not know that your body is a temple of the Holy Spirit, who is in you, whom you have received from God…" (1Cor. 6:19)

The construction process was lengthy, and there have been many attacks from the enemy on this temple, lots of damage done, at a lot of different times…… and there have been lots of restorations made. At one time, I thought the restoration came from the front end of a church-house aisle. I have come to the conclusion that true restoration comes only from the One Who created it to begin with. He built it, He re-builds it. Praise God.

Though I'm not there yet, He is in the process of restoring me to be what He intended me to be all along. Praise God He has mended damage done by the enemy, damage from past hurts, damage from sin. Some of the damages to this temple were done from the inside, my temple hasn't always been used as it was designed to be used. "…Therefore, honor God with your body." (1Cor. 6:20) I have not always honored God with my behavior. Very often, I've done the damage myself.

The enemy is persistent, he attacks on a regular basis. Some of his attacks are simply methods of deceiving me into tearing down the temple myself. He's a pesky rascal. He is defeated and he knows it for, "…. I am more than conqueror through Him who loved me. For I am convinced that neither death nor life, neither angels nor demons, neither the present nor the future, nor any powers, neither height nor depth, nor anything else in all creation, will be able to separate me from the love of God that is in Christ Jesus my Lord. (Rom. 8:37-39 personalized by me)

He continues to make those drive-by attacks and cause as much trouble as he can, gets me distracted, and when he can catch me off guard, he still gets an arrow thru or knocks a hole in the wall somewhere. That's ok. There is One Who restores me every single time. He is within, on the job at all times, helping me and restoring me. "I have heard the prayer and plea you have made before me; I have consecrated this temple..." (1 Kings 9:3)

BECOMING

There is a slogan among hair salons… "If your hair is not becoming to you, you should be coming to us." It's a catchy little advertising slogan. I've seen it printed on t-shirts and coffee cups. I don't use it, but during my quiet time, I sometimes hear it with just a little twist. "Connie…if what you see in yourself is not becoming to you, you should be coming to Me."

What is unbecoming in me is beyond my fixing it. And once He has addressed the unbecoming mess, there's always another unbecoming mess that becomes a problem. Just like my house, my temple needs cleaning regularly.

"What is my beloved doing in my temple as she … works out her evil schemes? (Jer. 11:15) And so, again, I find myself convicted by scripture. "… on the day… He comes to be glorified in His holy people and to be marveled at among all those who have believed. (2 Thessalonians 1:10)

When, not if, for be assured, He IS coming, to be recognized and acknowledged for all that He is., IN His holy people. And since I am His, that includes me. He is coming to be glorified in me. And if you're His, that means you too.

That process is begun. It is visible, or should be…for we "are being transformed into his likeness with ever-increasing glory." (2 Cor. 3:18) When He comes, it will be no longer be a matter of 'good hair days' and 'bad hair days'. For now, some days we look a little more like Jesus than others. On that day, He will be revealed in every one of us. Never again will we evaluate each other "…. from a worldly point of view." (2Cor. 5:16)

RETIREMENT

It's a biblical concept, but I wonder if we haven't distorted it. After the tribes of Hebrew people left Egypt, and while they were traveling thru to the land that God intended to give them, there was a portable structure called the Tabernacle that served as the place to meet with God. When the people moved, the Tabernacle was disassembled and moved with them, the structure itself and all the furniture and furnishings that served various purposes in the worship conducted there. When the people stopped again and made camp, the Tabernacle was reassembled and readied again for worship and meeting with God. One of the tribes of people, the Levi people, were designated to take care of everything concerning God's Tabernacle and were also to conduct the worship activities. If you were a Levite man, at the age of 25 you began to train for your work as a priest. At 30, you began to serve. ("Count all the men from thirty to fifty years of age who come to serve in the work in the Tent of Meeting." Numbers 4:3) At the age of 50, you retired. "The LORD said to Moses, "This applies to the Levites: Men twenty-five years old or more shall come to take part in the work at the Tent of Meeting, but at the age of fifty, they must retire from their regular service and work no longer. They may assist their brothers in performing their duties at the Tent of Meeting, but they themselves must not do the work...." (Numbers 8:23-26)

The difference in their retirement and what we think of as retirement if huge. The 50-year-old Levite priest retired only from taking down the structure and from the physical parts of the worship rituals. They didn't 'retire' and go back to the tent and sit in the recliner. Their retirement was becoming a supervisor instead of a laborer. Their retirement relieved them early from physical stress on an aging body. It allowed the older men to advise and counsel the upcoming workforce by on-the-job mentoring. Retirement in our culture sounds like a great thing. But I really doubt anyone enjoys not being useful to some body, some way, somehow. Maybe so, maybe no.... don't know if I'll ever find out!!!

LIMBO

Limbo... Have you ever felt like you were living in it...just suspended somehow, waiting?

Waiting to be a teenager. Waiting to be 21 years old, that 'magical 'legal' age.

Waiting to get married. Waiting to have children. Waiting for the children to be grown.

Waiting to have the house paid for. Waiting for retirement.

Waiting to get a doctor's report. Waiting for a treatment plan.

Waiting on some difficult situation to get better. Waiting on financial burdens to be lighter.

Waiting for next year when political offices change. Waiting on the next election.

Waiting, waiting, waiting....

Living in limbo while you wait, trying to figure out what to do, how to do it, what not to do, and how to keep from doing that, and waiting on promises. I often feel like I'm in limbo. There are seasons of my life when that feeling is a constant thing. There are times I want to do what the Thessalonians did, but Paul wrote to them, it's recorded and preserved in scripture, so I have been instructed against it. They believed in Jesus Christ, Who He is, what He accomplished. And they believed He was coming back to get them. So, they just pretty much quit the business of life, sat down, and waited in limbo for that to happen.

"Concerning the coming of our Lord Jesus Christ and our being gathered to Him... stand firm and hold to the teachings we passed on to you, whether

by word of mouth or by letter.... We hear that some among you are idle....
Such people we command and urge in the Lord Jesus Christ to settle down
and earn the bread they eat. And as for you, brothers, never tire of doing
what is right. If anyone does not obey our instruction in this letter, take
special note of him. Do not associate with him, in order that he may feel
ashamed. Yet do not regard him as an enemy, but warn him as a brother. (2
Thessalonians 2:1,15 3:11-15)

It is true. I am in limbo. Between eternity past, and eternity future. But I am
not to just sit and wait. I pray in agreement with Paul, "May the Lord direct
my heart into God's love and Christ's perseverance. (2 Thessalonians 3:5
personalized by me)

BREATH

Ever feel like you can't breathe, feel like you are suffocating, like the air you breathe in just isn't enough somehow, and you find yourself sighing over and over? I often find myself doing that. I just don't always breathe right. Don't breathe deeply enough.

When God formed the first human, Scripture says "He breathed the breath of life into him. And the man became a living person." (Gen.2:7) "The heavens were made when the LORD commanded it to happen. All of the stars were created by the breath of his mouth." (Ps. 33:6) God created life and every facet of our reality. God sustains life and every facet of our reality.

Don't be fooled. You don't do it. Government doesn't do it. Education doesn't do it.

A wealthy economy doesn't do it. Medicine doesn't do it. Not even religion does it.

He does.

"When You turn Your face away from them, they are terrified. When You take away their breath, they die and turn back into dust." (Ps. 104:29)

A look into history will show that when the blessings begin to be withdrawn, when things get tough and the tough can't seem to bring about restored blessing, people begin to pant and search for God, begging for help. Time and time again, He has brought restoration and healing. How I praise Him for His mercy, and the perfect love He offers. My human nature is incapable of that perfect love, I am slow to extend love to those I deem undeserving. Thank You Lord God that you do not have a heart like mine. And thank You Father that you have said, "I will not find fault with my people forever. I will not always be angry with them. If I were, I would cause their spirits to grow weak. The very breath of life would go out of the people I created." (Isa. 57:16)

The breath of life within me is more than the oxygen my lungs process for maintaining this flesh. The real breath within me is what He breaths out. Some days, I choose not to breath it in. Some days I choose to ignore the breathe He provides, and choose to choke and spew on whatever is available, and be assured, the enemy of my soul provides alternatives to the breath of life from God.

Today, I choose life. Today, I choose to breath in, what He breaths out. "God has breathed life into all of Scripture. It is useful for teaching me what is true. It is useful for correcting my mistakes. It is useful for making my life whole again. It is useful for training me to do what is right. By using Scripture, I can be completely prepared to do every good thing" (2 Tim. 3:16-17 personalized by me)

Call me a Bible banger. Call me a religious finatic. Call me a Jesus freak. Call me whatever you like. He calls me friend. (John 15:15) I breath oxygen and have a heartbeat and pulse because He created human life, a life so very different from plant and animal life. Because of His breath, I breath the breath of God as I inhale what He has said, what He has done, and as I "Receive The Holy Spirit…that He breaths on me …" (John 20:22 personalized by me)

Don't be satisfied with anything else than the life made available and sustained by the very breath of God.

OPPOSITION

I heard it said somewhere, "The positive response to Paul's teaching stirred up opposition to him." The positive response?!? Brought opposition?!? Man, that'd make you want to quit wouldn't it?

When you have some success at what you are attempting to accomplish, it'd be nice simply to not have to listen to negative responses, much less be faced with resistance and obstacles. Human nature is so often ugly, and our enemy doesn't miss many opportunities to make trouble.

At one time, the apostle Paul had been passionate about stamping out the movement of what was then known as 'The Way', that being the way of Jesus Christ. He was passionate, but he was dead wrong. When he met Jesus, he found out how horribly wrong he'd been, then began the mission of his life.: to tell anyone he could get to listen, that Jesus was the Christ, the Messiah, the Son of The Most High God. Jesus was the remedy and cure for the cancerous sin nature in mankind. The sin nature that Paul himself struggled with. (Romans 7 records Paul's testimony about that very thing) God had equipped Paul for all this. He had the best of education. He was a talented communicator. He had some political advantages because he was a Roman citizen. He had lots of success. He preached the story of salvation all across his world. He convinced lots of people, made lots of converts, trained lots of other people to do the same. But it was never easy. It didn't begin easy, and it never got any easier. There were opposing voices even within the believers who loved him. There were attempts to stop him. Permanently.

I thank God right now that he wasn't stopped. I thank You Lord God for recording and preserving these stories in scripture. Thank You for showing me that even Paul had to bear up under opposition, opposition even from within the circle of friends. Thank You for showing us how he met struggles and overcame them. Thank You Lord that you never left him without Your help and the assurance of Your Presence with him.

I am so very thankful for these words our brother Paul penned, "So, if you think you are standing firm, be careful that you don't fall! No temptation has seized you except what is common to man. And God is faithful; he will not let you be tempted beyond what you can bear. But when you are tempted, he will also provide a way out so that you can stand up under it." (1Cor. 10:12-13) I think Paul knew what he was talking about. I think he probably gives us some great advice here. Anyone is prone to fall. Everyone faces difficulty. Each of us must choose good over evil, but God will never leave us alone in a situation. He is present. He sets a boundary around us. He offers an escape. "…All you need to remember is that God will never let you down; he'll never let you be pushed past your limit; he'll always be there to help you come through it." (1Cor. 10:13 The Message)

FATHERED

One of Webster's definitions is 'he who creates

I attended a baby shower recently, my nephew has fathered a child. We are all excited, my sister especially. This will be her first grandchild. It is a boy. My nephew and his wife are anxious to see and hold this new creation. They are to be the parents, not just children of their own parents. Fathering doesn't stop there. Planting the seed is the easy part. It's the rest of the story that is challenging. In fact, the rest of the story is the most vital part.

Those of us who follow Jesus call God our Father. God most certainly created., He created everything. You. Me. And little Eli, who is yet to be born from his mother's womb. "Before I formed you in the womb I knew you..." (Jer. 1:5) He continues in fathering us. Just as little Eli will be nurtured, so does God nurture us.

Jesus Christ ushered in our new birth. The most vital birth, "what counts is a new creation..." (Gal. 6:15) "Therefore, if anyone is in Christ, he is a new creation; the old has gone, the new has come!" (2 Cor.5:17) Being born a human child starts the process. Our parents love us and guide us along the way as we grow up, teaching, mentoring, correcting, disciplining.

Being re-born and becoming a mature child of God is also a process. In a perfect world, human fathers always do the right thing. (sadly, we don't live in a perfect world, not since Eden.)

"Flesh gives birth to flesh...but the Spirit gives birth to spirit." (John 3:6)

"For you have been born again, not of perishable seed, but of imperishable, through the living and enduring word of God." (1 Peter 1:23)

Thank You Father for continuing to father me, for nurturing, teaching, mentoring, correcting, even for the discipline. Thank you for this new life coming into our family. Bless these young parents, give them wisdom and guidance as they take responsibility for this tender new life.

FUTURE

Do you wonder about it, ever wish you could see into it? There are people who claim to do that, and people who pay money to hear what they say. I think most of them are just great con-artists, people who have formulated some general scenarios to spout, most of them pleasant of course. But I think some of them may have some power. Power from a power source that is certainly not of God. Evil in fact.

Scripture has quite a bit of advice about this kind of thing. Simply put… just don't have anything to do with it. If it is not clearly of God, just don't go there. God has given His Word, divinely inspired and recorded, preserved and kept thru the ages. He has given His Spirit to aid in understanding it, recalling it, and applying it. He reveals His truth to us, layer after layer, if only we go to Him with an open and honest heart, asking and expecting. we pay no price. He has paid the price, and it was great.

Oh, I've heard the argument, "I don't really believe it, it's just fun…harmless fun."

Well, maybe you think so. But God seemed to take it pretty serious. "…he consulted mediums and spiritists. He did much evil in the eyes of the LORD, provoking Him to anger." (2 Kings 21:6)

Serious enough to be in a list like this: "Let no one be found among you who sacrifices his son or daughter in the fire, who practices divination or sorcery, interprets omens, engages in witchcraft, or casts spells, or who is a medium or spiritist or who consults the dead. Anyone who does these things is detestable to the LORD" (Deut. 18:10-12)

Make no mistake, God is God. There is no other. But Satan is real, and though his trump card of death is defeated for the child of God thru Jesus Christ, he is real and he is dangerous. He is not harmless. And he is not fun. Don't fall for the deception that dabbling in his realm is recreational. He intends to steal, kill, and destroy you. (John 10:10)

TRUTH

"...the truth will set you free." The words of Jesus, recorded in John 8:32.

There are many ways to be enslaved. There is only one way to be truly free. Often, there are difficult choices to make, many hard things to admit and to deal with.

The enemy is always on the scene to accuse and shame. Satan offers many counterfeit choices. He is the father of lies. He encourages us to live in his lies, he shames us, encourages us to hide the ugly truth, as if that changes it somehow.

Jesus never shames. His Hand is always extended. His desire is that we live in truth and in freedom. But He will not accept anything but absolute truth from us. He forces us to be truthful with Him....and with ourselves.

"So, if the Son sets you free, you will be free indeed." (John 8:36) What lie do you hide? What shame do you live with? Will you be free today?

INTEND

Webster says "To mean; to design; to purpose, that is, to stretch or set forward in mind." Over and over I have come across the same theme, the same message.

Nobody intends to screw up their life. Nobody means to have their once wonderful, romantic marriage turn sour. Nobody means to become financially destroyed. Nobody means to become addicted to drugs or alcohol. The list could go on and on and on.

Nobody means to be a sinner. I don't mean to be one, but try as I may, I am one.

Thank you again Lord, for your forgiveness, for your outstretched Hand, Your Spirit within me that enables me to learn from those things and move forward. Thank You for Your amazing ability to bless me even out of my own poor decisions and wrong attitudes when I truly repent and turn AWAY from them, and turn TO You. Thank You for the amazing way you have used those things to grow my faith in You. How I love You for that.

The book of Joshua gives an example of provisions and protection that God put in place for people who had 'didn't intend to' things in their life. "A person shall escape for refuge to one of these cities, stand at the entrance to the city gate, and lay out his case before the city's leaders. The leaders must then take him into the city among them and give him a place to live with them. "If the avenger of blood chases after him, they must not give him up--he didn't intend to kill the person; there was no history of ill-feeling. He may stay in that city until he has stood trial before the congregation and until the death of the current high priest. Then he may go back to his own home in his hometown from which he fled." (Joshua 20:4-6)

God's Heart has never changed. No matter what wrong thing has happened to us, no matter what poor decisions we have made, no matter how devastating the consequences of those choices, His Heart's desire is to restore us, heal us, and use even the wrong thing in the process. He is God. And He can do it, He WANTS to do it. But we have to make the move. We must turn and go to Him. He is our city of refuge. He is our Healer.

ALE THEUO

Aletheuo is a Greek word that Paul uses in his letter to the Ephesians as he writes about the nature of the Christian church. He uses it again in his letter to the Galatians, challenging and correcting them in some of their conduct. In both cases, it is translated into our English word 'truth'. (Eph. 4:15) "Instead, speaking the truth in love, we will in all things grow up into him who is the Head, that is, Christ."(Gal 4:16)"Have I now become your enemy by telling you the truth?"

It is hard to speak the truth in love. It is easier to speak it in anger. I've done both so I speak from experience. Speaking truth in anger has no care for the damage it may do. Speaking truth in love is concerned about the healing it might bring. I have friends who will speak the truth in love to me. Sometimes, it's not easy to hear it. I have friends who hold back from speaking the truth to me. Sometimes, it's not easy to speak it. I am thankful for those friends who don't want to hurt me with the kind of truth that is not fun to hear. But I am doubly thankful for those few who will speak the truth to me in love, and challenge me to change a wrong attitude or action. And when they do, I want to respond in the same way. In love.

HALLELUJAH

The word hallelujah is a command to praise the Lord. The word is derived from the Hebrew words hālal and Yah . Yah is a pronoun for God, a shortened form of Yahweh, which is often translated "LORD." hālal is a verb that means to praise, to commend, to boast, to shine.

The word most often means praise and is associated with the ministry of the Levites who "…were also to stand every morning to thank and praise the LORD. They were to do the same in the evening." (1Ch. 23:30)

The Levitical priests were God praising, worship leaders. You and I are not Levites, but we too "are a chosen people, a royal priesthood, a holy nation, a people belonging to God, that you may declare the praises of him who called you out of darkness into his wonderful light." (1 Peter 2:9) We should be God praising, Jesus loving, worship leaders.

Jesus Himself said, "Go into all the world and preach the good news to all creation. "(Mark 16:15) The Message reads: "Go everywhere and announce the Message of God's good news to one and all." Hallelujah. Let's praise God. Let's speak His praises to any and every single person whom will listen.

POOR

Reading what is often referred to as The Beatitudes, this passage of scripture record teachings of Jesus that seemed to be a list of contradictions.

"Blessed are the poor in spirit, for theirs is the kingdom of heaven." (Matt. 5:3)

How can you be blessed by being in an obvious negative situation? How can you be happy by being spiritually poor? What does it look like to be poor in spirit?

It is a common thing to find the Christian way of life in complete contradiction to that of the natural world. Spiritual and natural rarely, if ever, follow the same course. Eternal kingdom values and temporary worldly values are so very different. The kingdom of God is nothing like any kingdom of this earthly realm. Wealth and power are important in our world. But what we consider wealth and power are only deceptions. ANY amount of prosperity here, fails to measure up to the hope and joy found in utter dependence on God instead of outward circumstance.

The way of the world says 'feel good about who you are, be confident, be assertive, even aggressive.' Jesus' way is to embrace the truth about who I am, a spiritual beggar incapable of fixing what is wrong deep within my spirit. Accepting that truth about myself, I find myself blessed beyond measure, called a daughter of The Most High God, a citizen of His kingdom, standing as an heiress to the eternal kingdom of heaven.

The more I know the character and love of Jesus, the more I realize the absolute poverty of my own spirit. How merciful He is to extend such grace to this spiritual beggar.

FRUIT

"No good tree bears bad fruit, nor does a bad tree bear good fruit. Each tree is recognized by its own fruit. People do not pick figs from thorn bushes, or grapes from briers." (vs. 43,44) The whole idea of fruit inspecting bothers me. I don't relish the idea of anyone inspecting my fruit. Yet I am to bear fruit.

"He cuts off every branch in me that bears no fruit, while every branch that does bear fruit he prunes so that it will be even more fruitful...This is to my Father's glory, that you bear much fruit, showing yourselves to be my disciples." (John 15:2,8)

Each tree is recognized by the fruit it bears. A peach tree will always have peaches on it, if there is any fruit. Never apples. Never blueberries. Never acorns or pine cones. But the peaches may or may not be great quality or quantity. There must be a lot of work and attention given to a peach tree if you expect to pick good peaches from its branches. Pruning, water, fertilizer, correct sun. Frost can destroy the chance of fruit. Bugs can ruin any fruit that grows. Birds and worms can beat you to the taste test.

"Remain in me, and I will remain in you. No branch can bear fruit by itself; it must remain in the vine. Neither can you bear fruit unless you remain in me. I am the vine; you are the branches. If a man remains in me and I in him, he will bear much fruit; apart from me you can do nothing." (John 15:4,5)

Immediately after Jesus talked about the fruit bearing tree, He said this about the heart. "The good man brings good things out of the good stored up in his heart, and the evil man brings evil things out of the evil stored up in his heart. For out of the overflow of his heart his mouth speaks." (vs.45)

I am reminded not to trust my own heart. "The heart is deceitful above all things and beyond cure." (Jeremiah 17:9)

Only God can change a human heart. "Create in me a pure heart, O God, and renew a steadfast spirit within me." (Ps. 51:10) Only God can enable me to bear good fruit. "...Neither can you bear fruit unless you remain in Me." (Luke 15:4)

Albert Barnes had this to say, "The Savior gives the proper test of their character. People do not judge of a tree by its leaves, or bark, or flowers, but by the fruit which it bears. The flowers may be beautiful and fragrant, the foliage thick and green; but these are merely ornamental. It is the "fruit" that is of chief service to man; and he forms his opinion of the nature and value of the tree by that fruit. So, of pretensions to religion. The profession may be fair; but the "conduct" - the fruit - is to determine the nature of the principles.

Lord, help me to bear good fruit. Prune even though it may be painful, protect from what might destroy or disable fruit bearing, and keep me ever attached to Your lifegiving Vine.

RETALIATE

Webster says it is to return like for like. We all know the golden rule, 'Do unto others as you would have them do unto you'. (Mt. 7:12) Often, we choose to understand it as 'Whatever others do to me, that's what I can do to them'. We want to justify our own desire to retaliate. Life gets difficult. Relationships get complicated. People are people, and with sin natures. We live in a fallen world, with fallen people. Some of them redeemed, some not. People don't always do the right thing. I don't always do the right thing. But I am not given freedom to retaliate. If we were, where would it end?

It can end with me. Right here. Right now, I continue to seek, to listen and to hear, then follow the Holy Spirit that is within. I am assured that He is there… "God has said, "Never will I leave you; never will I forsake you." (Heb. 13:5, Joshua 1:5)

"Those who live according to the sinful nature have their minds set on what that nature desires; but those who live in accordance with the Spirit have their minds set on what the Spirit desires." (Rom.8:5) I resolutely and repeatedly set my mind on Jesus, moment by moment choosing to believe His way and choosing to obey. Constantly, I am on the battlefield of flesh vs. spirit.

LIKE THIS...

οὕτω. It is pronounced hoo'-to. It's a Greek word that means 'like this'. Jesus used it when He spoke the words recorded in Matthew 6:9. ""This is how you should...." Jesus lived a perfect life. He fleshed out a perfect example of 'how you should.' (makes me think again of that WWJD thing.)

We have some of that recorded in the narratives of scripture. One of the 'how you should' topics is about praying. Our enemy would have us deceived about praying. He convinced Eve in the garden that she had misunderstood God. He made her question God's instructions and His motive, and Eve failed to communicate with God about the issues to get some clarity.

Let us not fall into that same trap. Our enemy is as real today as then. He is still a liar. He is still a deceiver. His intent is still to cut us off from our Creator God. Jesus' teachings in this passage instructs us about prayer. I have studied it phrase by phrase more than once. It is rich. As always, Jesus is The Teacher, and He is Master of it.

When seeking that God opens my understanding to deeper levels, opens my eyes to see relevant and personal applications, I look again to my Lord Jesus to teach me 'how I should..' pray.

FATHER

πατη

patēr/pat-ayr' Father, 'the one by whom one is begotten', Progenitor, ancestor.

"Our Father, which art in heaven…" (Matthew 6:9)

I did a cross stitch some years ago with lettering that said 'Anyone can be a father, it takes someone special to be a daddy'. It is true. Unless there is a medical fertility problem, any man can father a child, but only because God has created life and ordained procreation.

I find it remarkable that the language of the beginning of this prayer has Jesus instructing us to call God 'daddy'. Jesus never minimized God's majesty or holiness, but even in the awesomeness of our God, He is our daddy. He is all-powerful, omnipotent, omnipresent, and a million other things, but He is our pater. Our Daddy. OUR Daddy, Jesus'….and mine. And yours if you choose.

God's position, character, and nature have never changed. But our position has changed. We are adopted. God is holy. He is majestic. But He is also loving, caring, nurturing, and oh so personal.

Father God, my heavenly Daddy, thank You that you are approachable. Help me to be increasingly familiar with You, grow my relationship with you to deeper levels, cultivate in me a trust even beyond the trust of my earthly daddy, make me to live in Your love and know it as being even more real than the love of my earthly father.

CHRISTMAS

MARY, DID YOU KNOW?

Again, at Christmas time, I find myself trying to put myself in Mary's place. Young, common, the future settled... Or so she thought. Her life was planned out. Her future had been decided. She would be married to Joseph and live happily ever after. Then............

"Do not be afraid, Mary, you have found favor with God. You will be with child and give birth to a son, and you are to give him the name Jesus." (Luke 1:30-31)

I wonder, how much courage did it take to announce the news the angel brought to her? I wonder, who did she tell first? I wonder, how long did she wait to tell it? Did she wait until she was sure she really was with child? Or did she immediately believe, and without reservation, share the angel's news right away? How precious that God made sure that Joseph had no unanswered questions. Joseph wasn't asked just to take Mary's word for it. What a comfort it must have been to Mary for Joseph to share in the divine revelation of the coming Messiah she carried. I bet they compared notes about what their angel looked and sounded like, was it the same one, or different...

Mary had her world turned upside down. Yet, she didn't go into a tailspin. Incredible (God knew not to pick someone like me, I'd have definitely gone into a tailspin...)

I think Mary probably shed plenty tears, wondering about what lay ahead, hearing the whispers, feeling the stares. But there was no turning back. She did nothing but go forward in trust.

I was once young and certainly common. At one time, I too thought my future was settled. It sure has taken some turns I didn't expect. How thankful I am that God continues to reassure me with His Presence. Mary didn't know her life would turn out like it did. But she knew her Child was The Messiah. None of us can know what our life will turn out like. But we can know Him, Who was the Christ Child. He is the great I AM. And He has my future. Eternally

WHAT?!?!!

I don't worship angels, and I don't assume that they are at my beck and call. (they aren't)

At Christmas, I think about their roles in the story of Christmas.
The messenger sent to Mary.
The messenger sent to Joseph
The messengers sent to the shepherds.

Imagine having been an angelic being in the Presence of The Triune God and being sent to humans to announce to humans that The Word of that God would become one of them. God Himself would become human…. To save them from their fallen human condition.

"WHAT?!?"

"You? The God of the universe, Creator of it all…going to that planet and becoming a ……..a human?"

They were sent to announce and smooth the way. Peter writes that angels 'desired to look into' the very things that he was reporting in the letter he was penning. (1Peter 1:12) Angels were interested in the gospel message.

Angels have no Savior. We, however, do.

Thank You Lord Jesus. (…. sure am glad I'm not an angel)

FAVORED

Mary was highly favored. She was chosen to be the birth mother of deity. Probably in her teens, an angel appeared to her to give her the incredible news.

I haven't seen an angel (that I know of…), but I've been given some incredible news. "…. He hath made me accepted…" (Eph.1:6 KJV, personalized by me) Both 'highly favored' and 'accepted' are translated from the same original word 'charitoo'. I am highly favored.

Mary received the Seed of God into herself.

I have received the Spirit of God into myself.

I am not His mother, He is my Father.

I do not share my human condition with Him, He shares His perfect holiness with me.

"When I believed, he marked me with a seal. The seal is the Holy Spirit that He promised." (2Timothy 1:14 personalized by me)

"The Spirit marks me as God's own…" (Eph. 1:14 personalized by me)

"He has given me the Holy Spirit as a down payment. The Spirit makes me sure of what is still to come…" (2Cor. 5:5 personalized by me)

I'm not a god, and I'm certainly not God. I'm not an angel, and I'm not perfect. But I am a child of The Most High God. I will "Guard the truth of the good news that I was trusted with. Guard it with the help of the Holy Spirit who lives in me…" (2Tim. 1:14 personalized by me)

"I know the One I have believed in. I am sure He is able to take care of what I have given Him. I can trust Him with it until the day He returns as judge. I will follow what I heard as the pattern of true teaching. Follow it with faith and love because I belong to Christ Jesus." (2 Tim. 1:12-14 personalized by me)

I am highly favored. Hallelujah.

WISH LISTS....

At Christmas time, we hear a lot about wishes. Children have long lists, often very expensive ones. I begin my wish list. It will NOT be a regret list. It won't be a list of things I wish I hadn't done or said. A wish is a desire. What is it that I really desire?

The words recorded in Psalm 37:4 have long been a very personal message to me......"Delight yourself in the LORD and He will give you the desires of your heart." The message in that verse is not a matter of how to get what you want. It isn't about kissing up to God so He'll give us everything on our wish list.

It IS, however, about the desire of our hearts being met. How? Where from? Certainly, not the North Pole or the fancies of department stores.

The wishes of my heart will never be realized by anything I can do. I can't buy it, you can't furnish it. I wish to know Him better than I know Him now. Not so He will give me anything. But because He already has. He has given me life eternal......I wish to know Him as never before.

WISH FOR DISCERNMENT

I wish to be more discerning.

I want to recognize right from wrong. Immediately.

I want to recognize good from bad. Instantly.

I want to recognize the vital from the trivial. Consistently.

I want to have my conscience trained.

I want my senses to be alert.

I want my mind clear and focused.

I want my body responding to my spirit and not my flesh.

I want my spiritual eyes to be keen.

I want my spiritual taste to be for truth.

I want to distinguish what is pleasing and what is provoking to my Creator.

I want to recognize what is helpful, and what is hurtful to my body, my spirit, my soul.

I want to recognize temptation before it gets to me, long before I become trapped or involved.

I want to use scripture as it is intended by God, not to suit my own purposes.

"O LORD, you have searched me and you know me. You know when I sit and when I rise; you perceive my thoughts from afar....... you are familiar with all my ways. Before a word is on my tongue you know it completely, O LORD."(Ps. 139:1-4)

".... Keep your servant also from willful sins; may they not rule over me.... May the words of my mouth and the meditation of my heart be pleasing in your sight, O LORD, my Rock and my Redeemer." (Ps. 19:13,14)

I live in a body of flesh. But I am a spiritual being and I have a soul. Personal sin is not just offensive to God, it is hurtful to me. What is displeasing to Him is even more so because of the effect it has on me, His creation. My sin hurts Him....and me. Even if I don't discern it at the moment.

I wish to be more and more discerning.

WISH FOR CALMNESS

I wish to be calm.

Listening to the well-known Christmas carole, "Silent Night" makes me wish to always be calm. Oh, I like a little excitement sometimes, (…but… never, ever, drama !!) There is just nothing that will ever replace a calm heart. Nothing compares to a rest filled spirit. God has made it possible for me to be calm…. He has provided the possibility of rest. for me, and for all believers, and for you if you choose to receive it…

I sit at His feet, and know calmness. "…all is calm…"

I feast on His recorded Word and get new glimpses of His majesty, "glory streams, from heaven afar…"

I revel in His love for me, His forever outstretched Hand, even in the face of my sin and imperfection, "with the dawn of redeeming grace…"

"Christ, my Savior, is born…"

LYRICS

"…. while mortals sleep, the angels keep their watch of wandering love…"

Another beautiful Christmas carol…angels hovering over the Christ child, The Holy One Himself, dressed in human infant flesh.

Angels are not at our disposal. They can be, and are, sent by God to minister to us, but only to serve His purposes and carry out His will. Certainly, not ours.

I'm really glad I'm not an angel. Angels obviously can choose poorly. " …. the angels who did not keep their positions of authority but abandoned their own home…." (Jude 1:6)

"God did not spare angels when they sinned. Instead, he sent them to hell. He put them in dark prisons. He will keep them there until he judges them." (2Peter 2:4)

But there is no offer of redemption to them. Satan and his rebellious group were cast out. There is no Savior to angels.

Jesus stepped out of His deity within the Godhead, not to become an angel. He didn't enter into the angelic realm, angels can't reproduce. There are no baby angels. But God's created humanity procreate. He chose to birth Himself into our race, become like us, to live the perfect life that we forfeited in The Garden incident.

He lived the perfect life that I cannot because of the sin nature passed on to me from my ancestors. He shares in my heritage thru His mother's blood, formed in her womb, birthed from her body. All humans "…. have bodies made out of flesh and blood. So, Jesus became human like them in order to die for them. By doing that, he could destroy the one who rules over the kingdom of death. I'm talking about the devil. Jesus could set people free who were afraid of death. All their lives they were held as slaves by that fear. It is certainly Abraham's children that he helps. He doesn't help angels. So he had to be made like his brothers in every way." (Hebrews. 2:14-17 from The Message)

I wonder if angels die. I wonder why it is that in scripture, when they manifest themselves, they are always portrayed as men, never female, and why do we always see feminine figurines or pictures. I wonder what things they 'long to look into' (1 Peter 1:12) I wonder what they will be judged about, and what it will be like to judge them…because "Don't you know that we will judge angels?" 1Cor.6:3)

I wonder about a lot…. we aren't told a lot. Just enough to make me really glad I'm not an angel. (…. I know, I know…. you all already knew I'm not one…)

OFFERING

"I beseech you therefore, brethren, by the mercies of God, that ye present your bodies a living sacrifice, holy, acceptable unto God, which is your reasonable service." (Romans12:1)

I don't think there is one of us that would jump to say our body is 'holy'. But the 'therefore' of verse 1 refers back to the preceding 11 chapters of Paul's message in the book of Romans. Paul wrote those chapters explaining about the situation of all humans, our ruined condition….and God's rescue.

We often jump right to the 'duty', right to what we should 'offer'….and never really come to understand the doctrine taught…. that HE is the one that makes our bodies holy. Nothing I can ever do or not do, will in any way make me holy. Not one single thing or a hundred things…

If God places me in His Son, I am holy….

Not because of things I eliminate…

Not because of words I don't say anymore or places I don't go anymore…..

Not because of any kind of behavior modification.

The "therefore" of verse 1 is a first step…a first choice to finding God's will and walking in it, walking behind His Son Jesus, Whom we follow. Choosing to do that is really the only thing we have to offer God.

He created every single thing that is a reality to you and I. Nothing of it is really mine, I have nothing He has not provided. The paper (money) that we lay in the offering plate is just a tool that WE have devised to USE what HE has given us in the first place. The only value it has to Him is the attitude of our hearts when we offer it back to Him. We either offer it freely and with joy, or out of meaningless duty.

Is our money all we offer Him? During the season of Christmas, we hear songs about the wise men bringing gifts to the infant Jesus. I'm sure those valuable gifts came in handy to two poor parents, displaced from their homes, separated from family and support systems. The gift was valuable, and the gift was used. But I wonder what a big smile it brought to God's heart to have these 'wise men' travel such distance, just to meet Immanuel, "God With Us". The priority was to find The Promised One. The offerings were the least of it I think...the true gifts they brought were within. The worship of the newly born King of Kings.

What do you understand about what He has given you? "The One who is highly honored lives forever. His name is holy. He says, "I live in a high and holy place. But I also live with anyone who turns away from his sins. I live with anyone who is not proud. I give new life to him. I give it to anyone who turns away from his sins. (Isa. 57:15) What do you bring Him? A little of your money? An hour or two of your time?

"The sacrifices of God are a broken spirit.... a broken and contrite heart, O God, you will not despise." (Ps. 51:17)

Living sacrifices.....I am a living sacrifice. Are you?

Like me, do you have a tendency to squirm around on the altar?

Like me, do you regularly climb off?

Today, I bring an offering of worship to my King. No one on earth deserves the praises that I sing, Jesus, may You receive the honor that You're due...Oh Lord, I bring an offering to You.

WATCH OUT

•♫♫♫••♫♫♫•*•♫♫* "You better watch out !"....*•♫♫♫••*•♫♫•*•♫♫*

That lyric is heard a lot at Christmas time, especially in homes with children. I've used it many times when my boys were little.

I 've sung:

•♫♫♫•"...Santa Clause is coming, to town."*•♫♫♫•*

many many times as a reminder to 'be good', and not that I'm pleased that I did it, sometimes I sang it as a threat. Today I would change the lyrics!

•♫♫♫• "You better watch out....Jesus Christ is coming, again." *•♫♫♫•*

That isn't a threat, it's a promise from scripture that you can be sure of. Whether you are 'naughty' or 'nice'. Whether you've been 'bad' or 'good'. He sees you. He knows. And He is coming.

Surer than Santa Clause....

OFFERINGS 2

'♫♫♫•What can I bring Him, poor that I am♫♫♫•'....

Voluntary giving something to God ...what can I possible give to God? Everything I have comes from His Hand in the first place. Everything in my reality is His. Yet, He has given me dominion over the realm of my life. What can I possibly add? What God might lack, He could speak into existence just as He spoke into existence every single thing you and I have ever known. What He might want, He could certainly have. But would it all be worth having?

Again, I marvel at the love of God for me...and I marvel that the only thing He wants that He cannot make, is my choosing Him over all else.

The blessing of our marriage has been the freely given commitment to each other. I've never forced my husband to stay. I've never manipulated circumstances 'so that' he will love me. He chooses to do so. And I am secure in that. I daresay he would say the same thing.

God loves us, wants our love in return...but will not force our choice. It grieves Him that some do not choose Him. He is sorrowful that they will suffer because of it, and has gone to great measures to be sure we know WHAT we are choosing when we do not come to Him. "...tell the people, 'This is what the Lord says: See, I am setting before you the way of life and the way of death...' ..." (Jer. 21:8)

"...I have set before you life and death, blessings and curses. Now choose life, so that you and your children may live, and that you may love the Lord your God, listen to His Voice, and hold fast to Him. For the Lord is your life...." (Deut. 30:19,20)

"I am the way and the truth and the life..." (words of Jesus in John 14:6)

Good or evil.

Life or death. T

Those are the only two choices.

"...as for me and my house, we will serve the Lord." (Joshua 24:15)

SANTA

That sweet man with the big soft tummy and big soft heart, love for everyone, gifts to share, joy to bring... I wonder if some people don't think of our God like they think of Santa. The Sacred Santa of heaven, the One Who loves everybody, wants to fill our every need, fill us with happiness and joy.

Oh, and He does!!

But not in the way we expect it.

Often what we expect is warped from the disease of sin that we all share. Often our image of God is just that...an image of OURS. A wrong image.

I was never guilty of thinking of God as Santa-like. For me it was opposite, my image was a frowning unhappy old guy with a giant flyswat raised in waiting...waiting to swat me when I messed up. That too was a wrong image.

No, God is not a Santa.

But He IS the one who decides. What is 'naughty and nice' is determined by HIS Word, by What HE says. He is Shopet...Hebrew for judge. He judges, He decides, He governs.

"Rise up, O Judge of the earth..." Psalm 94:2

"You have come to God, the judge of all men...."Hebrews 12:23

But there is a list .A very important list. Just one. And it is written in what scripture calls the Book of Life, and 'if anyone's name was not found written in the book of life' (Rev 20:15), that person will not see 'the city that does not need the sun or the moon to shine on it, for the glory of God gives it light...' (Rev.21:23)

"Nothing impure will ever enter there, nor will anyone who does what is shameful or deceitful, but only those whose names are written in the Lamb's book of life.' (Rev. 21:27)

Forget Santa's list. My name is written in the Lamb's Book of Life. Written in red.

Thank You Jesus.

SEES

We sing a song at Christmas, "He sees you when you're sleeping...." Santa sees if you're sleeping and he knows if you're awake.

Well, God is not a Santa. He does, however, see. He is El Roi....Hebrew for 'the God who sees me." Psalm 33 tells us that He looks down from heaven to see all humankind. He observes all our deeds.

You think Santa is watching? I can assure you that our God is....

"The eyes of the Lord are everywhere, keeping ...watch on the wicked and the good." Proverbs 15:3

EVERYWHERE

Santa can visit every house on planet earth in one night.

God is omnipresent. He is in every place at all times. He does not come to visit a believer, He comes to remain.

God is YAHWEH SHAMMAH...Hebrew for 'The Lord is there'.

And yes, He is real.

WORKSHOP

Santa has elves to help in his workshop who make things and then carry out Santa's plans to deliver them.

God is YAHWEH TSEBAOTH, Hebrew for 'The Lord of Hosts.' His workshop is the universe.

He has every single thing, both material and spiritual, at His disposal. His angelic helpers far outnumber Santa's elves, according to the prophet Elisha. "Those who are with us are more than those with them" (2 Kings 6:16).

This Lord of hosts came in Person. "For to us a child is born, to us a son is given, and the government will be on his shoulders. And he will be called Wonderful Counselor, Mighty God, Everlasting Father, Prince of Peace.' (Isaiah 9:6-7) Hallelujah

PROVIDE

We give Santa a list of what to provide under our tree.

God is JEHOVAH JIREH, Hebrew for 'The Lord provides'.

Matthew 6:32 tells us that our God knows what we need even before we do...
and verse 30 tells us that if God takes care of the fields, He will surely take
care of us ! Our... problem is we get 'needs' and 'greeds' mixed up !!

What is on your list this year?

BANNER

There are many things that symbolize the Christmas season to us. Trees, holly, mistletoe, lights. YAHWEH NISSI is Hebrew for 'The Lord is my Banner'. At Christmas time, I want my banner to be the nativity, the birth of that YAHWEH TSEBAOTH Who came in Person just for me. And you. The Lord is my Banner, Exodus 17

PEACE....

At Christmas time, I like to read 'The Night Before Christmas' to my grand-daughters. The book is put on our coffee table at Christmas, and is read often before it disappears after Christmas is over.

"I heard him exclaim as he drove out of sight, Merry Christmas to all and to all a good night!'.

Our God is JEHOVAH SHALOM, Hebrew for 'The Lord Is Peace. He gives much more than a good night, He brings 'the peace of God that transcends all understanding'. Philippians 4:6-7

I pray you know His peace. Not just during the Christmas season, but every moment of every day.

LEADS

Santa has a red-nosed reindeer that leads Santa's sleigh around the world on Christmas Eve.

JEHOVAH ROI, Hebrew for 'The Lord is my Shepherd' leads us beside quiet waters, in paths of righteousness, thru the valley of the shadow of death, to springs of living water...'(Ps. 23)

He 'carries us close to His heart.... (Isaiah 40) I pray that you are a sheep of His pasture.

OLD

I often lightheartedly say that I am old and tired. That becomes more and more true with each passing day !! Older and tired-er !!

Santa doesn't seem to get any older, and does anyone know where he came from? And who are his parents?

EL OLAM is Hebrew for 'The Eternal God'. He has no beginning, no end, and is the same yesterday, today, and forever. According to Isaiah 40:28, He is everlasting, never grows tired or weary, and no one can fathom His understanding.

He IS. And I am His. That fact is indeed hard for me to fathom...that He cares for me.

OPPORTUNITY

MIQWEH YISRAEL is Hebrew for 'Hope of Israel', the One Who saves those who trust in Him...

The Christmas season is the Christians' opportunity to 'go into all the world'(Mark 16:15) with the message of IMMANUEL, Hebrew for 'God with us'.. What better opportunity do we have to speak His name than at CHRISTmas time? What better time to speak of the Christ, the Messiah, the Savior of the world? He is The One it's all about.

The One Isaiah said would thwart the enemy's plan..(8:10)..

The One the angel said would save His people.(Matthew 1:21)...

Father, open our eyes to see the opportunities to speak Your Name and tell Your message of salvation. May we see those opportunities BEFORE they unfold, not in hindsight...not wishing we had spoken, but empower us to recognize the time, enable us to be bold and courageous, that we might act in obedience, immediately, cooperating with Your Holy Spirit, acting as Your instrument to bring the Good News of Jesus Christ to those He chooses to put in our path.

He is come. HALLELUJAH, praise the Lord.

HEAR

♫♫♫•'Do you hear what I hear♫♫♫•.....'

I love the message of the familiar Christmas carol. PROPHETES is Hebrew for prophet, a proclaimer of a divine message. In Dt.18 the people did not want to hear or see God anymore, they were afraid.

God promised to send a Prophet...One Who would speak the words of God, One from among them, they would not be fearful of Him.. That Prophet is Jesus the Christ. His arrival was common, He invoked no fear...he entered the world a tiny helpless infant. He perfectly communicates God's Word to us (Heb.1) Do you hear Him? Will you hear Him?

ALIVE

As you hear the Christmas carols and bells, do you hear LOGOS, the Voice that calls us to light and life? Do you listen to the LOGOS that was with God the Father in the beginning?

Do you know The LOGOS that became flesh?(John 1)

This LOGOS IS God's creative life-giving Word!! Just as at Creation, He speaks and it is. Life and Light. HALLELUJAH, Praise the Lord.

This Christmas season, when you see a decorative holiday light, think of THE Light. Jesus said HE is The Light of the world.

Listen carefully, turn your heart to hear His Voice beckoning you to share His Life. Just as He was born to die and live again, so are we born to die... Thru Him, we have the opportunity and invitation to die to sin, and be made re-born, made alive. .Alive.... to live eternally with Him.

JOY

"You will show me the way of life, granting me the joy of your presence...."
(Psalm 16:11)

For many, this time of year brings everything but joy. Many of us have experienced changes of life's circumstances. Traditions will be diffiult to keep, if not impossible. There will be people missing. Some permanently. Some have been snatched away, only to be seen again on the other side of this realm. Some have been rescued from suffering here, whisked away to an eternal life of no pain or sorrow. Sadly, there are some who will not know the joy of the Lord, never to experience His Presence. Eternally separated.

PARAKLETOS translates 'comforter'. Jesus sent this Comforter. (John 16:7) He comes, and when welcomed in, He says "I will not leave you comfortless: I will come to you." (John 14:16)

This Comforter is here to help us know Him and His purposes. "He shall teach you all things, and bring all things to your remembrance, whatsoever I have said unto you."(John14:26)

I pray that you will open your heart to Jesus afresh this Christmas season. I pray you will experience the Comforter in very real and practical ways, bringing you the promise of "...peace that is not logical." (Phillipians 4:7)

Speak His Name. Tell the joyful news. ALL people need to know and believe. .... else there will be another Christmas lacking joy for someone, somewhere, someday.

GIFTS

At Christmas, there are always so many gifts.Things we've wished for, things we expect to bring us joy. But real joy is not a gift, it is a fruit. A result.

"But the fruit of the Spirit is love, joy, peace, longsuffering, gentleness, goodness, faith..." (Galatians 5:22) This joy doesn't get old, the joy doesn't fade away...in fact, this joy grows and multiplies, birthing into our life peace, patience, kindness..... (not like the newest trend or latest toy)

Don't be tricked into expecting joy from inside a giftwrapped box. You will be disappointed time and again. Joy is a fruit of God's Holy Spirit, comes listed right after love...it is the love expressed to us by the gift, that is the joyful thing.

On the first Christmas, the greatest gift of all time was given. God Himself stepped into the flesh of a naked, helpless infant. God Himself stepped out of perfect glory into the setting of a smelly barn....and lost humanity. Happy? Oh yes!! And so very blessed. He has "redeemed us from the curse of the law..." (Galatians 3:13) "He has visited and redeemed his people..."(Luke 1:68)

"He has rescued us from the dominion of darkness..."(Col. 1:13)

Hallelujah!

SILENT

♫♪•*•♫♪ "Silent night....holy night..... ♫♪•*•♫♪

I'd like to know what was silent about it !!

Luke 2 tells about shepherds and flocks, then a PLETHOS of angels appear praising God. PLETHOS translates "a bunch"!! And they are not silent!! I doubt those shepherds and flocks were silent after that either!

And chidbirth in a barn?? Any mother out there think THAT was silent !?!

But it was holy. Praise God for that night.

Luke 2:17 lets us know for sure the shepherds weren't silent ....they "made known abroad the saying which was told them concerning this child."

PEACE

We sing about 'Peace on earth, good will to men.'

We make symbols. (I'm wearing the trendy 'peace sign' for the second o around!)

Lack of conflict.... Jesus has made it possible for us to have that with God, a way to remove the sin barrier. (Col.1:20) We can have a relationship with God that is free of conflict, made free of the curse of death, the consequence of sin. Jesus left glory and became man, perfect and sinless. That first Christmas morning was the arrival of our Savior, the perfect Lamb of God.

Our enemy uses every opportunity to cause conflict. Be aware of his tactics. He will present offenses, showcase them to us. It's a great bait. He knows how to dangle it just right. It is a choice. Even in righteous offense, even when we have a valid reason to be offended, we can bear it with the help of The One Who suffered the ultimate offense....and He was indeed totally innocent.

Determine that The Prince of Peace will reign, do not give the enemy opportunity.(Eph.4:27) That devil has no regard for special occasions he'll cash in on it. Do not allow him to steal the joy and peace of this Christmas time.

LORD

♫♩••*•♩♫♩••*•♩♫♫..'the little lord Jesus, asleep on the hay.'♫♩••*•♩♫♩••*•♩♫♫

KYRIOS translates 'lord'. I wonder about how loosely we use that word. Does it mean 'owner'? 'master'?. Or just 'sir'? Is He your Lord? The ruling force in your life? He IS Lord of lords. ("For the Lord your God is God of gods and Lord of lords, the great God, mighty and awesome, who shows no partiality and accepts no bribes." Dt10)

Everyone will know the truth of that. ("...every tongue will confess that Jesus Christ is Lord..." Phil.2:11) Simply calling Him 'lord' isn't enough ("Not everyone that saith unto me, Lord, Lord, shall enter into the kingdom of heaven; but he that doeth the will of my Father which is in heaven" Mt7:21)

Be certain that you have chosen Him to reign in your life. Be certain that He is Lord. Be certain that you follow His design for your life. He left the glory of heaven and went thru the agony of the cross for you. ♫♩••*•♩♫♩••*•♩♫♫And He will reign forever and ever.♫♩••*•♩♫♩••*•♩♫♫

Allelujah !!

BIG

..attention college kids!! The best 'big' ever!! Your sorority 'big' sister or brother may be great help and encouragement to you, but they are no match for this Big !! .

..He is the ALPHA KAI OMEGA.

The first, and the last. (Rev.22:13)

We celebrate His birth, but that event was not His beginning, only the beginning of the image of the invisible God.

He was present at creation.(Col.1 and John1)

He was born to die. (Isa53)

He is alive forever.(Rev1)

And I'm in...for my eternal lifetime He is my big

PRESENTS/PRESENCE

Christmas is the season of gift giving. Lots and lots of presents. All in pretty gift sacks with tissue spilling out the top, or wrapped in pretty paper with bright shiny ribbons and bows.

Given a choice, which do you prefer? Presents? Or His Presence?

When you worship, where is your focus? Your salvation? Or Your Savior? The gift? Or The Giver?

TRADITIONS

♫♪•*•♫♪ ♫♪•*•♫♪ I'll be home for Christmas…. you can count on me, please have snow, and mistletoe…and presents 'neath the tree….♫♪•*•♫♪♫♪•*•♫♪

It is great to be 'home'. It is great to carry on the traditions we have established…to do what we have always done…the way we have always done it. But as the circle of life grows, some things must necessarily change. The tradition becomes what you do THIS time. (…I often caution young parents: NEVER to do something you don't want to continue to do from now on!!! Fill a stocking once, you must fill it for years to come!!!…)

We have an enemy whose purpose is to 'steal, kill, and destroy'. (John 10:10)

We have a Savior Whose purpose is to 'give life in all its fullness.' (John 10:10)

This is a season of celebration. Let us purpose to stand against the enemy assault, for be assured, the enemy will attack at our most vulnerable time. He is an enemy. There are no rules of engagement, no honor to uphold. Our enemy is also a liar. "He was a murderer from the beginning and has always hated the truth. There is no truth in him. When he lies, it is consistent with his character; for he is a liar and the father of lies." (John 8:44)

As we find ourselves in new circumstances, distanced from loved ones, separated by time and space, let us not believe lies. Let us not be influenced by the enemy, but let us purpose that we WILL "Above all, love each other deeply…" (1 Peter 4:8) Love is not bound by time and space. It is not defined by tradition. Traditions are only manifestation OF love. Love's power is strong, and is pictured in the very life of Jesus Christ. Deity stepping into a woman's body, pushed thru a birth canal, living a human life, dying a horrible death. Because He loved us. The Eternal, Omniscient One has never been bound by time or space.

And He is Immanuel…. God with us.Hallelujah.

FOOD

At holiday time, there is always plenty everywhere we go...more than plenty. We will eat. And eat. But a few hours later, we will be empty and hungry again.

ARTOS ZOES translates 'bread of life'. Jesus IS this bread. (John6:48) Don't confuse your hunger pains. Recognize your spirit craving His Bread. ...He fills an emptiness and hunger that nothing else can. Permanently

LIGHT

Anyone who does not have Jesus Christ cannot appreciate Light, they only know darkness. To not know Jesus Christ is to live in darkness.

Ever ask a person born blind to describe light? It is difficult to describe light without knowledge of darkness. And impossible to fully appreciate the value of light having never known darkness.

Jesus is the Light of the world. Heavenly starlight was just a glimmer of the Light born in the stable that night.

♫♪ ♫♪•*•♫♪ ... "a star, a star, shining in the night, it will bring us goodness and light' ..'♫♪•*•♫♪ ♪

♫♫♪ ♫♪•*•♫♪ I once was lost, but now I'm found, was blind, but now I see'..♫♪•*•♫♪ ♫♪•*•♫♪

TO PHOS TOU KOSMOU translates 'light of the world'. "I am the Light of the world, whoever follows me will never walk in darkness but will have the light of life."(Jesus, John 8:12)

Have you experienced the discovery of His Light? Can you now describe Light because you've been rescued from darkness? May we not forget what a dreadful thing it is to live without His Light...may we never take for granted His birth, His Life, and His death. He came. He is coming again. Hallelujah.

CHILD

What can a child do? What power could a child possibly wield? "From now on, you and the woman will be enemies, and your offspring and her offspring will be enemies. He will crush your head, and you will strike his heel." (Gen. 3:15)

A Child was God's answer for humanity. All mankind was touched by the stain of sin, no longer innocent, no longer perfect, the relationship between man and The Perfect One forever broken.

Until The Child.

"For unto us a child is born, unto us a son is given: and the government shall be upon his shoulder: and his name shall be called Wonderful, Counsellor, The mighty God, The everlasting Father, The Prince of Peace." (Isa. 9:6) Hard concept. A Child will bear the responsibility of governing me? A Child will be the One to give me advice and counsel? A Child will somehow oversee my peace?

"For unto you is born this day in the city of David a Savior, which is Christ the Lord."(Luke 2:11)

"And the child grew, and waxed strong in spirit, filled with wisdom: and the grace of God was upon him."(Luke 2:40)

"And he preached in the synagogues of Galilee." (Luke 4:44)

".... you are to give him the name Jesus. He will be great and will be called the Son of the Most High. The Lord God will give him the throne of his father David, and he will reign over the house of Jacob forever; his kingdom will never end." (Luke 1:31-33)

Hallelujah!!

PONDER

"Twas the night before Christmas, when all thru the house..."

"...the time came for the baby to be born"(Luke 2:6 NIV)

This Eve of Christmas, what will your activity be? Both of my sons were born around 9a.m. after a night of labor. Every year, I remember the day and the evening before that night of labor. I recall the activities of the day. I especially recall the emotions of that first birth...the un-known. What will it be like...will everything be ok...can I do this...should I have accepted this responsibility...

"Mary treasured up all these things and pondered them in her heart." (John 2:19 NIV) I.have no doubt that every Eve of Christ's birth, Mary re-lived the trip to Bethlehem on that donkey, every closed door and every 'sorry, we don't have room for you', every scent of that barn.

Thankful for Joseph, who could have walked away but didn't.

Remembering the labor. The pains, the blood, the pushing.

No proper way to bathe the newborn, no family to 'OOOooooo, and aaaaahhhhh'

The face of the Child! the first cry, the first suckle... the thoughts and wonderings of what the future held for her baby. Ponder indeed.

We too have much to ponder. May we all ponder this Eve of Christmas. Immanuel, God with us.

WHITE

♫•*•♫♫♪•*•♫♪I'm dreaming of a white Christmas ♫•*•♫♫♪•*•♫♪

Though your sins are like scarlet, they shall be white as snow". (Isa.1:18)

Snow may fall on you this Christmas. I've seen no snow, but I am reminded of my cleansing. I don't know of anything that's whiter than snow. It's about as white as it gets I think....

"Cleanse me and I will be clean, wash me, and I will be whiter than snow"(Ps.51:7) Whiter? It all began when God left the perfection of heaven, stepped off His throne and into the flesh of an infant human. Just to make me whiter than snow. THAT is something to make merry about. Thank You, Jesus.

Happy Birthday Lord.

IMAGINE AND EXPECT

Imagination... does anyone else play out the day in your head before it happens? How perfect it will be? What might go wrong? I do it because I am selfish. There, I said it. I might as well admit it,"The Lord searches every heart and understands every motive behind the thoughts.("1Chron.28:9) I want things how I want them.... but God doesn't always work the way I imagine.... even when He wants the same things I do.

Expectations...did you have them? Were they met? Disappointed? Pleasantly surprised? Were you properly prepared? If so, what did you do to prepare? Jesus said when we put His purposes first, He takes care of the rest. (Matt6:33) I struggled to depend on Him, trusting Him to tend to the details...and He did. Magnificently. As ...He always does.

NEW YEAR ..

As one year ends and we're about to enter a new year, I wonder...is anything really new? Solomon says no.(Ecc.1:9)

Time is not new. Measuring it is not new. Filling it is not new...no matter what you fill it with. Measured time...hours, days, months, and yes...years... is not new.

But eternity will never be old.

Things that have eternal worth are the only things that matter. The only way this coming year will be different from the last will be determined by our relationship with The Creator. Not stuff. Not image or appearance. Not information and knowledge. "Fear God and keep His commandments..."(Ecc.12:13) Solomon should know, He tried it all...and found success in his efforts but found no fulfillment from the success...no value. Make it your business to know His will for your days and years. Seek Him with an undivided heart, and He will be found. (1 Chron. 28:9)

EXERCISE

At the beginning of a new year, we hear a lot about exercise. There are dozens of infomercials about exercise equipment that will supposedly make exercise easier or more effective. There are commercials for pills to swallow or concoctions to drink.... But the bottom line is, exercise is work. It takes on purpose, disciplined activity. Strenuous activity. No pain, no gain, (or should I say loss?)

I came across this passage from The Message: "Now pass on this counsel to the Christians there, and you'll be a good servant of Jesus. Stay clear of silly stories that get dressed up as religion. Exercise daily in God—no spiritual flabbiness, please! Workouts in the gymnasium are useful, but a disciplined life in God is far more so, making you fit both today and forever." (1 Timothy 4:6-8)

Like staying clear of those machines that make promises as big as the price tags on them, I am instructed to be wise about my spirituality. I can't buy something and sit it in a room of my house and my body automatically be in better physical shape. Neither can I buy a Bible, or a case of them and automatically be in better spiritual condition. Going to a church building won't do it. Only exercising the muscles of my heart and mind with the Word of God will make my spiritual condition more vibrant and healthy.

Exercise daily...in His Word. Don't wait till January 1st, begin right now. This minute. Don't make a goal that is unattainable, don't set yourself up to fail. One verse that conveys a message of truth from Him is better than mindlessly reading several chapters. Read, ask Him to speak to you thru the printed page. And expect to hear Him. He is faithful.

SALE

At certain times of the year, it seems as if everything is on sale. You have your eye on a costly item? Don't want to pay the price? Just wait til it's on sale.

What we need most is something we can't purchase...never could, never will be able to. It will never be on sale...in fact it's the most expensive thing to ever exist. Whether you know it or not, it is the only thing that will fill your need, bring you comfort, contentment, and total peace. It is right standing with God, paid for in full by the blood of Jesus Christ. (Rev.1:5) It is the greatest need you will ever have.

Jesus offers to fill that need for us completely, we need only accept the gift. It is the deal you can't afford to pass up and if you do, you will never know the joy of His salvation and you will regret that for eternity.

HARMONY

I spent some time teaching my grand-daughter piano and voice. One lesson included just a touch of the concept of harmony. God created harmony. He created the instrument we call 'voice'. In singing, we use our voices in different ways, creating harmonies that can stir every emotion God made in us. Some voices sing the melody...the soprano, or lead. Some voices add other tones that harmonize, we call them alto, tenor, baritone, or bass. The lead may carry the melody, but it is not fully complete without the other parts.

The voice is an instrument, and we must learn our own particular voice, discover the function of it, identify it, explore its use...and train it. The voice that is regularly used becomes more capable and sure...able to produce sounds that were not possible before. It is more dependable, less likely to squeak out off-key or crack and make you want to hide, never to sing again!!!

There is other harmony as well...the harmony of His Body, the church. "...the body is not made up of one part but of many'.(1Cor.12:14) Here too, we must learn and train....learn who we are in Him, learn what part of the melody is ours to sing. "...they form one body...So it is with Christ." (1Cor.12:12) We must learn He has created in each of us, a part of the harmony...a place and purpose. 'God arranged the parts in the body, every one of them, just as He wanted them to be' (1Cor.12:18) He did not leave you out. 'There are different kinds of service, but the same Lord' (1Cor.12:5) 'Those parts of the body that seem to be weaker are indispensable" (1Cor.12:22) You may not sing the lead... but the song is not complete without your voice

BLESSED

What do you think of? Got a mental list yet? House? Job? Cars? Stuff of all sorts? Maybe health? Family? Friends? How about this...'Blessed are you when men hate you, when they exclude you and insult you and reject your name as evil, BECAUSE of the Son of Man.'(emphasis mine Luke 6:22)

I've been there...it didn't seem like much of a blessing. Maybe we should examine our definition Makarios means 'blessed' in the original language of this passage. Its definition includes the concept of being approved by God and marked by a fullness from God, and it indicates the state of the believer in Christ. You see, the most valuable thing we can have is His approval. Yet we are not capable of earning it, even when we make all sorts of resolutions about our conduct. If that were possible, the simple Ten Commandments would have done the trick.

So...where does that leave us?

Lost...without His approval, that's where. UNLE SS we get help. And we certainly need help...(especially when 'men hate you and exclude you and insult you and reject your name as evil...' Amen ??)

Luke wasn't saying that we are blessed BECAUSE we are hated and insulted....he says we are blessed by God in spite of it!! Blessed because we choose His way over our own or that of the culture around us. Who cares what anybody says when God gives His approval?! Oh, His standards are indeed high, but He helps us! "His divine power has given us everything we need for life and godliness through our knowledge of Him...He has given us His very great and precious promises, so that through them you may participate in the divine nature and escape the corruption in the world caused by evil desires." (2Peter 1:4) You notice that this hinges on our knowledge of Him? And SO often, we have little or no knowledge, and even more often we have the WRONG knowledge. (my opinion...)

Who is He to you? He has given promises. Do you know them?

WAR

The conflicts go on and on. Jesus said 'do not be alarmed..' (Mark13:7) War does not surprise Him. Neither does famine and earthquake. (vs.8) The conflicts and the devastations are global, common to all humanity... and we feel so powerless. But we are not. We can donate time, donate money to provide physical help, those things are important. "...if anyone gives even a cup of cold water to one of these little ones because he is my disciple, I tell you the truth, he will certainly not lose his reward." (Matt.10.42) But the most pressing battles are spiritual. 'What profit is it if you gain the whole world, and lose your own soul?' (Mark 8:36) '...though we live in the world, we do not wage war as the world does.'(2Cor. 10:3) We have His power available to us. 'The weapons we fight with are not the weapons of the world...they have divine power to demolish strongholds." (2Cor.10:4)

We have a weapon that has no earthly match. '...take the sword of the Spirit, which is the word of God.'(Eph. 6:17) His Word as recorded in our Bible is not just a bunch of ink and paper. It is our only weapon. Have you picked it up? Do you know what it is capable of doing? (Heb.4:12)

SHAKE

I can't fathom the terror of the earth shaking beneath me. My mind knows the truth about this world, it does not offer security. He has told me in scripture that all created things are temporary and unsure. (Heb.12:27) Yet I realize that I place much confidence in them. The 'real' things are not the things I see and touch, the 'real' things are the things of God, the spiritual realities. He is unshakable. I haven't experienced an earthquake. Neither have I experienced the sudden loss of a spouse, or a child…or a fire destroying the place I call 'home', shaking the foundation of life here on this ball of dirt we call Earth. Neither am I in physical battle against a cancer that threatens to shorten my stay.

I hope those things are not in my future, but if they are, I want to walk thru them in unshakable trust that He holds my eternal future in His loving Hands. I would want others to see His love evidenced in me as I have seen it in all its glory, displayed in the lives of those who DO walk thru these shakings, hand in Hand with Him.

When shaking comes, only what can NOT be shaken remains. When the future is so unsure and loss is so great, a future built on Him remains steady and sure, even in the suffering and loss. "…since we are receiving a kingdom that cannot be shaken, let us be thankful, and so worship God acceptably with reverence and awe…" Hebrews 12:28 He is so good.

WEAR

I have a bit of spring fever I guess. I'm ready to change out some boots for sandals and ready my wardrobe for warmer weather. What will I wear this spring? Add a new color when I replace some of last years stained t-shirts? Will I go with a trendy look, worn-out ragged jeans and tattoo-inspired t-shirts? Or maybe a classic look with dark jeans and polo shirts? What will I wear… Shallow huh? But be honest, you think about it too. Every time you are preparing to go somewhere the question looms. What to wear.

Planning ahead and being responsible are good qualities to cultivate. Being organized and prepared in every facet of life is a benefit. But despite all my organization, all the preparations and thinking ahead, if I am not wearing His righteousness and His spiritual armor, I might as well be naked on a desert. In fact, until He rescued me, I was. 'In a desert land, He found her, in a barren and howling waste. He shielded her and cared for her and He guarded Her as the apple of His Eye." (Deu.32:10 gender changed by me) Now I am clothed in clothing I could not purchase. '…He has clothed me with garments of salvation and arrayed me in a robe of righteousness.'(Isa.61:10) God made Him who had no sin to be sin for me…so that in Him I might become the righteousness of God.'(2Cor.5:21 pronouns personalized by me)

Jesus said '..do not worry about your life, what you will eat, or about your body, what you will wear. Life is more than food, and the body more than clothes.' (Luke 12:22,23) My priority must be His purposes, His Kingdom ('seek His kingdom and all these things will be given to you' v.31). I must be dressed and ready for HIS service.('be dressed and ready, keep your lamps burning' v.35)

So today…I 'stand firm, with this belt of truth buckled around my waist..'(Eph. 6:14)… that He is sovereign, and that He chooses to value and love me. How can I not return His love and live every moment basking in it? How can I not clothe myself daily in Him, 'not by works of my righteousness, but according to His mercy…' (Titus 3:5) 'Behold, I come as a thief. Blessed is he that watches and keeps his garments, lest he walk naked and they see his shame.'(Rev.16:15)

Thank You Lord Jesus, for paying my debt and not only covering my shame, but removing both the shame and guilt. Thank You that I am blessed in keeping watch, that 'having been baptized into Christ, I have put on Christ.' (Gal.3:27) and am no longer naked and ashamed, but clothed in Your garment of righteousness.

CLOTHES

They really do tell a lot sometimes. In the story of Lazarus, his were graveclothes. I remember the times I've chosen the clothes for a burial garment. I remember going to purchase a new one for my father-in-law. And I remember the years I walked around with my graveclothes on. Yikes!! Yes, I wore them for years, dressed up in the finery of my good behavior. Graveclothes are what dead people wear, and I was dead... a breathing, heart-beating, walking, talking, dead person. They are everywhere, people who just think they are alive. Jesus provided a new garment, a garment finer than any of mine, perfect in fact.

Perfect... I never accomplished that myself but He did. He offered it to me time and time again. I said I accepted it, but I never put it on, I couldn't figure out how it fit. Then, in frustration and utter defeat, I quit trying and accepted the clothes I had on. I continued to wear them, tried to make them look as good as possible... (even washed them in the baptistry a couple times), and went on with my existence.

I even tried to put my clothes on other people. Mine looked a little bit better than theirs, I thought. But they usually rejected them, choosing to wear their own grave clothes. Then one day, in the middle of a stormy time of my existence, when all I could say was 'Help me." ...He called me out.

Oh relax, I didn't hear a Charlton Heston voice say my name, but since that day everything changed. Just as Jesus said 'Loose him and let him go' after He had called Lazarus out of the grave, He has loosed me. I'm not wearing the grave clothes anymore. "...she will be dressed in white and I will never blot out her name from the book of life, but will acknowledge her name before My Father and His angels." Rev. 3:5 Hallelujah

DESIRES

There was an occasion when a cousin was trying to fulfill his mother's desires for her funeral. Years ago, she had given me a list of songs. I know…strange, you'd have to know her. It seemed so important to her that she made her desires known about her funeral. The songs, the order, who spoke and who didn't, like she was planning a party. The funeral services don't matter to her now, in my opinion. But they matter to her family. It brings a certain amount of comfort to do as she wished.

There will be sadness. It is ok to be sad. Jesus Himself wept out of the emotions of His humanity. (I remember my aunt drilling us on Bible trivia… what's the shortest verse in the Bible? "Jesus wept." John 11:35)

Jesus' tears were shed at a time when a friend lay dead, the family mourning. They questioned why Jesus hadn't come and made Lazarus to recover from his illness. "Lord, if You had been here, my brother would not have died." (John 11:32) Jesus asked where they had put Lazarus' body. "Come and see…" they replied." (v.34), and they led Jesus to the place of their grief. They believed that he would 'rise again in the resurrection at the last day.' (v.24) They were not hopeless in their grief. But hopeful grief is still grief, still bitterly painful.

So where is the place that holds your pain and grief? Where is it that you need to say to Jesus 'Come and see.'? He has said, "Did I not tell you that if you believed, you would see the glory of God?" (v.40) You can't call yourself out from behind that stone, but He can. And He IS calling you. But you have the option of staying behind the stone. Listen for Him…" Come to Me, all of you who are weary and burdened." (Matt. 11:28)

WIND

Wind is a force you cannot see. We only see the evidence of it. I wonder if there is anyone that does not believe in wind. Absurd you say? Well, people claim to not believe in God, yet they believe they stand on a planet, they believe we have seasons because this globe tilts and moves in space around a sun. They believe all the evidence. Hundreds of things people accept as absolute truth, yet they doubt the Master Design Creator?

God IS infinite, and there are a lot of things that will always be mysterious, things that are out of the realm of our reality…other-worldly things…things we can't see. But look at the evidence!! Like wind. "Who has gathered up the wind in the hollow of his hands? Who has wrapped up the waters in his cloak? Who has established all the ends of the earth? What is his name? and the name of his son? Tell me if you know!" (Prov. 30:4). I know. His Name is "I AM". (Ex.3:14) His Son is called Jesus. (Mt.1:21) "…we fix our eyes not on what is seen, but on what is unseen. For what is seen is temporary, but what is unseen is eternal." (2Cor. 4:18)

I haven't seen God…nor have I put my eyes on the Face of Jesus. But the wind of His Spirit has blown into my life, it has blown away a lot of debris, knocked out a few dead branches, blown away a lot of "stuff", only to rebuild what is new and eternal. Jesus said, "Wind blows wherever it pleases. You hear its sound, but you cannot tell where it comes from or where it is going…" (John 3:8) "..so it is with everyone born of the Spirit."

LISTS

Do you make them? I do. Seems if I get it written on a list, I can release it from my mind, depending on the list rather than my memory. If I send someone to buy things for me, I make a list. I'm in good company, God made a few lists. The first one I think of is that list of ten things He wrote. ('Moses was there with the Lord...and He wrote on the tablets...the Ten Commandments' Ex. 34:28) THAT is a list, and if you haven't really considered all those ten things, it would be worth your time. It's an impossible list to fill though. He knew that when He made it...but we didn't. We had to learn that it was impossible, that was the purpose of the list. ('no one will be declared righteous in God's sight by observing the law, rather, through the law we become conscious of our sin.' Romans 3:20)

Jesus filled that list perfectly. (...I have not come to abolish the Law, but to fulfill..'Matt.5:17) What is simply amazing is that He is so gracious to credit to us, what HE did to fill that list, He did all the work and we can gain reward. Amazing grace indeed.

There are other lists. Lists of behavior that offend God. I find myself listed somehow in all of them. And am so thankful for the Amazing Grace of Jesus Christ and His payment for my offenses.

One of the things on that list of Ten things. 'Honor your father and your mother,'(Ex. 20:12) I notice there are no conditions attached. I don't get to pick and choose when or if I honor them. I am not told to obey them instead of God, and never in disobedience to God, but I am not given the option of deciding they don't deserve my honoring them.

'kabed'=to be heavy. This is the word that is translated honor. It carries with it the idea of importance. Parents are important. Even bad parents are important, but how my heart hurts for those who did not have the nurturing they needed. I grieve for those who are alone in their struggles. The mother in me wants to step into those situations and try to make up for it. But there is no making up for it. Not by me, or you. But there is help. 'When my father and my mother forsake me, then the Lord will take me up.' (Ps. 27:10)

The very best thing we can do for adults who have been let down, disappointed, abandoned, forsaken by parents, is point them to The Perfect Father. Even the most devoted parent among us lets our children down, failing on some point. 'God is not a man, that He should lie' (Num. 23:19) Hallelujah.

Paul has a great list. "…whatever is true, whatever is noble, whatever is right, whatever is pure, whatever is lovely, whatever is admirable…if anything is excellent or praiseworthy…think about such things.'(Phil. 4:8) This list really helps to re-program wrong thinking. When I have those 'kakos dialogiamos'/ evil thoughts, the Holy Spirit will often remind me of this list, and if I do not quench His whisper, He helps me to re-direct my thinking to whatever is true, noble, right, pure, lovely, admirable, excellent, or praiseworthy

Another list:

'…from within, out of your hearts, come evil thoughts, sexual immorality, theft, murder, adultery, greed, malice, deceit, lewdness, envy, slander, arrogance, and folly. All these evils come from inside and defile you.' The words of Jesus Christ as recorded by Mark in 7:22. Think you're not on that list? If so, the arrogance got you. Let's consider the list.

Consider that first thing…'evil thoughts'. 'kakos'= evil. It includes hurtful, bad, harmful, malicious, injurious, ill, worthless.

dialogiamos=thoughts. It means internal consideration, imagination, reasoning, to reckon thoroughly, to deliberate by reflection or discussion, cast in mind, consider, think. So,when someone cuts you off and grabs that parking space you were headed for, and you think how they deserve a flat tire when they get out of the store with $100 worth of groceries, including ice cream and milk, and its hot July weather…THAT is a 'kakos dialogiamos', and you made the list.

FORECAST

On the day of this writing, the forecast is for cold weather, it will likely get icy around here in a day or two. The stores will probably be packed today. People will 'stock up' on things. We won't want to run out of milk and eggs, or bread, or whatever tops your list of important items. We want to be prepared, right? We will make all sorts of preparations, buy more groceries than we really need, fill the tanks with gas, bring the firewood in under shelter. After all, the prediction is for snow and ice.

Propheteia=prediction in Greek, and nbula=prediction in Hebrew, the original languages of scripture. Predictions. Prophecy. I wonder, do we pay more attention to the weather-man on television than we do to the One Who is Creator and Master over it all.

'In the beginning, God created...' (Gen.1:1) 'lightning and hail, snow and clouds, stormy winds that do His bidding...'(Psa. 148:8) 'He spreads the snow like wool and scatters the frost like ashes. He hurls down hail like pebbles. Who can withstand His icy blast?' (Ps. 147:16) '...the Lord hath His way in the whirlwind and in the storm, and the clouds are the dust of his feet...' (Nahum 1:3) He changes the times and seasons. (Dan. 2:21)

This is the God we serve. Give Him more consideration than the weatherman. Give His forecast some serious thought. He has gone to such great lengths to help us be prepared. The book we call the Bible is full of predictions and advice. How long since you held one in your hand, how long since you asked Him to reveal the message it contains...and it does have relevant messages for each of us, every day. Go ahead and stock up, but hear the words of Jesus... 'Don't hoard treasure down here where it gets eaten by moths, corroded by rust, or stolen by burglars. Stockpile treasure in heaven, where it's safe.' (Matt. 6:19 The Message)

BIRTHDAY

If you're reading this, you had one. Do you remember it? Of course not, but it happened. Obviously.

I remember lots of days when a birth took place. The day of this writing is my baby sister's birthday, but honestly, I don't remember it. I was 15, and on another planet perhaps. But it happened. Obviously...

We are all born from the womb of our mother. 'Flesh giving birth to flesh...' (John 3:6) There is absolutely no other way to have a human existence than to be born of a woman. That existence is more limited than we are comfortable with realizing. "Man born of woman is of few days and full of trouble... springs up like a flower and withers away...' (Job 14:1)

But, 'He has made everything beautiful in its time. He has also set eternity in the hearts of men...' (Ecc. 3:11). Eternity is in the hearts of men, God put it there. We all have that basic desire to live. That's why human beings cling to life in the face of devastation. We WANT to live!! Oh, there are people who exhaust all their fleshly resources, having built their hope on self or other people, or "stuff", only to be disappointed and let down. With no hope, they forfeit their life in defeat. Jesus said '...the thief comes only to steal and kill and destroy, I have come that they may have life, and have it to the full. (John 10:10) Sometimes we believe the enemy's lies about an escape. There is an escape for the human condition, and it IS death..."we died to sin....all of us who are baptized into Christ Jesus are baptized into His death...buried with Him through baptism into death...raised from death ...to live a new life...united with Him like this in His death...our old self crucified...freed from sin..." (Romans 6: 2-18)

I love my life. Oh, I have stressful times, sad times, frustrations come and go. I get weary, angry, disgusted. My life is not all beauty and fun. But eternity is in my heart, and I'm aware of the promises of God, and the power of God to fulfill those promises in me. See, I had another birthday, different than the one that involved my mother. This birth involved my Father. 'Spirit gives birth to spirit.' (John 3:6) ' My new life is not like my old life. My old birth came from mortal sperm, my new birth comes from God's living Word, a life conceived by God Himself.' (1 Peter 1:23 The Message) I don't recall the calendar date. But it happened. I hope it is obvious.

CONNECTION

Isn't it frustrating when you need to make a call, and your phone tells you 'no service' or 'failed connection'? The metal walls of the store you are in interfere with the signal, or the mountains are too high they cut off the signal all together, or you're simply so far away from a tower there is no signal at all. Been there? Yep...me too.

It's especially frustrating when the call is vital, you need to get an important message thru to someone or you need help. We are so accustomed to our easy communications, but they fail occasionally, and we are shocked and frustrated, even scared sometimes. Our communications are built around a system: towers, little tiny devices we call cell phones, and invisible things called digital signals. They all work together to keep us invisibly connected to each other.

Ever call God and feel like you're got 'no service'? Ever thought you just didn't know how to pray at all, that you don't have a contract with Him for 'service'? Or pray about something and seeing no answer think you just failed to make a 'connection', that your prayers don't reach His ears?

Sometimes in prayer time, I find myself NOT praying at all, but thinking about what I need from the grocery store tomorrow or some such thing. I call that a 'dropped call', and I'm the one who dropped. God does not fail. And the truth is, He's even interested in my grocery list!!

This is not a perfect analogy, but it gives us a reference point. When we use a cell phone, we must operate within the system. Our location is important. When we want to communicate with God, our location is important. We must be praying WITHIN His will. THAT is our main problem. We often talk to God about things strictly based on our perspective. What we desperately need is to see from HIS.

Jesus deliberately chose to pray within The Father's will. "...if it is not possible for this cup to be taken away...may Your will be done.' (Matt.26:42) He didn't relish the idea of spikes being hammered thru His hands and feet, but He saw from The Father's perspective, He saw the big picture, what was at stake overall. The decision was, save Himself from the circumstances, or save every person throughout time who would choose to participate in His death instead of being responsible for their own sentence of death and separation from God.

'...this is my prayer...that your love may abound more and more in knowledge and depth of insight, so that you may be able to discern what is best....' (Philippians1:9) I am again encouraged and filled afresh with love and adoration because of the words of Jesus as recorded by John in chapter 17. I encourage you to read this chapter for yourself. Pay close attention to verse 20...because if you believe in Him, Jesus personalized this for you. Put your name in it...He did.

TANGLES

As a hairdresser, I deal with lots of tangles. Some hair is in really good condition and the tangles will comb out easily. Some hair needs lots of conditioner and several minutes to soak before the tangles can be removed. Occasionally, I have to cut out a tangle. Some people, especially children, don't keep their hair brushed. They brush the top layer, leaving the underneath to knot in tangles so twisted that it's painful to remove them. Maintenance is vital.

Life gets tangled. It is just part of the human condition. There will always be maintenance because 'all have sinned' and sin 'easily entangles us'. (Rom. 3:23 & Heb. 12:1) Just like brushing hair to keep the tangles out, we must take personal responsibility to 'walk in the Light'…to 'confess our sins'. (1John 1:7,9), to 'put off the old self, to be made new in the attitude of our minds' (Eph. 4:22-24), '…stop thinking like children, …in your thinking, be adults…' (1 Cor. 14:20)

I could go on and on with scripture that encourages and instructs us to ON PURPOSE 'not give the devil a foothold' to tangle up our life. (Eph. 4:27) Sounds like a daunting task, impossible really.)

My grand-daughter has long thick hair. She doesn't brush it except right on the surface. As a result, it gets matted and tangled underneath. So, her mother helps her, I help her. We try to be gentle, but sometimes it hurts.

God knows my life is like her hair, matted and tangled underneath. I try to keep it smooth. But the best I can do is keep the surface tangle-free. If I can even manage that. So, He helps me. He has sent '…The Comforter…to guide me into all truth and show me things to come…'(1 John 16: 7, 13). He 'teaches me all things and reminds me of everything He has said…' (John 14:26). He 'guarantees my inheritance.'(Eph. 1:14). ..that I will be 'acceptable to God (tangle free)…'(Rom. 15:16).'God made Him who had no sin (tangles) to be sin for me, so that I might become the righteousness (perfectly tangle-free) of God.' (2 Cor. 5:21) He is the very Presence of God within me, (2 Tim. 1:14), helping to brush and keep out the tangles. (Titus 3;5)

It is a daily, hourly, every moment choice, to appropriate either His power or mine. Do you need help with your tangles? He is willing and able. It sometimes hurts a little, though so worth it!

REMOTE CONTROL

When the battery for our TV remote control is low, it doesn't respond properly. Sometimes believe it or not, I just decide to walk over and do the controlling myself. Impatient or irritated, I make a statement of my ability to control the TV myself. I do have a remote control that can control EVERYthing, the TV, the video player, the satellite receiver, but it gets stuck away somewhere or lost in the recliner.

'...my Savior...has the power to bring everything under His control, transforming my lowly body to be like His....' (Philippians 3:21) No batteries are required, His power really does keep going and going, but I have the option of not using it. I can stuff it away

'...Quench not the Spirit.' (1Th. 5:19) '...the holy Scriptures...are able to make you wise for salvation through faith in Christ Jesus. All Scripture is God-breathed and useful in...training in righteousness...to be thoroughly equipped...' (2 Tim. 3: 15-17) The manual will never be exhausted. It will always be fresh and relevant, teaching me how to use this Remote Control in more and more ways, but I have the option of not reading it.

REMOTE CONTROL 2...

Our satellite equipment quit working properly. The service man came and installed new equipment, which included a new remote control device. It is different from the old one. Now we must learn how to use it. I suppose we could just get up and change the channels by hand, but like you, (admit it, you're the same way...), we want to sit across the room in our easy chair and change the channels.

We are discovering some new benefits from this remote control, things other than simply changing channels. I'm hoping it will control everything so we can do away with the other equipment controllers. We haven't read all the manual yet, so I'm not sure.

He has 'given me everything I need for life and godliness through my knowledge of Him...' helping me to '..add to my faith, goodness and knowledge, self-control and perseverance, godliness, brotherly kindness.... and love.' (2 Peter 1:3,6) This Remote Control will address every area of life, sending the Signal that selects the very best programming. But I have options for all sorts of programming. I get to choose.

We have a lot of things blocked on our TV, opted out of several channels that are available. Our Remote Control advised us against many of them. '...whatever is true, honest, just, pure, lovely.....think on these things...' (Phil. 4:8)

'...the Spirit of truth...will guide you into all truth...He will show you things to come...'(John 16:13) THIS is remote control, but I have the option of not using Him . Do you have Remote Control? Do you read the Manual? Do you appropriate His Power Source, or use your own? It is available to you, but you too, have the option of not using it.

PERSONAL

My God is personal. (not remote) '...The Lord my God will go with me. He will never leave me. He will never forsake me.' (Deut. 31:6 and Heb. 13:5) 'You are near, O Lord..' (Ps. 119:51) '...it is good for me to draw near to You, I have put my trust in You..'(Ps.73:28) Need some personal, reliable help? Where are you looking for it?

It's hard to stop listing scriptures that tell how faithful He is, and how much help He offers. He is THE Friend of friends, The Wise Counselor. (Isa. 9:6) The narrative of scripture tells such a beautiful story of His love. From creation, to salvation...perfect self-sacrificing love.

Why is it so difficult to grab hold of? Do we think it's too good to be true? After all, most of us have learned the hard way what it is to be forsaken by someone we called friend. We've all been hurt by bad advice. When we think of our Creator God in terms of what we know of human beings, comparing Him to us...we are making Him into an image. Our image! And He is not like us! 'God is not a man that he should lie...or change His mind.. He does not speak and then not act. He does not promise and not fulfill.' (Num. 23:19)

I tried personally to tend to my own behavior. I attempted to 'fix' all the wrong things in myself. The wrong attitudes and bad behavior kept popping its ugly head up. '...law (rulekeeping) made nothing perfect.' (Heb. 7:19) Oh, I'm not 'fixed' yet, it's a work in progress. I am 'being transformed by the renewing of my mind.' (Rom. 12:2) 'Not that I have already obtained all this, or have already been made perfect, but I press on...forgetting what is behind and straining toward what is ahead...' (Phil. 3:12,13,14)

While He is faithful, I am not always. I sometimes turn a deaf ear to His Whisper. I brush off His Hand, choosing my will over His. (Even though experience has taught me that He always, always, always, knows best!) But '...as for me, it is good to be near God. I have made the Sovereign Lord my refuge. I will tell of all His deeds.' (Ps. 73:28) 'Teach me your way, O Lord, and I will walk in your truth. Give me an undivided heart, that I may fear your name...for great is your love toward me...' (Ps. 86:11,13) He never forces His will. It is a personal choice. Ask Him for an undivided heart. Be honest. Completely. With yourself and with Him. Make it intimate...and personal.

SHADOW

On the day of this writing, somebody will watch to see if a groundhog sees his shadow. What's the deal with being scared of a shadow? A shadow is simply the darkness that is cast by placing a body between light and what the shadow is cast upon. Why be concerned about a shadow?

There is one shadow we are all concerned about. 'Even though I walk through the valley of the shadow of death, I will fear no evil, for you are with me.' (Ps. 23:4) Oh, you may not think about it much if you're healthy, especially if you're young, but when something happens to endanger your life, you are very much concerned. When the doctor has some bad report, you are concerned about staying alive. When your child falls, and comes up bloody and screaming, you're concerned about the shadow of death. Those are times when the shadow of death shows up, and when we see it, we wish for a way to escape. Like the groundhog, we want to stay away from it. Just as the groundhog causes the shadow he sees, we've caused this shadow of death.

'...you must not eat from the tree of knowledge of good and evil, for when you eat of it...you will surely die.' (Gen. 2:17). If Eve hadn't picked it, if Adam hadn't joined her, even if every human being since that time had been perfect in obedience...I'd have done it.

I've chosen the knowledge of evil often. Finding out for myself, disobedient, only to find out God was just protecting me when He said 'don't. Ever since that day in The Garden, death has loomed, shadowing our lives. Because there is sin between us and our Perfect Creator God, we all will die. There is no hole to crawl in, no escaping this shadow. Unless...

'I tell you the truth, whoever hears My word and believes Him Who sent Me has eternal life.... he has crossed over from death to life...' (Jesus' words in John 5:24) 'all of us who were baptized into Christ Jesus were baptized into HIS death...' (Rom. 6:3 emphasis mine). '..be faithful even to the point of death and I will give you the crown of life.'(Rev. 2:10) Our bodies will die, they are corruptible. Perishable. But, 'in a flash, in the twinkling of an eye...we will be raised imperishable and all be changed...clothed with the imperishable...immortality...death swallowed up in victory.' (1Cor. 15:52-54) "...death came through a man, the resurrection of the dead comes also through a man...in Christ, all will be made alive...as in Adam, all die. so, in Christ all will be made alive.' (1Cor. 15:21,22)

The groundhog runs back into his hole in the ground. I run to the empty tomb of Jesus Christ. Death is defeated, and I've accepted the escape offered. This body is wearing out, and it will stop working someday. The heart will stop pumping the blood, but my life is eternal. This body that will perish in a grave one day, will be replaced by one as glorious as that of Jesus Christ when He came out of His tomb.

WAR

It is real. It is here. You and I are IN it. "...this is no afternoon athletic contest that we'll walk away from and forget about in a couple of hours. This is for keeps, a life-or-death fight to the finish against the devil and all his angels." (Eph. 6:12) The Message) 'Be prepared. You're up against far more than you can handle on your own. Take all the help you can get, every weapon God has issued, so that when it's all over but the shouting, you'll still be on your feet.' (Eph. 6:13 The Message)

Are you prepared? Do you make it your business to stay prepared? The enemy has no shame, he will surely notice if you are not, and he will take advantage of the opportunity. He will attack when you are most vulnerable. There is no honor found in him. He 'prowls around like a roaring lion looking for someone to devour'...so, 'be self-controlled and alert' (1 Peter 5:8)

The natural response to the awareness of danger is to seek protection. We will never succeed in protecting ourselves from this enemy. He has the upper-hand, he won it in The Garden incident. It's that curse of death, and we can't defeat death, remember?

I have been saved from that curse but the war goes on. The attacks still come. Daily. I need protection. 'Give me aid against the enemy, for the help of man is worthless.' (Ps.60:11)

There are many battlefields. The frustration and anger that show up in the workplace. The behavior we display when a neighbor annoys us. The addictions that hold us captive. The attitudes of disrespect and dishonor to other people. The self-righteousness and pride in our hearts. Dishonesty. Gossip. Neglect. Putting ANY thing or ANY one above God. There is no place, no moment that we are not standing on a battle ground.

Are you fighting? Or are you surrendered? I want to fight. I have protection, and I have One weapon. "Put on the full armor of God so that you can take your stand against the devil's schemes...take up the Sword of the Spirit..." (Eph. 6:11,17) Get your Sword, and look at this armor closely....

ARMOR

Do you have pictures of King Arthur in your head? (He's a myth, by the way.) A handsome knight in shining armor? (A righteous vigilante, putting down evil-doers for his queen?) Romantic huh?

Armor looks uncomfortable to me. Heavy. Bulky. Restrictive. David would not wear Saul's armor when he went out to meet Goliath. Why? You tell me. 1 Samuel 17 tells the story. Take up your Sword of The Spirit (Bible) and see for yourself.

Ephesians 6:11 advises me to "put on the whole armor of God". Not part of it, the whole thing. And it doesn't advise me to come up with my own outfit. It tells me to put on God's armor. Why? 'So I may be able to stand against the wiles of the devil.' (verse 11)

OK, so what is this armor? Eph. 6:14 begins to tell us about it. Don't take my word for it. Open that Sword of The Spirit and see for yourself.

First of all, STAND. Decide you're going to in fact PUT this armor ON. We can talk about what a good idea it is, but that doesn't give us even a tiny little bit of protection. So, will you decide? Will you begin to arm yourself against the very real enemy?

Next, we must "…have the belt of truth buckled around our waist.." There IS absolute truth. If you have no consistent views of truth, you are an easy target for the adversary to successfully attack. Ask God right NOW to help you to see. Ask Him to remove the scales from your eyes so that you are not deceived or blinded by the enemy's lies. What God says IS. Period. Absolute.

In the time period this scripture was written, people wore long flowing garments, men and women alike. It was vital, when battle came that those garments not be a hindrance. A belt, sometimes called a girdle, would be worn to secure all the garments in place. The loose parts would be gathered up and fastened inside the belt.

Truth keeps all our 'self' grounded and in place. Truth keeps us from being tangled up in the 'stuff' that surrounds us on every side, the struggles, skirmishes, and outright war that we face. Truth keeps the fleshly/human part of us standing firmly, supporting us, so that we all fight on the same ground, for the same side. The enemy wants us divided, wants us confused about what IS true and right. That's one of his best tactics. I detest him for it.

Armor. God had one tailor made for me, and He has one for you, if you'll wear it.

BREASTPLATE...

Batman wore one with six-pack abs made into it. Remember? My breastplate doesn't give me abs, but it protects the vital parts of me...my heart. There's a table of contents in the front of your Bible to help you locate the books, Ephesians is in the New Testament section. Look at chapter 6, verse 14. "...with the breastplate of righteousness in place..."

Why does scripture use this picture to illustrate something to us? Just what IS righteousness anyway? And a breastplate?? Come on...Batman's breastplate turned bullets and protected him from blows to his ribs. (Fictional) Police have garments that serve as breastplates, they call them bullet-proof vests. They offer protection from attacks helping to slow down or stop a piece of lead screaming thru space, shot from a lawbreaker's gun. I think it's made of something called 'Kevlar'. (Reality)

Dikaiosune = righteousness in the original language of scripture. The word dikaiosune has to do with character. Innocent, holy, absolute rightness. It was once spelled 'rightwiseness'. So, we are to 'put on' this thing to protect us, this thing called righteousness. Think you can fill that description? I can't !! I am not innocent, far from holy, and absolutely never absolutely right!! So how can I wear something I don't have?!!?

Here's The Good News, the absolute best news you'll ever hear. I quote it from The Message translation "...anyone united with The Messiah gets a fresh start...God settled the relationship between us and Him...He put the world square with Himself through the Messiah Jesus...God put the wrong on Him who never did anything wrong, so we could be put right with God." (2 Corinthians 5:17-21)

There my friend is my rightwiseness. There is the only absolute right character you'll find in me. My only innocence. Nothing holy in me except from Him. I want it firmly in place every single day. I have never accomplished it, try as I might. HE accomplished it, and HE continues the work in me to rid me of the stains and residues of sin, the stuff that keeps me from being innocent, holy, and right.

It is an on-going process, will be until I draw my last breath in this body. My breastplate of righteousness is always on. My heart is not just set right with God, but was changed. I want what He wants. And even when I don't really, I WANT to want what He wants. He protects me in that way, drawing me to Him rather than letting me be content out of His perfect will.

My breastplate doesn't give me six-pack abs. But it makes me look perfect to God. He sees perfection…the perfection of Christ. And knowing THAT protects my heart.

SHOD

People with horses know that term well. I'm not a horse, but I like being well shod. Most people do, especially us girls, we like shoes. There is a purpose for being shod, it is to cover the feet and make us able to take steps without subjecting our tender flesh to the bare ground. The older I've gotten, my choices have changed, the emphasis becomes more on comfort and purpose rather than style and appearance. When I go on a day's shopping trip, I take in consideration the amount of walking, and I make sure I'm shod accordingly.

Every Christian should make similar considerations daily, we should be 'shod' appropriately, for we are shopping with Jesus, looking for others who will choose His offer. "He is not willing that any should perish, but that all should come to repentance." (1 Peter 3:9) He has already bought me, paid the price, I'm just waiting to go home with Him. Meanwhile, He is within me, with me every moment of every day. He's not walking around in flesh anymore, He is RE-presented to the world now thru the flesh of His children. "Christ is in you..." (Col. 1:27) That's me...and you, if you're His.

So what about the foot-gear in the armor we've been discussing? '...your feet shod with the preparation of the gospel of peace...'(Eph. 6:15). The common soldiers of that day were shod with a type of sandal or 'caligae'. They were strapped around the instep and ankle, with thick soles studded with protruding nails that kept them standing firmly in the sandy ground. In the very real spiritual war that is going on all around you and I, we must be shod. But not with a spiked heel. We are to be shod and prepared with 'the gospel of peace'. We can't achieve any victory without this important basic piece of equipment. (...shoes DO make the outfit!)

The gospel/good news/message IS peace. Peace with God instead of conflict with Him. He is perfect, we are not. FAR from it in fact! Conflicts (sin) exist in our relationships with each other. There is conflict between us and God. Conflict destroys personal peace and peace with others, family, friends, spouses, neighbors, strangers, other nations...it gets to be a really awful mess. Painful. Hurtful. Damaging. There is a solution to the problem. Reconciliation has been made possible.

Peace with God will bring personal peace and peace with one another. Ephesians 2 has a lot to say about this. "In Christ Jesus, you who were far away, have been brought near...He Himself is our peace, Who has...destroyed the barrier, the dividing wall of hostility...making peace...to reconcile... them to God through the cross, by which He put to death their hostility." (selected verses)

How you are shod will tell off on you. Is the gospel of peace what keeps you grounded, standing firmly, able to stand against enemy assault? Or is it your flesh? Your tender, vulnerable, bare feet?

SHIELD

I wear a raincoat as a shield against falling drops of water. It keeps my clothes dry, therefore keeping me warm instead of chilled to the bone. I have a plastic shield I use in my microwave. I put it over the food to keep it from splattering. My shields are of water-proof material and microwave safe plastic. What about the shield in this armor of God? "...take the shield of faith, with which you can extinguish all the flaming arrows of the evil one." (Eph. 6:16)

Don't get off the point here, don't zoom in on that faith word yet. (I'm not sure I can tackle that one!) We need to understand why we have a NEED for a shield, and what we use it for. We are being told in this scripture that there are 'flaming arrows' from 'the evil one', warned that we are in harm's way, and we need a shield between us and these methods of attack. We have to have a way to put out these 'flaming arrows'. (I have images of Calvary forts and Indians, on the western movies that often play in our living room.) The Indians' flaming arrows may or may not have been real, but the ones our enemy uses are very real.

The wrong thoughts that pass thru my mind, but get caught and thrown out as I use my shield. The opportunities to do what I know I should not, I use my shield of faith to turn them down. The occasions I want to lash out and return the attack, I raise my shield to protect myself, refusing to hurt another person unnecessarily. The fear that plagues me, I raise up my shield to keep it from penetrating my heart. The burning questions I struggle with, I raise up my shield to put out the fire of doubt and unbelief that my enemy would like to see steal my joy and destroy me. All the 'what if's, I raise my shield to knock them down, remembering the promises of God.

I must on purpose raise up my shield. It's up to me. It doesn't raise itself. The shield used in Biblical times was usually made of light wood covered with several layers of leather hides with a rim of brass. Some shields were covered in metal, making them heavier and harder to use for long periods of time. The wood was vulnerable to fire but lighter and easier to maneuver in battle.

Leathers were kept rubbed with oil to protect them and help keep the surface smooth so that arrows or darts would not penetrate easily. (anointed with oil!)

Our shield is made of faith. That's a really big word. The writer of Hebrews says it is "being sure of what we hope for and certain of what we do not see." (Heb. 11:1). My faith is not in my faith. My faith is in the God of the universe, the Creator of everything in my reality and beyond. HE, my friend, shields me from any flaming arrow my enemy hurls. "Thou O Lord, are a shield around me." (Ps. 3:3

HELMET

At the time of this writing, it was recently Superbowl Sunday. If you know me very well, you will know I have issues with football. I'm not a big fan. Today, I smile at God's timing, He is so cool, so good at what He does. I've spent all this time reflecting on armor, the equipment He tells us to use to defend ourselves against the very real attacks of our very real opposition. The last piece of protective armor is 'the helmet of salvation.' "…let us put on…the hope of salvation as a helmet." (1Thes. 5:8) "Take the helmet of salvation…" (Eph. 6:17) "…press on toward the goal to win the prize for which God has called me heavenward in Christ Jesus." (Phil. 3:14) (…listen to all this football language! Doesn't God have a sense of humor?!) "…make it my goal to please Him…" (2 Cor. 5:9) "…receiving the goal of my faith, the salvation of my soul…" (1 Peter 1:9)

Let's clear up our thinking about this hope thing though. Hope = 'elpis' in the original language of scripture and it means to anticipate with pleasure, to expect with confidence, desire something good with the expectation of obtaining it while not yet an actuality. It is difficult to stay in a battle when there is no hope of victory. This is not a big 'what if'. This is not an impossibility. But, "thanks be to God! He gives us the victory through our Lord Jesus Christ." (1 Cor. 15:57)

Daily putting on this helmet of salvation protects my mind. This hope protects me when my understanding is being assaulted. The enemy wants me to have poor understanding. He will twist truth so that I MISunderstand. He wants me to have poor judgment. He wants me to be confused and uncertain. He would have me live in fear and insecurity, or horribly misuse and misapply the grace that God has extended. But I have received "…the Spirit Who is from God" (1Cor. 2:12) I have possession. "…the promised Holy Spirit… guarantees my inheritance until the redemption of those who are God's possession…" (Eph. 1:13,14)

HE is "the source of eternal salvation for all who obey Him." (Heb.5:9) The opposing side plays rough and dirty. I have protective gear to wear because the opposition wants to take me down any way possible. The helmet is a vital part. It is crucial to protect my mind, and God Himself provides that protection.

I have possession, and I have the promises of God. I am assured victory. How about you? Are you on God's team? Are you suited up? Are you protected with His gear, or relying on your own? Your apt to be injured without it. Are you in the game, or on the bench? He needs all players on the field, He really wants to run the scoreboard up. "...look at the fields, they are ripe for harvest." (John 4:25)

SWORD

Have you noticed all the pieces of the armor we've looked at are for protection? Did you notice there's nothing for the back side? We are to stand, not run. Standing implies a continued action. We are called to face the assault. We have protection, and we have one weapon to fight with. "Be prepared. You're up against far more than you can handle on your own. Take all the help you can get. Truth, righteousness, peace, faith, and salvation are more than words. Learn how to apply them. You will need them throughout your life. God's Word is an indispensable weapon." (Eph. 6"13-17 The Message)

We are not to fight with our idea of what is right, (truth), but His. We can't fight armed in our own good behavior (righteousness), but His. We don't overcome what we face while sitting on our hands, simply on the strength of faith. "faith without deeds? Can such faith save?" (James 2:14) We have to act on what we say we believe. We are provided what is necessary to secure ourselves, but we are still vulnerable and will never take out the enemy without this one weapon He provides for our armor. The Sword of the Spirit, God's Word.

God's Word. Communication from the Almighty. What God has said has been recorded for us by a host of different writers, in 3 different languages, under all sorts of circumstances, from every social rank, kings to peasants, highly educated to absolutely no education, Jews and Gentiles, most of them completely unknown to each other, living over the space of some 1600 years, all telling the same story, the relationship between God and man, how it started, what went wrong, and God's rescue. The redemption story.

What God says IS. Period. He said "...let there be..." (Gen.1) and there WAS. He is the same God. What He says packs a powerful punch and the opposing forces can NOT over-rule His say-so.

What satan can and does do, is deceive us about what God has in fact said. (...we make it easy when we haven't a clue what He said in the first place!)

The first sin was a result of not being sure of what God had said. Satan asked Eve, "Did God really say, 'You must not eat from any tree in the garden'?" (Gen.3:1 NIV)

Read the complete story for yourself, see how that happened. Learn the tactic the serpent used. He uses it still. Look for God's Word in that story, what DID He say?

Satan's agenda is to keep us ignorant of what God has said. He wants to make us believe his version (lies) of what God has said. That devil will try to make us question and doubt God's character, doubt His intent, question what He has said and why. God has a reason for what He has said, always always a good reason, and for our ultimate good.

You can't fight without something to fight with. You'll get slaughtered standing against an enemy with no weapon to take that enemy down. You may manage to stand a short while, but you'll not stand long. The enemy will certainly use his weapons. His weapons are a distortion of God's Word. You are wise to find out the truth of what God says.

REFLECTION

I work standing in front of a mirror. I'm so accustomed to it, I seldom see my own image there. But it IS there. There are reflections of ourselves in a lot of places if we look for them. We are reflected in our children. Simply the face of a child often reflects who the parent is, the image being so similar. Often, we see ourselves reflected in the behavior of our children, sometimes not a pretty reflection.

Our actions and words are reflections. (I am convinced that we act on what we REALLY believe, not on what we SAY we believe.) Words are important, but actions speak much louder. "As the body without the spirit is dead, so faith without deeds is dead...show me your faith without deeds, and I will show you my faith by what I do." (James 2:26, 18)

Sometimes the mirror is true, sometimes it's distorted. Sometimes I just wish for the excuse of a distorted mirror, giving me an excuse for the reflection I see. It's not pretty sometimes, often in fact. But I've become more able to look at the ugliness I see reflected because only when I acknowledge it can it be changed. We are prone to not really look, to only look from a distance, or look quickly and turn away, ignoring what we see, even pretending we look entirely different. "Anyone who listens to the Word but does not do what it says is like a man who looks at his face in a mirror, and after looking at himself, goes away and immediately forgets what he looks like." (James 1:23,24 NIV) "But suppose you take a good look...keep looking at it...don't forget...but act...' (James 1:25 NIrV)

I can change a lot standing in front of my mirror. I'll be changing my own reflection in front of a mirror in a few minutes as I ready for the day ahead. I can change your reflection to a degree, with shears, a brush and a blow dryer. But only the Lord can remove the real ugly, the ugly that goes all the way to the spirit. "Examine yourselves..." (2Cor. 13:5)

I need to prayerfully look at my reflection. I don't want to have "eyes that could not see..." (Rom. 11:8) My desire is to reflect Jesus Christ. His image is perfect, and He shows me what I really look like. I am thankful He doesn't leave me to my own skill to make improvements, for my image is beyond flawed, beyond my capacity to improve. "Let perseverance finish its work so that you may be mature and complete, lacking nothing." (James 1:4) "I have put on the new self, which is being renewed in knowledge in the image of the Creator"(Col.3:10)

It is a work in progress.

MIRROR

There are distorted mirrors that make us look taller and thinner, wider, or strangely curved. A perfect clean mirror will reflect a perfect image of what stands before it. Often, we don't like what we see.

What we call The Ten Commandments mirrors something to me that's not pretty. When I look at this "thou shalt/thou shalt not" list closely, I become keenly aware of how disfigured I am. "...through the law we become conscious of our sin." (Rom. 3:20)

Are you brave enough to look into that mirror with your eyes really open? We will start with a simple one. "Thou shalt not steal."(Ex.20:15) There's no thief reading this right? No bank robbers I'm sure. The word translated steal is 'ganab' in the original language. It means to secretly bring, to obtain by stealth, the implication to deceive, to thieve literally or figuratively. Think you're innocent? So, you're 100% honest on your tax forms? You have never passed on some unkind, untrue, or unnecessary remark, that takes away someone's good reputation. What about that item that was mispriced, you knew it, but that young kid working as a salesclerk didn't. What about the stuff you bring home from work, that stuff the company pays for, provides for you as you work there, and you take it home to provide for your family, saving yourself the cost of purchasing it yourself? Maybe you didn't correct that person who thought it was you that did that great thing, you just kept quiet and let them think it. Dozens and dozens of things to list.

This mirror shows my face. I'm guilty. Perhaps I'm the only one though...or maybe you're not looking into this same mirror. Maybe you're looking into a distorted one. You know, one that makes you look taller and thinner. Better than you really do.

Think I'm being legalistic? I am. That is what law is. Legal. God's purpose in issuing law is served when we really begin to see how guilty we are of breaking them. Only then do we really see our predicament and our great need of rescue. When God looks, He sees all that stuff...unless I'm covered by His Son. Then He sees Jesus, the One and Only Perfect One. Thank You Lord for Your amazing grace. I'm a thief.

SNOW

Seldom do we see the amount of snow that blankets the landscape at the time of this writing. Leaving work yesterday, it seemed early. A blanket of white covering everything makes just a tiny bit of light bounce and reflect until it almost looks like daylight even when the sun has long since set, even when clouds hang low, weeping out fluffy white flakes. Every little speck against a backdrop of this snowy whiteness stands out starkly, the contrast so great. A footprint thru to the soil beneath, a tire track, a patch of snow that has been soiled with a spilled drink…every little thing shows up against the pure white snow.

I think about how disfigured and imperfect I am. When I examine myself against a simple ten-part standard, I fail miserably. Black…dirty…so ugly against the pureness of God. It serves the purpose God intended…it makes me see how badly I need a Savior.

I can't get myself pure when I can't even follow ten simply stated guidelines. Do you see any black ugliness in yourself? "Come now! Let us reason together…" (Isa. 1:18) That is God speaking thru the prophet Isaiah. Engage yourself, enter into the conversation He initiates.

He continues, "…though your sins are like scarlet…they shall be as white as snow."

Imagine a bright red against this backdrop of snow. What a contrast! My sin shows up. Like a huge bright red stain on this pure white landscape of snow, my sin shows up.

The Good News is that the scarlet blood of my Savior "purifies me from all sin" (1 John 1:7) I am "justified by His blood…"(Rom. 5:9)

White as snow, He "suffered outside the city gate to make me holy through His own blood." (Heb. 13:12) Whiter than snow, "...wash me and I will be whiter than snow." (Ps.51:7)

How could anything possibly be whiter than this snow....

COVET

We don't use that word. Maybe you use it, but it's not in my vocabulary normally. I do know it's one of those 'thou shalt not' things. Chamad=covet in the original language. In the verb form, which is the acting out of this thing called chamad, it means to desire passionately or intensely, to take delight in something delectable. It expresses the idea of finding pleasure in something. So why is it a 'thou shalt not? Is our God just mean and nasty and intends for us to not enjoy anything? "Thou shalt not covet thy neighbor's house, nor thy neighbor's wife, not his manservant, nor his maidservant, nor his ox, nor his ass, nor any thing that is thy neighbor's."(Ex.20:17) "Don't set your heart on anything that is your neighbor's."(Ex.20:17 The Message)

You see, it's not that we should not find pleasure, we're just not to find it in the wrong places. Having the great house is ok as long as we are not taking what we want from someone else. Are we sure the desire for the great house is not out of a wrong heart motive? And who is a neighbor? Looking for a loophole?

Jesus addressed that very thing in Luke 10. My conclusion is that my neighbor is anyone within the realm of my existence and opportunity of influence. Wherever the ripple effect of my decisions go, whoever it touches, that is my neighbor. I am not to undermine any other person in order to further the desires of my own heart. This 'thou shalt not' has to do with our wanting and even planning to have what is someone else's, and even getting it by whatever method necessary, at their expense.

An extreme example is David's coveting the wife of another man, and what David was capable of doing to have her. The story is told in 1 Samuel 11. "... David said ' put Uriah in the front line where the fighting in the fiercest, then withdraw from him so he will be struck down and die." (vs.15 NIV)

Whew! I'd surely not do anything that awful, would you?.

Then the Lord answered my prayer about revealing to me the sin in my own heart so that I might truly repent and turn away from it, asking Him to forgive and remove the guilt. He did. It is ugly. I am so thankful that He will remove the ugliness and grow me up in the process. You'll have to examine your own heart prayerfully in His Presence. If you know His love, you'll feel safe doing that. It's not a pleasant thing to look on purpose at the ugliness within yourself. But I believe it is necessary for spiritual growth. God knows every detail of it anyway, it's us that refuse to acknowledge the presence of it within us. We are the ones who hide our eyes and pretend it's not there. We pretend that it will not be noticed, or will somehow go away and never effect our lives. Wrong. So wrong…

LOVE

The day of this writing is Valentine's Day. Love is in the air.and the banner of love has been flying high. Restaurants are full of couples, and stores are cashing in on the opportunity to sell merchandise designated for your 'valentine'.

"…He has taken me to the banquet hall, and his banner over me is love." (Song of Solomon 2:4) The entirety of Solomon's book is a romantic love story. It has lots of rich lessons for us, lessons about our relationships as husband and wife, and the love relationship that God has for us. The relationship that God WANTS us to be completely engaged in and committed to. I've been married to my valentine since 1974. He treats me like a "lily among thorns" (Song of Solomon 2:2) He makes me feel treasured and beautiful. I am secure knowing his love for me. "How great is the love the Father has lavished on me, that I should be called a child of God! And that is what I am !" (1 John 3:1 personalized by me) I am secure in my marriage, my husband puts me as his top priority, nothing out-ranks me except God Himself.

How much more secure I can be in the love of God. "His banner over me is love." (Song of Solomon 2:4) God has stopped at nothing to communicate His love for me. Jesus left the perfection of heaven to step into a body of slowly dying flesh, just to communicate the love of God, to dwell among us, and to restore our relationship with Him back to the way it was, perfect and complete.

"Taste and see…the lord is good.." (Ps. 34:8) "Whoever is wise, let him heed these things and consider the great love of the Lord." (Ps. 107:43) How I pray you really know Him, I pray you know His character and His perfect love for you. He is so good.

PERSONAL TRAINER

A personal Trainer is a person who works one-on-one with a client to plan or implement an exercise or fitness regimen. People hire them when they want to lose weight or change their body condition but can't seem to accomplish it by themselves for whatever reason. Maybe they don't work at it every day as they need to. Maybe they don't perform the exercise correctly, opting instead for an easier way that doesn't really stretch the muscle much. (...that's me, if there is an easier way, I will find it.)

Sometimes more weight needs to be added. Other times, the weight needs to stay the same and the endurance level needs to be increased. Or maybe raise the tilt on the treadmill, same pace, same distance or time, but more uphill. I don't like any of it. I am sure I would like the result.

I have different kind of personal Trainer. I don't pay Him. He offers Himself to me freely. I love the results He has accomplished in me, never want to go back to the shape I was once in. But sometimes I want to quit and just stay in 'this' shape. He pushes me on. He allows me a break now and then, a time to "rest in the shadow" (Ps. 91:1), but He does not allow me to quit. Even more, He does not allow me to WANT to quit for very long.

He "renews my strength" and helps me to "run and not grow weary, walk and not faint." (Isa. 40:31 personalized by me) I often say that I am old and tired. But "He energizes those who get tired, gives fresh strength to dropouts. For even young people tire and drop out, young folk in their prime stumble and fall. But those who wait upon God get fresh strength. They spread their wings and soar like eagles, they run and don't get tired, they walk and don't lag behind." (Isa. 40: 29-31 The Message)

I'm thankful for the faith muscles that I have. I trust The Trainer when He adds a little weight, or increases the incline of the hill, or pushes me for another lap. He has shown to me that He knows what He's doing.

PRETTY

Pretty is as pretty does. When I was younger, I heard my grandmother and countless others say this. I knew they were advising me to behave properly, be nice, be polite, smile and say please and thank you, etc. etc. etc. "The Lord does not look at the things man looks at. Man looks at the outward appearance, but the Lord looks at the heart." (1 Samuel 16:7)

I've spent the last 35 years doing what I can do to improve appearances. Shaping a haircut to compliment and balance a face, using color to brighten a face, covering up the natural signs of aging (gray hair!! shudder....) I've practiced my craft, I've gotten a lot of education, know a lot of 'stuff' about what I do, how to do it and why. But only the outward appearance is changed. And while it is true that the outward appearance affects the way we feel about ourselves, it doesn't really change anything that is inside us. It doesn't change who we are. I can change appearance, but only God can change a heart. And He is so very good at what He does.

CHEQER TABAWN

Cheqer tabuwn in Hebrew means finding out knowledge. Isaiah says that we cannot fathom God's knowledge or His understanding. "Do you not know? Have you not heard? The Lord is the everlasting God, the Creator of the ends of the earth...His understanding no one can fathom."(Isa. 40:28) But I try.

I'm not the smartest gal around, but I'm smarter than I was. I'm not the wisest, but I've gained in wisdom. I don't understand everything, but I understand a great deal more than I once did. "The fear of the Lord is the beginning of wisdom. All who follow His precepts have good understanding..." (Ps. 111:10)

Fear was the beginning. Thank You, God, that fear isn't all there is. I 'll never know as much as God knows. But I have knowledge OF HIM. "...if I call out for insight and cry aloud for understanding, if I look for it as for silver and search for it as for hidden treasure, I will understand the fear of the Lord and find the knowledge of God. For the Lord gives wisdom...He holds victory in store...He is a shield...He gaurds the course...He protects the way..." (Pro. 2, selected passages, personalized by me)

I must "turn my ear to wisdom and apply my heart to understanding." Seems that often I listen for only what I want to hear. "...since you would not accept my advice and you spurned my rebuke, you will eat the fruit of your way and be filled with the fruit of your scheme..." (Prov. 1:31 NIV) Ouch.

Better leave my schemes out of it, ya think? "Trust in Me with all your heart and lean not on your own understanding, Connie. In ALL your ways acknowledge Me, and I will make your paths straight." (Pro. 3:5 personalized by me)

BIRTH DAY

August 19th is mine. It is also what I call my mother's 'birthing' day, the day she gave birth to me. I have two birthing days. Two sons, healthy baby boys, born just a few minutes before nine o'clock in the morning after a long night of hard labor, 6 ½ years apart. Every year when those birth days come around I re-live the hours before, during, and after…remembering.

Oh the day of my birth, my mother was alone in an army hospital hundreds of miles away from any family or friend except for my daddy, and he wasn't allowed in the room. (things are so different now, thankfully) My mother was there, going thru childbirth for the first time, not knowing what to expect, alone with the pains except for strangers. Thank You God that You were there with my young mother.

I don't remember that day, but it happened. Obviously. I also don't remember the day of my spiritual birth. I remember the day I was baptized, two of them in fact.

I remember times of repentance, times of knowing His Presence intimately. I recall definite times of change, times when I was certain that I knew His direction and answers, times when His Voice was almost audible to my ears and not just to my spirit. I don't remember the moment of my spiritual birth. But it happened. Obviously.

"He gave me birth through the word of truth, that I might be a kind of first fruit of all He created." (James 1:18) "Praise be to the God and Father of my Lord Jesus Christ! In His great mercy, He has given me new birth into a living hope through the resurrection of Jesus Christ from the dead, and into an inheritance that can never perish, spoil, or fade." (1 Peter 1:3,4)

There was a long time that I questioned my spiritual birth and my salvation. Am I saved? Have I been re-born? I don't remember an event, perhaps it is different for you. And that's ok, even great! For me, it was a process.

Somewhere along the way, I was "born again, not of perishable seed, but of imperishable, through the living and enduring Word of God." (1 Peter 1:23) Somewhere along the way, amid my struggle to re-create myself, trying to 'fix' all that was terribly wrong, I got out of the way long enough for God to do His work in me. I got tired enough to surrender the fight, accept that I was defeated in the battle against sin, keep the desire to have victory over it, yet look for victory from The One Who died to offer it to me. Hallelujah, What a Savior! Thank You Lord Jesus on my birthday, for Your birthing me, whatever that date was.

It happened. It is obvious to me.

FIT

Do you? I heard someone say they didn't. I know that feeling. I'm not sure when I stopped feeling like I didn't fit. Makes me wonder if somewhere along the way I began to fit, or if I just stopped caring that I didn't fit. Someone once told me about a missing piece of a puzzle, a piece that she needed to complete the picture of herself. She searched for a long time for that missing piece.

To fit, I think we first must know who we are. I can't fit unless I know the shape of my piece of the puzzle. I won't fit into your puzzle piece's place. I must find my own place, and to find it, I must examine what it is I'm searching for, what is it that I am trying to find a 'fit' for.

Jesus didn't fit. Even though by His very breath, the stars were created. "By the word of the Lord were the heavens made; all the host of them by the breath of His Mouth." (Ps. 33:6) Even though by His Word, light became. "…God said 'Let there be light', and there was light." (Gen. 1:3) He was responsible for the creation of every part of our reality and beyond, He made our world, yet did not fit in it. "He was in the world, and the world was made by Him, and the world knew Him not." (John 1:10) It was not always so. God The Father created perfect fit, intimate relationship between God and man.

"…the Lord God, walking in the garden in the cool of the day…God called unto Adam, and said to Him, 'where are you?'" (Gen.3:8) God came to walk with Adam in the cool of the day! Everything God made was once perfectly fitted. "God saw all that He had made, and it was very good."(Gen. 1:31) Then the choice was made to know evil, the choice was made to decide for self rather than obey. Because sin was present, the perfect fit was spoiled. Everything that was once good, now had evil in the mix.

That is exactly why I didn't fit. I didn't understand it, but I felt it. I sensed the very real truth that something was dreadfully wrong. I was not what I was meant to be. I was not meant to be any of the things that I saw as I searched for that missing piece and searched for the place where I fit. I felt it until He did the work of re-creation in me, when I "received the Spirit Who is from God that I could understand what God has freely given me." (1 Cor.2:12 personalized by me) I felt it until I found Him in such a personal way, that I no longer fell for the deception and lie of the enemy, no longer looked outward for where my puzzle piece fit. I felt it until I looked upward to Him and then inward to His Spirit, The Holy Spirit that is now present within.

I don't fit…HE does. He fits perfectly into that gaping hole in my soul. And because of that perfect fit, I don't care that I do not fit anywhere else.

HOPE

Hope is the desire of some good, with the expectation of obtaining it. 'I hope so' hope and 'I know so' hope are different. What kind do you have? How do you answer the familiar question, 'If you die today, will you spend eternity in heaven?' Do you have a god that 'might' be able to save you? Is that your hope?

Do you have enough willpower to correct what is wrong yourself? Is your own performance your hope? Do you serve The God Who is able and willing? Is your hope in Him?

Do you hope you have hope, or do you KNOW you have hope?

"I ask God to give you the spirit or wisdom and revelation, so that you may know Him better. I pray also that the eyes of your heart may be enlightened in order that you may KNOW the hope to which He has called you.... His incomparably great power for us who believe..." (Eph. 1:18 emphasis mine)

GLORY

Glory. Is it an ego trip? Scripture says a lot about glory, especially about the glory of God. I once thought God had a really big ego that needed fed. Why else would He have so much to say in His Word about bringing Him glory?

I'm faced often with challenging situations and difficult choices. Most of them would be so easy to make were I not a follower of Jesus Christ. Every time I make a decision and follow through with actions in line with what Jesus would do, I bring Him glory. (...remember WWJD?..) In those difficult times I have opportunity to display the Character of God, IF (big if..) my choice is made from His Truth, IF I am doing it because it is right, IF it is because He has called me to do it, and IF I recognize that it is thru the power of His Holy Spirit that I am enabled and empowered to do it.

"If you ever see any fruit of righteousness in me, you can be sure that it is because thru Jesus Christ, my love has abounded, my knowledge and depth of insight has abounded, if I am able to discern what is best, it comes thru Jesus Christ, and you need to be attracted to God because of what He might show you thru my life". (Php. 1:9-11 my personalized version and Paul's prayer for us)

There are many times I'd sure like to be Jonah, run the other way, pass my judgment, and hold back Gods love and mercy from somebody else. Yep, some days my name is Jo-netta. Sigh….

God doesn't need glory. We need to see it. God's doesn't need glory. I need to reflect it. My glory at its best is still not attractive, only 'filthy rags'. (Isa. 64:6)

"Help us, O God our Savior, for the glory of Your Name. Deliver us and forgive our sins for Your Name's sake." (Ps. 79:9) "I can do everything through Him Who gives me strength." (Php. 4:13)

OLDER

We count the years. We expect. We dread. We expect our children to roll over, then crawl, then walk. On and on the list goes as our babies get older. Then we dread the day they leave, even though we expect it, even pray for it. We dread the years piling up on us, dread the aches and pains, the health issues, the wrinkles. Even though we expect to get old, even want to live to be very old, we dread. We expect to take care of our children. We expect to take care of ourselves. But do we really do either? Without what God provides, we are utterly helpless. "Listen to Me, you whom I have upheld since you were conceived, and have carried since your birth. Even to your old age and gray hairs I am He, I am He Who will sustain you. I have made you and I will carry you. I will sustain you and I will rescue you. To whom will you compare me or count me equal?" (Isa. 46:3-5)

We are deceived by Satan's lies that we have any power at all. The only thing we have is choice, and with that choice, we choose so poorly sometimes. We choose to "pour out gold...hire someone...make a god and lift it up on our shoulders and carry it, set it up where it stands and can't move from that spot. Though we might cry out to it, it does not answer and cannot save from any trouble." (vs. 6-7 my paraphrase)

I never want my trust to be in money. I don't want to try to buy what only God can really provide. There is no security outside of Him. I never want my trust to be in any thing or any system. We set up things that supposedly make us secure, or even things that supposedly make us 'righteous' or 'saved', then we must sustain it, we must carry it as it gets heavier and heavier. No thing and no system can make one iota of difference in any eternal way. There is no security outside of Him.

As I get older I want to pray regularly with David, "O God, You have taught me from my youth...now when I am old and gray headed, Oh God, forsake me not until I have shown Your strength to this generation and Your power to everyone that is to come." (Ps. 71:7-8)

I'm older than I was. But I am not as old as I want to be. I want to be more and more useful as I grow older, not less. I long to watch and count as my children grow older. I expect to see God do mighty things in their lives and expect Him to work through them as they too grow older. "I have no greater joy than to hear that my children walk in truth." (3John 1:4)

CONCEALER

We girls use them to hide some flaw that our foundation won't cover. I've never had a lot of problems with my skin, even as a teenager. But every now and then my skin decides to gift me with a zit. The area under my eyes seems to get darker and darker, not to mention baggier. So, concealer is my friend.

We can hide a lot of imperfections and not just with cosmetics. We all have methods of covering them up. We are quite good at putting on the mask, hiding, pretending. It's an old strategy, it began in The Garden with a fig-leaf. (Gen.3:7)

The hiding is such a waste of energy. "Nothing in all creation is hidden from God's sight. Everything is uncovered and laid bare before the eyes of Him to Whom we must give account." (Heb. 4:13) We are much better off to embrace the truth, responding to the guilty feelings by running TO Him instead of away. Besides, "He will bring to light what is hidden in darkness and will expose the motives of men's hearts...", anyway. "There is nothing concealed that will not be disclosed..." (Matt. 10:26) We are believing a lie to think we can conceal any little thing from Him. We can conceal it from others but there is absolutely no advantage in doing it. It changes nothing for the better, in fact, it may lead to our own heart believing the lie of the enemy and even becoming calloused, even worse, hiding God's Face from us. "... your iniquities have separated you from your God, your sins have hidden His Face from you..."(Isa.59:2) "There's nothing wrong with God, the wrong is in you. Your wrongheaded lives caused the split between you and God. Your sins got between you so that He doesn't hear." (same passage, The Message)

Here is my goal...I want to get rid of the concealer. I want to feel no need to hide. "Keep your servant from willful sins, may they not rule over me."(Ps. 19:12) "May the words of my mouth and the meditation of my heart be pleasing in Your sight, Oh Lord, my rock and my Redeemer." (Ps. 19:14) It's a work in progress, a daily, moment by moment choice, throwing away the urge to conceal, embracing truth, even when it's ugly, and running TO the One Who "...restores the joy of salvation...and grants me a willing spirit..." (Ps. 51:12)

DISCOVERY

Webster says it is to make known, bring to light, to find something, first sight. Columbus is said to have discovered America. This continent was already here, Columbus didn't create it. This continent had people on it, it wasn't a discovery to them. Just to Columbus.

Have you ever discovered anything? When we study scripture for ourselves, we discover. We can learn by listening to preachers, but that's hearing what they have discovered. We can learn by reading books and commentaries, but again, that is hearing what someone else has discovered. The best preacher is the Holy Spirit of God. "...The Counselor, the Holy Spirit, Whom the Father will send in My Name, will teach you all things and will remind you of everything I have said." (John 14:26) "The anointing you received from Him remains in you, and you do not need anyone to teach you. But as His anointing teaches you about all things, and as that anointing is real, not counterfeit, just as it has taught you...remain in Him...Continue in Him..." (1John 2:27)

Coupled with an open Bible and open heart, He turns us into a walking, talking, living, breathing commentary. Teachers are great. Research material is great. But without the power of the Holy Spirit of God, it will be lifeless, powerless information. There is absolutely nothing like discovering Him for yourself. And when you do, you can't help but tell it.

What have you discovered about Him, for yourself, that you can relate to someone else? Open your bible, open your heart, and go to the throne of God in prayer, ask Him to teach you. He will.

"When the Friend comes, the Spirit of the Truth, He will take you by the hand and guide you into all the truth there is..." (John 16:13 The Message) "I turned my mind to understand, to investigate, and to search out..." (Ecc. 7:25) "...the Lord searches every heart and understands every motive behind the thoughts. If you seek Him, He will be found by you." (1Ch. 28:9)

DO IT

Nike says just "do it". Ever had someone ask you how you "do it"? Ever wonder how someone can get thru what they get thru? Ever wonder if they will? Is it a matter of putting your ears back, your head down, and just pushing thru? Perhaps sometimes it is. Often, it is a matter of calling on a Power greater than self.

There are periods of life when obligations pile up and we don't know just how we are going to "do it". There have been occasions that I have interceded for someone who has a burden of sorrow I've never experienced, I wondered how she would "do it". I asked God to show out thru her circumstances, to be so actively evident in her life, helping her to cope, enabling her to go on, it is an opportunity to show Your stuff Lord. Just "do it" for her, then everyone will see that she has Your extra-ordinary, super-natural ways of dealing with this burden. That's when He whispered to me...I will "do it" for you Connie, but only if you allow me. You can insist on "doing it" yourself, but you can't sit down and quit when you run out of your own resources, you have to stay on the field even then, and allow me to "do it"... even and especially when you cannot.

Often, I have been hearing the accuser (Rev. 12:10), and I'm so relieved to identify that, for Satan can no longer accuse me before God. I am washed in the Blood of The Lamb. But he still accuses me. He still lies. He still twists truth. He is a devil. His purposes will NOT be accomplished thru me... Lord, please make my eyes and heart to see his lies and activities. What may be accomplished thru 'me' and 'my' obligations, will be accomplished thru the extra-ordinary, super-natural Power of the Holy Spirit of God. It is not for my glory. No longer will I retreat because of that accusation from the enemy.

What is it that God wants to accomplish thru you that you draw back from? Are you retreating because of fear of failure, or fear of fame? Either one is a tactic of the enemy to hide the glory of God, and to keep us in bondage. God forbid.

BITTERSWEET

I use a bittersweet chocolate in baking. It looks yummy, but by itself, it's really pretty yucky. Bitter. A square of that chocolate mixed with appropriate amounts of other ingredients will produce a perfectly delightful dessert. Sweet. The dessert can't taste as it does without that bitter ingredient.

Life is certainly like that. The delightful is often gained by having some bitter experiences in the mix. But no matter how bitter, God is able to sweeten. "Though I…see trouble…many and bitter, You will restore…You will bring me up…You will increase…and comfort.." (Ps. 71:20)

It takes all the ingredients for my recipe. It takes that bitter chocolate else the whole thing is a failure. Life is certainly like that. "Surely it was for my benefit that I suffered…" (Isaiah 38:17) In every struggle, I want to expect the benefit. I want to recognize every sweet thing that comes from the bitter. I want to praise Him, before, during, and after.

REASON

To justify. Convince. To argue and be right. I confess. It is important for me to be right. I know...I'm the only one. Right?

I can justify my need to be right. I can argue until I convince you or until you convince me that I'm really NOT right, but in fact, YOU are right. Whichever it is, the key and the value in it, is the reasoning together. We are so much better off when we can do this reasoning/arguing with an honest heart searching for truth instead of just for the sake of being the winner. Winning is empty if the truth has been lost in the battle.

We have a false victory. When anger comes in, the devil is usually the victor. "Come now, let us reason together," says the Lord." (Isa. 1:18) God invites us to come to Him with issues, argue the thing out, reason together with Him and find solutions. When we come to Him with an honest attitude, not hiding, not masquerading or pretending, He will reveal truth. Even though it's often not pretty and usually hard to accept, the truth is indeed the truth whether we accept it and embrace it or not.

Job reasoned together with God. When all the disaster fell, Job went to God with all his questions, "I desire to speak to the Almighty and to argue my case with God." (Job 13:3) His friends had all the answers, or so they thought, but Job went to God. Job was right about a lot of things, but he also found out he wasn't nearly as good nor nearly as smart as he thought he was. "...surely I have spoken of things that I did not understand...my ears have heard of you but now my eyes have seen you...and I repent in dust and ashes." (Job 42: 3-6)

I want to always be willing and eager to reason together with God. Not to have my status verified, but to honestly seek truth

ROOTS

I love roots. Roots help me pay my bills. As a hairdresser, I see lots of roots. I make a living covering up that gray that peeks thru or the dark that demands to be seen. (Some girls are just really blonde on the inside and need a little help being blonde on top.)

God made us perfect, without sin. What we were on the outside, matched what we were on the inside...perfectly. We were intended to exist in that condition, but a bad choice was made and we all now suffer the imperfections. Now, what we are on the inside is marred, (sin nature) and what is manifested to the outside is imperfect. Praise God that He has a method of changing that and restoring us to what we were created to be.

Choosing to change our dark hair to blonde requires maintenance. (Changing the appearance of it does not change the natural of it) In the same way, while we are in this life, it is a daily, moment-by-moment process of maintenance.

Maintenance. Choosing. I mean the daily, sometimes moment-to-moment choices that we are faced with. (Joshua's challenge in Joshua 24:15 "Choose you this day whom you will serve") The choices we make are vital. One day, on THAT DAY, there will be no more "maintenance", no more changes needed, no more choices between good and evil, no more temptations, no more mistakes, no more regret. "...in the twinkling of an eye..we will all be changed."(1 Cor. 15:52) Until then we must maintain, or call it persevere. "Perseverance must finish its work so that you may be mature and complete, not lacking anything." (James 1:4) After THAT DAY there will be no maintenance. No contrasting root line, the growing out will stop. We will be made fully mature, lacking nothing. And we'll be that way forever

BEAUTIFUL ROOTS

Roots are where all beauty and strength come from. You just can't be beautiful without being strong FIRST. The most talented hairdresser can't make beautiful hairstyles from malnourished abused hair. Psalm 1 gives us a great word-picture of beauty and strength. "Blessed is the man who does not walk in the counsel of the wicked of stand in the way of sinners of sit in the seat of mockers. But his delight is in the law of the Lord, and on His law, he meditates day and night. He is like a tree planted by streams of water, which yields its fruit in season and whose leaf does not wither. Whatever he does prospers."

A tree grows strong and beautiful when it is close to a source of water. We are wise and 'blessed' when we plant ourselves near the source of life. We want beauty and strength in our hair AND in our heart.

Strength manifested in a beautiful head of hair, or strength manifested in a beautiful peace-filled, joyous, loving life, the beauty grows out of that strong place. Beautiful hair comes from a strong healthy scalp, well nourished. It stays beautiful when we tend it and care for it properly. It doesn't stay pretty if neglected or abused.

So it is with our lives. We stay strong when we are well nourished.

STRAIGHT

We offer a service in our salon for curly, frizzy hair that makes it possible for you to have straight hair without trashing it with chemicals or fry it with a flat iron every day. Oh, if only we could get our lives straight so easily. But we can't lay out a few dollars and walk away with a straightened out mess, even for a few months.

God never wanted all the kinks in our lives. He still doesn't, but we insist on twisting truth, bending His standards, and wrapping ourselves around all sorts of stuff. Changing the truth of God for a lie never has changed truth. "Instead of believing what they knew was the truth about God, they deliberately chose to believe lies." (Rom.1:25) Taking detours instead of the straight path only causes us prolonged periods of learning. We can wander in wilderness, twisting around and traveling in endless circles, getting nowhere, or we can get through it in a much shorter time just following right behind God as He leads us straight thru. We can't drive around a storm of life, but we can be delivered through it. Safely. Even stronger and better. We will never straighten out the mess of human life, not without Divine Intervention. "Oh, what a miserable person I am! Who will free me from this life that is dominated by sin?" (Rom. 7:24 NLT) Thank You again my Jesus.....

READY

A grieving friend said she thought she was ready for what was inevitable. A loved one faced the end of a long battle. The end was near. This friend thought she was prepared for that news to come, news that it was over, her loved one gone, the end come.

Praise God that of all the people who tried to be ready, the one who left was ready. Praise God is was not an end, it was the first moment of eternity. The battle is over. The struggle has stopped. The pain is gone. Forever. Hallelujah!!!

Knowing what lies ahead, are you ready? If not, what are you waiting for? God has "…set eternity in the hearts" of each of us. (Ecc.3:11) Eternity is the surest of sure things. Our hearts long for a perfect place. A perfect world is only to be found in His perfect rule, in His perfect kingdom, in His heaven.

"Listen to the call, the gospel call today, get in the glory land way." Be ready my friend. You may not face the terminal threats of cancer, but don't be deceived by the devil's lie. You do face death.

ALARM

We have been awakened in the early morning to our smoke detector going off. When that sounds, take heed...your house may be on fire. We didn't have a fire, we just needed new batteries, but we got up and checked the house.

What alarms do I ignore? What do I suffer that might be avoided if I'd just heed the warning? In scripture, Jesus has issued a 'take heed...' many times. Luke 17:3 issues a 'take heed' about forgiveness. I am to recognize sin and confront it, but in Mark 4:24 He addresses how I measure. He reminds me of the mote in my brother's eye and the beam in mine. (Matt.7:3)

I could list dozens, but even if we could hear all the alarms, even if we respond to every threat, we can never defeat sin and death. We cannot fix the problem of humanity, but we can live without feeling alarm.

"The peace of God which transcends all understanding will guard my heart and mind in Christ Jesus." (Phil.4:7) I take that personally. My heart and mind feel no alarm.

(I'm hearing the old hymn 'Living By Faith' in my head....)

FRIENDS

Our culture calls lots of things friendship, but having a true friend is a treasure, and being one is not easy. It is a relationship that requires commitment and work. On Facebook, we collect friends and number them. People request to be your friend, and we have the option of accepting or rejecting. I rejected a request last night, it made me wonder if I do that in 'real life'.

"Every man is a friend to him that gives gifts". (Prov.19:6) Do I look for friendship only from those who have something to offer me in return, when it's beneficial for ME, when I am comfortable with it?

Jesus calls us friend. If we look for benefits from friendship, He is THE ONE. But it's a relationship and requires commitment and work. "... You are my friends when you do the things I command you". (John 15:14MSG) That would be a tall order without His grace, without being connected to Him, for He is the PowerSource. "...apart from Me, you can do nothing". (John 15:5)

Lord help us be good friends to each other.

HALLOW

I think about that word a lot at Halloween. There is very little hallow about Halloween, except maybe if it falls on Sunday, the day that should be hallowed to God.

Hallow isn't a word we use much, unless we are reciting what is known as The Lord's Prayer, "Our Father Who art in heaven, hallowed be Thy Name...." Psalm 23 To hallow something is to give it a higher purpose. It means to set it apart for a special use, dedicate to a special purpose. I wonder if we really hallow God's Name, I fear we speak His Name rather flippantly sometimes. Do we grasp how holy He is? How utterly perfect? How complete and absolutely other than we are?

Let us purpose ourselves to counting and naming the blessings that God has granted to us. In that familiar fall season, let us make it our goal to hallow Him and give thanks to Him, "...proclaiming aloud Your praise and telling of all Your wonderful deeds" (Ps. 26:7) I challenge you, be specific. No broadbrush strokes...not just "I'm thankful for my health, for my family, for my freedom etc." All those things are certainly things to be very thankful for, but I challenge you to articulate and spell it out.

I'm thankful too for my health. I'm thankful I don't sit somewhere this morning, like many are doing right NOW, with a needle in my arm, injecting me with chemotherapy to fight a cancer raging in my body. Yet, I am thankful that there are ways to fight cancer, and I pray right now for those who DO sit in those therapy rooms, those who are fighting for longer physical life, that God will bring healing to them thru that treatment, that He will remove fear, I pray that if that person does not know Him as Savior, that He will put some bold child of God in their path to speak His Name and His message of salvation, so they may know the joy of His salvation and have a secure eternal life, as well as a longer physical life.

I'm thankful for my health. I'm thankful that my hands have served me for 40+ years doing the work that I do. I'm thankful they don't hurt worse than they do. I'm thankful they are not gnarled with arthritis, and I pray right now for those who do battle that pain. I pray for that one who on cool damp fall days, hurts because of it. I know many who do.

Thank You, Father, for my strong body. The body that birthed two sons. The body that is fit and able to work and play. This body I offer afresh to You this morning, as a living sacrifice, take my everyday ordinary life, consume me, use me, show Your glory, have Your will and way, accomplish Your purposes. You are God...You are holy...Hallowed is Your Name.

HOCUS-POCUS

Hocus-pocus...defined is nonsense words or phrases used as a formula.

Ever been abandoned? Abandon means to thrust off. Leave alone. To be unused.

I never thought about God abandoning anyone. But, "You have abandoned Your people, the house of Jacob..." (Isa. 2:6) I think of abandonment as an unjust thing. But is it ? Is there a time to just back off, leave someone alone to do as they choose, or even do as they insist in rebellion?

"God, You have walked out on Your family Jacob because their world is full of hokey religion, Philistine witchcraft, and pagan hocus-pocus." (Isa. 2:6 The Message)

I am convicted. God allows me choice. Even when I choose hokey religion and hocus-pocus. "The arrogance of man will be brought low and the pride of men humbled. The Lord alone will be exalted in that day..." (Isa. 2:17)

So I ask myself, where is the hocus-pocus in my life? Is my religion hokey? Do I use phrases and formulas?

"Search me, O God, and know my heart. Test me and know my anxious thoughts. See if there is any offensive way in me, and lead me in the way everlasting." (Ps. 139:24

THANKFUL

Webster says it's an adjective, that means it describes. I found a list of words that have similar meaning in our language: Grateful, gratified, satisfied, contented, pleased, appreciative, You get the idea. "Enter into His gates with thanksgiving and into His courts with praise. Be thankful unto Him, and bless His Name." (Psa. 100:4) The Hebrew word 'yadah' is translated thankful in that verse. The use of that word showed an action or motion in their language, as well as an acknowledgment.

I am convicted about my decision to be 'thankful'. That still small voice asked, "Are you really, Connie?" Thinking about the word 'wrath' because of some questions in a Bible lesson, I thought I'd write that I was thankful for God's wrath, because His wrath is birthed out of His complete holiness and His perfect love for me. He loves, He disciplines, and I want to appreciate the value of that discipline. But do I really? Or do I just know I should, and I wish that I did in fact appreciate the discipline? Am I really thankful for it? Are you?

I challenge you to examine your heart as well. We do not want to be in a downward spiral like the Romans that Paul wrote to,"The wrath of God is being revealed from heaven against all the godlessness and wickedness of men who suppress the truth…although they knew God, they neither glorified Him as God, nor gave thanks to Him, but their thinking became futile and their foolish hearts were darkened…" (Rom.1:18,21)

I don't want to just acknowledge God, I want to treat Him like Who He IS. I don't want to simply recognize the reasons I should be thankful, I want there to be an action on my part, a motion, an exhibition in my life somehow, somewhere, that I do know from Whom all blessings flow,

Praise God from Whom all blessings flow,
Praise Him, all creatures here below,
Praise Him above, ye heavenly hosts,
Praise Father, Son, and Holy Ghost.
Praise God, The Father, Who's the Source,
Praise God, The Son, Who is the course,
Praise God, The Spirit, Who's the flow,
Praise God, our Portion, here below.

Amen.

COTTON

I'm thankful for cotton. Have you ever heard the term fabric snob? I like that term. I think I might be one, I like nice fabrics. I love good cotton fabrics. Expensive silks and cashmeres are ok, satin I can pass, but a good cotton is hard to beat in my opinion. If you don't think so, try sleeping on a nice high thread count sheet for a few nights, then go back to a 200 thread count set! Your skin will tell you the difference.

I think it's ok to be a fabric snob. Scripture has a lot of examples of fine linens. The Proverbs 31 woman had fine garments, carpets, bed coverings, and she is said to be the "wife of noble character, worth far more than rubies". God created beauty. He made the first garments, they were "garments of skin". (Gen. 3:21) He gave many instructions about weaving fabrics and making things. "Weave the tunic of fine linen, make the turban of fine linen...the sash to be the work of an embroiderer..." (Ex. 28:39) The priests garments must have been very beautiful. Fine fabrics, beautiful colors, ornately decorated, you should read the descriptions for yourself. (Ex. Chapters 28&29, Lev. chapters 8,&16)

My High Priest owned one thing of any value. He had a plain, seamless, woven garment. He watched as Roman soldiers gambled over it. I happen to think His mother made it for Him, and I think it was cotton. A very high thread count, soft, comfortable, cotton.

WHISPERS

I'm thankful I can still hear a whisper. On an occasional morning, I hear a whispered 'bye' from my husband as he leaves for work. I rouse from deep sleep to hear it, and I wonder now how many whispered goodbyes I've not heard from him as he quietly leaves me snuggled down to sleep until my own alarm rings. A few days ago, an old classmate friend voiced a thankfulness for the whispers of his special needs grand-daughter. He told me of his thankfulness that God empowers him to understand this special child. I pray he understands every one of her whispers.

I wonder how many whispers I don't hear. I wonder how many I ignore, brush aside, how many are whispered amidst the stormy situations of my day only to be missed because I am listening only to the rage of the storm.

I am thankful that God speaks in powerful ways, in miraculous ways. But oh, how I love hearing His whispers! How precious it is to hear that still small voice speak to my spirit, calming my fears, reassuring and rescuing me. "… then a great and powerful wind tore the mountains apart and shattered the rocks before the Lord, but the Lord was not in the wind. After the wind, there was an earthquake, but the Lord was not in the earthquake. After the earthquake came a fire, but the Lord was not in the fire. And after the fire came…a gentle whisper. When Elijah heard it, he pulled his cloak over his face and went out and stood…then a voice said to him…" (1 Kings 19:11ff) Thank you Father for the whispers.

OPTIONS

I am thankful for options. Well…sometimes. God gave me options. We refer to it as free will. It stinks sometimes, at least in my experience. Sometimes I find myself praying to Him asking that He change my options, and to change what I find myself opting for!! Often my desire is for something I know I should not have the desire FOR in the first place! Often, when I am faced with a choice, I hear His Spirit whispering to me '…. might ought to rethink your options Connie, that one is not best…don't fall for a lie again…you do have an enemy, he is the father of lies and a deceiver…trust Me on this…'

So many times, I have been slow to learn. Many times, I wish I didn't have to choose…. I wish I didn't have to be responsible for choosing the right option. Man, it gets really hard sometimes. But, if God had not created as He did, if He had not given us that free will, we would not be capable of loving Him… only required to serve Him. We would not have a gift to give Him, He would control us completely without any other option for us. What good would that be?

Love is not love at all if it is not given. My husband loves me, and I am not always very lovable. He stays in our marriage NOT because he doesn't have another option. He comes home every day, he loves me even when I'm grouchy…. even when I'm sad, even when I'm angry. He opts to do that. (Thank God!! and thank you sweetheart….)

"Find your delight in the Lord. THEN He will give you the desires of your heart…Commit your life to Him…" (Ps.37:4) God asks us to commit ourselves to Him, entrusting every decision to His authority. He gives me information in scripture, revealing to me His character. I cannot trust Him if I don't KNOW Him. As I continue to get to know Him, my trust grows, my surrender becomes more and more complete. My security becomes more and more unshakeable in times of waiting.

I have learned from my options, I've chosen poorly often. I've learned that God is faithful to act, even though He must often wait until I've used up all my other options before coming to Him in full surrender, opting for His guidance.

HARMONY

Someone once asked me what Southern Gospel music is. I immediately think of harmonies. God created harmony. He created the instrument we call voice. In singing, we use our voices in different ways, creating harmonies that can stir every emotion God made and placed within us. Some voices sing the melody, the saprano, or lead. Some voices add other tones that harmonize, we call them alto, tenor, baritone, or bass. The lead may carry the melody, but it is not fully complete without the other parts.

The voice is an instrument, and we must learn our own particular voice, discover the function of it, identify it, explore its use and train it. The voice that is regularly used becomes more capable and sure, able to produce sounds that were not possible before. It is more dependable, less likely to squeak out off-key or crack and make you want to hide, never to sing again!

There is other harmony as well, the harmony of His Body, the church."...the body is not made up of one part but of many'. (1Cor.12:14) Here too, we must learn and train. We learn who we are in Him, learn what part of the melody is ours to sing. "...they form one body...So it is with Christ." (1Cor.12:12)

We must learn that He has created in each of us, a part of the harmony, a place and purpose. '...God arranged the parts in the body, every one of them, just as He wanted them to be' (1Cor.12:18) He did not leave you out. '...There are different kinds of service, but the same Lord' (1Cor.12:5) '...Those parts of the body that seem to be weaker are indispensable" (1Cor.12:22)

You may not sing the lead...but the song is not complete without your voice.....

FORECAST

At the time of this writing, the weather forecaster says that it will likely get snowy around here in a day or two. The stores will be packed soon. People will 'stock up' on things. We won't want to run out of milk and eggs, or bread, or whatever tops your list of important items. We want to be prepared, right? We will make all sorts of preparations, buy more groceries than we really need, fill the tanks with gas, bring the firewood in under shelter. After all, the prediction is for snow.

Propheteia=prediction in Greek, and nbula=prediction in Hebrew, the original languages of scripture. Predictions. Prophecy. I wonder, do we pay more attention to the weather-man on television than we do to the One Who is Creator and Master over it all.?

'In the beginning, God created...' (Gen.1:1)

'lightning and hail, snow and clouds, stormy winds that do His bidding..'(Psa. 148:8)

'He spreads the snow like wool and scatters the frost like ashes. He hurls down hail like pebbles. Who can withstand His icy blast?' (Ps.147:16)

'...the Lord hath His way in the whirlwind and in the storm, and the clouds are the dust of his feet...' (Nahum 1:3)

He changes the times and seasons. (Dan. 2:21)

This is the God we serve. Give Him more consideration than the weatherman. Give His forecast some serious thought. He has gone to such great lengths to help us be prepared. The book we call the Bible is full of predictions and advice. How long since you held one in your hand, how long since you asked Him to reveal the message it contains? It does have relevant messages for each of us, every day.

Go ahead and stock when the weatherman issues cautions, but hear the words of Jesus… 'Don't hoard treasure down here where it gets eaten by moths, corroded by rust, or stolen by burglars. Stockpile treasure in heaven, where it's safe…' (Matt. 6:19 The Message)

CONNECTION

Isn't it frustrating when you need to make a call, and your phone tells you 'no service' or 'failed connection'? The metal walls of the store you are in interfere with the signal, or the mountains are too high they cut off the signal all together, or you're simply so far away from a tower, there is absolutely no signal at all. Been there? Yep, me too. It's especially frustrating when the call is vital, you need to get an important message thru to someone or you need help. We are so accustomed to our easy communications, but they fail occasionally, and we are shocked and frustrated. Even scared sometimes. Our communications are built around a system, towers, little tiny devices we call cell phones, and invisible things called digital signals. They all work together to keep us invisibly connected to each other.

Ever call God and feel like you're got 'no service'? Ever thought you just didn't know how to pray at all, that you just don't have a contract with Him for 'service'? Ever pray about something and seeing no answer, think you just failed to make a 'connection', that your prayers don't reach His ears?

Sometimes in prayer time, I find myself NOT praying at all, but thinking about what I need from the grocery store tomorrow or some such thing, I call that a 'dropped call', and I'm the one who dropped. God does not fail. The truth is, He's even interested in my grocery list !!

This is not a perfect analogy, but it gives us a reference point. When we use a cell phone, we must operate within the system. Our location is important. When we want to communicate with God, our location is important. We must be praying WITHIN His will. THAT is our main problem. We often talk to God about things strictly based on our perspective. What we desperately need is to see from HIS.

Jesus Himself deliberately chose to pray within The Father's will. "...if it is not possible for this cup to be taken away, may Your will be done." (Matt.26:42) He surely didn't relish the idea of spikes being hammered thru His hands and feet, but He saw from The Father's perspective. He saw the big picture, what was at stake overall. He could save Himself from the circumstances, or save every person throughout time. He chose to save those who would choose to participate in His death. He chose to be responsible for their penalty of sin. Instead of being responsible for their own sentence of death and separation from God, he endured that death sentence

'...this is my prayer...that your love may abound more and more in knowledge and depth of insight, so that you may be able to discern what is best...' (Philippians 1:9)

I am again encouraged and filled afresh with love and adoration because of the words of Jesus recorded by John in chapter 17. I encourage you to read this chapter for yourself. Pay close attention to verse 20 because if you believe in Him, Jesus personalized this for you. Put your name in it. He did.

WIRELESS

It's a fascinating concept. The little machine across the room from me can print out whatever I type on my laptop, just by my pushing the 'Print' button. No wires connecting it, it's completely separated from the brain of this computer. How does that happen? How can information and data be transferred thru thin air? Imagine all the data that's floating around you right now. If you had a receiver to process each different one, it might fill up the room! The information is there, but it must have a proper receiver.

In the spiritual realm, God's Spirit is present and is "…able to do immeasurably more than all we ask or imagine, according to his power that is at work within us…" (Eph. 3:21) We aren't connected to Him by special lineage. We are Gentiles, not Jews, (but praise God that "…Gentiles are heirs together with Israel, members together of one body, and sharers together in the promise in Christ Jesus." Eph. 3:6) We don't get connected by doing some particular activity. "…not by works," (Eph. 2:9) We don't SEE this connection. "No eye has seen… but God has revealed it to us by his Spirit. The Spirit searches all things, even the deep things of God." (1Cor. 2:10) He chooses us to receive. "For God did not appoint us to suffer wrath but to receive salvation through our Lord Jesus Christ." (1Thes. 5:9)

So the question is, "Will you?" Will you be a receiver to re-present Jesus Christ? Will you respond to His wireless request? Will you let Him transform you, changing you so that you document and display the power of His saving grace? I am not hardwired to God. But there is a definite wireless connection. I don't push the 'print' button and have Him do my bidding. He presses mine. His desire is that my life duplicate the life of His dear Son.

The print job is in progress. "And in Him you too are being built together to become a dwelling in which God lives by his Spirit." (Eph. 2:22)

RESPOND

When in a difficult situation, facing conflict or uncertainty, maybe even a threat, how do you respond? Or do you? Often I think we don't. Instead of responding, we react. And there's a big difference.

To react, according to Webster, is to resist the action of another body by an opposite force. To respond, is to answer; to reply. I believe it is much easier to react than to respond. I also believe as followers of Christ, we are called not to react, but to respond. Our mission is to imitate Jesus. We are to have taken off the " ..old self with its practices and have put on the new self, which is being renewed in knowledge in the image of its Creator. "(Col.3:10) That old WWJD has a lot of profound truth.

Let us purpose in our minds and hearts to respond purposefully in every single thing, for HIS purpose, led by the Holy Spirit, depending on Him to defend and protect us, trusting Him to supply all our needs and even bless us far beyond our needs. "God can do anything, you know--far more than you could ever imagine or guess or request in your wildest dreams! He does it not by pushing us around but by working within us, his Spirit deeply and gently within us." (Eph. 3:20 The Message)

We must remember, He does not work things out like we do. In my experience, it never 'looks' like He is answering or sometimes even paying attention! And almost never within my time frame!! My task is simply to live in this moment, making RIGHT choices, behave as HIS child, in my now...and trust Him to work everything out.

I believe that it will always be for my good. "The moment we get tired in the waiting, God's Spirit is right alongside helping us along.... He knows us far better than we know ourselves...That's why we can be so sure that every detail in our lives of love for God is worked into something good. God knew what he was doing from the very beginning. He decided from the outset to shape the lives of those who love Him along the same lines as the life of his

Son. The Son stands first in the line of humanity he restored. We see the original and intended shape of our lives there in Him. (Romans 8:26-29 The Message) "But what does it matter? The important thing is that in every way... (every word, deed, and response,) Christ is preached.(imitated WWJD) And because of this I rejoice. Yes, and I will continue to rejoice, for I know that through your prayers and the help given by the Spirit of Jesus Christ, what has happened to me (every difficult situation and hard response) will turn out for my deliverance." (Phil. 1:18-19 The Message with personal application by me)

ALARM

We woke up one night to our smoke detector going off. When that sounds, take heed...your house may be on fire. Relax...we didn't have a fire, just need new batteries. But we got up and checked the house.

I wonder what alarms I do ignore? And what do I suffer that might be avoided if I'd just heed the warning? In scripture, Jesus has issued a 'take heed' many times.

Luke 17:3 issues a 'take heed' about forgiveness. "Take heed to yourselves. If your brother trespasses against you, rebuke him. And if he repents, forgive him." I am to recognize sin and confront it.

In Mark 4:24 He addresses how I measure. "Take heed...with that measure which you measure, it shall be measured to you..." He also reminds me of His advice about the mote in my brother's eye and the beam in mine. ("...why do you look on the splinter that is in your brother's eye, but do not consider the beam that is in your own eye?" Matt.7:3)

I could list dozens of 'take heed's and warnings, alarms to be recognized. Yet, even if we could hear all the alarms, even if we respond to every threat, we can never defeat sin and death. We simply can not fix the problem of humanity. But we can live without feeling alarm.

"The peace of God which transcends all understanding will guard my heart and mind in Christ Jesus."(Phil.4:7) Yes, I take that personally. My heart and mind feels no alarm. (I'm hearing the old hymn 'Living By Faith' in my head.... ♫♪♩•*•♪♪...♪♩•*•♫♪♪♩I'm living by faith, feel no alarm...♪♩•*•♫♪♪♩•*•♫♪.♪♩•*•)

WHOLE

Webster says it means all, not part, but the entire. We are instructed to put on the 'whole armor' of God. (Eph. 6:11ff) Panoply in classical Greek, is the full armor of a heavy-armed soldier. It is the word that is used by Paul here in his letter to the Ephesian Christians, teaching them truths about spiritual battles. You can be assured that you are in spiritual battles. If you aren't aware of a struggle, perhaps you've just surrendered. Every choice, every decision, every attitude, every action...all of them have spiritual implications. Concerning this armor of God, which of these have I decided not to put on today. What part of the armor have I decided I don't need? Are the things that I complain about a result of not being properly protected? Am I intentionally putting on what He gives and USING it?

"God is strong, and he wants me strong. So, I must take everything the Master has set out for me, well-made weapons of the best materials. And I must put them to use so I will be able to stand up to everything the Devil throws my way. This is no afternoon athletic contest that I'll walk away from and forget about in a couple of hours. This is for keeps, a life-or-death fight to the finish against the Devil and all his angels. I will be prepared, I'm up against far more than I can handle on my own. I will take all the help I can get, every weapon God has issued, so that when it's all over but the shouting I'll still be on my feet." (Ephesians 6:10-13 The Message, personalized by me)

I purpose to inventory my armor, beginning as Paul did, with truth. "Stand firm then, with the belt of truth buckled around your waist" (v.14) Do I have that belt buckled on me? Is it encompassing me? All the way, my entire life, all situations, all realms? Is it HIS truth? Or my version of it? All of it, or just part...whole? Part of truth is not sufficient. I must accept all of God's revealed truth. I must put that truth to use, and I must recognize what is truth about myself.

It is often not pretty. It is always difficult. Yet it is always safe to do so, with my Savior, the Lord of my life.

IMAGE

"Do not set up an image for yourself…" That is a directive from The Creator God recorded in Leviticus 26:1.

At one time, I thought I had that command aced. You'll find no 'graven images' in my house. I don't have 'idols', I never 'bow down and worship' them. But then He began speaking into my life and addressing my images. There were lots of them as it turned out, my own image being set up quite high.

I deal with image every day. Creating images is my job. Changing images, altering them, enhancing them. Yep, it's what I do. It pays my bills. There is nothing wrong with creating a better self-image. In fact, I think God intends for us to care about how we look, to ourselves, and the image we project to other people. But I wonder if the image I often see projected is indeed what it looks like it is.

Some young women look like they might be paid regularly for some very personal services. I wonder if they are anything at all like what they look like. Makes me pause to consider, what do I 'look' like? Am I what I 'look' like?

On the flip side of that, is the image I project what I really am? Or do I too 'look' like something I am not? I have come to the realization that it doesn't matter what I look like on the outside if the inside is marred.

And marred it is. With sin. Thank You Lord Jesus for removing that stain and taking the consequence of it. Thank You Creator God most of all, for changing me into the image of Your dear Son. (Romans 8:29)

I continue to be a work in progress.

CONFORMED

Scripture says I am being conformed, and it says I am not to be conformed. So…conform? Or not?

"For those God foreknew he also predestined to be conformed to the likeness of his Son, that he might be the firstborn among many brothers." (Romans 8:29) I like the plain language of this passage from The Message. "God knew what he was doing from the very beginning. He decided from the outset to shape the lives of those who love him along the same lines as the life of his Son. The Son stands first in the line of humanity he restored. We see the original and intended shape of our lives there in him"

Conformed = summorphos in the original language of scripture. It is a combination of 'sun' which gives a meaning of being soon, and 'morphe' which carries the idea of adjustment to shape and nature. So…I'm being conformed. To become like Jesus Christ.

Then there's this don't thing…"…be not conformed to this world.." (Romans 12:2) For a very long time I thought it was up to me. I was to change and adjust my shape and nature. I was to become like Jesus, and I failed miserably. Then, God changed the way I think. After exhausting myself in behavior modification and religious activity, screaming out to God "I can't do this!!", He made my spirit to hear Him say "I know Child. But I can."

It is a work in progress.

RENOVATION

We renovated our kitchen a few years ago. Boy, what a mess to live with that going on ! I'm sure glad it wasn't like the renovation going on with in me. "... put on the new self, which is being renewed in knowledge in the image of its Creator."(Col. 3: 10)

The word renewed in that verse is anakainoo in the original language. It means to renew or renovate. When we renovated our cabinets, all the doors were removed. I thought I was pretty organized in my kitchen cabinets. Until they took all the doors off. Man, what a mess.

Our Creator took all the doors off. Oh, it's not that He can't see what's behind them, it's me that needs to see the mess and allow Him to remove the clutter and renovate.

The kitchen is done. Cabinetry is beautiful.

The renovation within me, well..it is a work in progress.

HAPPY

Just what does it mean to be happy? Is being happy connected to other people? Situations? Circumstances? Is there a price tag attached? Or a location? Is it an emotion? Or a state of mind? Should we always BE happy? Do we have some right to be happy? What does it take so that we can in fact be happy?

There are dozens of scriptures that come to mind. A little searching turns up dozens more, too many to list, and certainly too many to brush aside. In defining this thing called 'happy', Maybe we should begin by eliminating what it is NOT.

"This poor man died, and was taken up by the angels to the lap of Abraham. The rich man also died and was buried. In hell and in torment, he looked up and saw Abraham in the distance and Lazarus in his lap. He called out, 'Father Abraham, mercy! Have mercy! Send Lazarus to dip his finger in water to cool my tongue. I'm in agony in this fire.' "But Abraham said...'Child, remember that in your lifetime you got the good things and Lazarus the bad things. It's not like that here. Here he's consoled and you're tormented." (Luke 16:22-25 The Message)

This rich man probably considered himself happy. Happiness we attain for ourselves can NOT be held on to. Listen to Solomon's advice: "Be happy...let your heart give you joy...Follow the ways of your heart and whatever your eyes see...but know that for all these things God will bring you to judgment..." (Ecc.11:9)

Whatever it is that defines that state of being 'happy', I purpose that for me, it is to be pleasing to my Creator and the ruling Force of my life. If God isn't happy...I certainly won't be for very long. And most assuredly not for eternity.

ACHE

Ever have an ache that you just can't describe? Not exactly pain, not exactly pressure, not exactly soreness, but very uncomfortable.

Sometimes my chest aches. Relax, it's not my heart. I've been thru the ER and all those tests to make sure. It's not a cough. It's not heartburn. It's not indigestion. They just call it anxiety. (...whatever THAT is!) So, I try to ignore it, find something to occupy my mind, some activity, or sleep and hope it's gone when I wake up.

This ache makes me think about that 'God-sized hole' that is in every human heart. Nothing can fill that space but Him. We try to fill it with 'stuff'. We try all sorts of distractions so that we don't think about it or feel it. Nothing works really. We are deceived for a while. A new car. A new dress. A new person. The emptiness returns. The ache.

We were created by a Creator Who designed us for a perfect world. We ache for it. We were Created by an Eternal Being Who created us for eternal fellowship. We search for it.

All over our world, in every kingdom of man, the quest rages. Efforts to find perfection, fix what has gone terribly wrong with our world. Wars rage as we search for peace. We ache for something we can't describe because it is completely other than we are. It does not exist within us. It will not be found any place. We prolong and even intensify our ache by our own tendency to choose the knowledge of evil rather than trust that He is always good and only good.

"He spreads out the northern skies over empty space; he suspends the earth over nothing. He wraps up the waters in his clouds, yet the clouds do not burst under their weight. He covers the face of the full moon, spreading his clouds over it. He marks out the horizon on the face of the waters for a boundary between light and darkness. The pillars of the heavens quake, aghast at his rebuke. By his power, he churned up the sea; by his wisdom he cut Rahab to pieces. By his breath, the skies became fair; his hand pierced the gliding serpent...And these are but the outer fringe of his works; how faint the whisper we hear of him! Who then can understand the thunder of his power?" (Job 26:7-14)

Oh, how I ache to understand and know Him more. One day, I will. "Now I know in part; then I shall know fully, even as I am fully known. (1Cor. 13:12)

PASTORING

According to a spiritual gift questionnaire, that's me. From my religious heritage, I immediately think 'preacher'. But is it?

"….he who gave some to be apostles, some to be prophets, some to be evangelists, and some to be pastors and teachers…." (Eph. 4:11-12) 'Pastor' is the Hebrew word 'raah'. It is a verb. It means to tend, to feed, to be a special friend. 'Poimen' is the Greek word. It is a noun. It is the one who tends and cares for.

There is relationship involved in this thing called pastoring. It isn't just a matter of throwing out a bale of hay, or strewing some corn. Neither is it a matter of preaching. If in fact this is an enablement I have been given, I am commissioned to use it. I am to 'go'. We all are. (Matthew 16:15)

It is our purpose to make disciples. With whatever He has provided to each of us, whatever He has gifted to every believer, we are to use in kingdom building. "….to prepare God's people for works of service, so that the body of Christ may be built up…" (Eph. 4:12)

Now, the next time I start preachin'… you know why.

EVANGELIST

TV preachers? Jimmy Swaggert? Billy Graham? Jeff Shreve? Whose face comes to mind at the term? euaggelistēs' is the original word that is translated as evangelist in our language. An evangelist has a full knowledge of the message of Christ and a passion to share that knowledge. Evangelists have the capability of explaining the mysteries of Christ, being enabled and empowered by the gifting of the Holy Spirit of God. "And he gave some, apostles; and some, prophets; and some, evangelists...For the perfecting of the saints, for the work of the ministry, for the edifying of the body of Christ..." (Eph. 4:11-12) It is a function, not an office. A purpose, not a position. A joy, not a job description. No pay check to take to the bank, but it makes one richer than anyone on earth. Ever. It begins now and will never end, and when shared, there is no dividing, only multiplied blessings!

"The mystery in a nutshell is just this: Christ is in you, therefore you can look forward to sharing in God's glory. It's that simple. That is the substance of our Message." (Col. 1:27b The Message)

Don't miss an opportunity to be the evangelist on the spot. Don't think that because you don't have a title or a certain personality that you can't do the work of an evangelist. Words may come, then again, words may not be needed. You may display the Word of God in action, the only Bible read by someone you see. You may need to step out of your box and trust God to put words on your lips, for surely you know someone that needs to understand the message of Christ and come to understand the Good News of redemption and salvation from the curse of sin and death.

"...keep your eye on what you're doing; accept the hard times along with the good; keep the Message alive; do a thorough job as God's servant." (2 Tim. 4:5 The Message)

And that's not Connie speaking to you, that is Brother Paul. I figure it's worth listening to!

WATER

I drink it. I cook with it. I bathe in it. I sit and look out across lakes filled with it. It soothes me, cools me, cleanses me. I've never experienced it bringing devastation. I find myself trying to comprehend the images of the power unleashed in a tsunami that happened just days before this writing. Just a crack and shift in one small place under a body of water on this planet, and the power that is unleashed is hard to imagine.

"For I am the LORD your God, who churns up the sea so that its waves roar— the LORD Almighty is his name." Isaiah 51:15 Did God make the earth to quake, did He send the tsunami wave? He certainly has power to stop it. So, He obviously allowed it to happen. I don't accuse God, but neither will I explain away what He has power to stop.

We read the stories about the plagues that Egypt suffered and wonder how they could explain all that away, how they could refuse to submit to The God of all creation. But they did.

We read how the Hebrews walked thru a rolled back sea on dry land, escaping a pursuing enemy army, and we wonder how they could ever again doubt The God Who set them free. But they did.

I thank Him today for His promise, "Never again will all life be cut off by the waters of a flood; never again will there be a flood to destroy the earth." (Genesis 9:11) My prayer is that somehow in this awful thing, our God will be revealed as the God He is and that all mankind will realize their absolute helplessness compared to the power He has at His disposal. I pray that in the heartbreak of this catastrophe, He will be found, and that He will restore and comfort.

POWER

Scientist have learned how to tap into a power they call nuclear. I marvel at how confident some of them are about being able to keep it harnessed even when the foundations beneath it are shaken. A bunch of smart guys take only a tiny bit of what God has created, use it in ways that produce huge amounts of dangerous energy, then when God's earth quakes, (for whatever reason), the thing that was an asset becomes a huge danger. Nuclear power plant melt down accidents are devastating.

"God blessed them and said to them, "Be fruitful and increase in number; fill the earth and subdue it "(Gen. 1:28). The world God created was given for man to inhabit and fill. How well are we doing that? I wonder if people don't get a little over confident about handling God's creation. (I think about being told as a child that I was getting too big for my britches.) "They did not remember his power..." (Ps. 78:42) Do we, like so many generations in the past, need to be reminded of His power? That He IS in fact in control, and not us? There is absolutely no power that we wield that is not granted from Him, (John 19:11) no gift (James 1:17), no authority (Rom.13:1). It is all really His.

Tapping into God's power sources is an intriguing thing to think about. Men do it in the physical realm all the time, but how miserably we fail in using the power that is available to us in the spiritual realm! There is so much power available to us thru the indwelling power of the Holy Spirit in every reborn child of God! Think about it...we have A Power Source who gives us HIS power. "For God did not give us a spirit of timidity, but a spirit of power, of love and of self-discipline." (2Tim. 1:7). Power to be obedient, bold enough to take a stand for His truth, a capacity to love beyond emotion, control over the natural sin infested impulses of this flesh, power and stamina to do what is hard, just because it is right...bringing visible glory to The God Who equips us.

"I pray that out of his glorious riches he may strengthen you with power through his Spirit in your inner being" (Eph. 3:16). Power to hang in there, knowing that it's not about here and now, but filled with hope for a blissful eternity. "May the God of hope fill you with all joy and peace as you trust in him, so that you may overflow with hope by the power of the Holy Spirit" (Rom. 15:13). Power to tell about Who He is and what He has done. "…. you will receive power when the Holy Spirit comes on you; and you will be my witnesses."(Acts 1:8).

I'd like to see a meltdown of His power in the Body of Christ. I'd like to see so much power unleashed within His people that the eyes of the entire world would be on Him…and not just a power plant in Japan.

FALLOUT

I remember being taught in the school classroom about protecting ourselves from nuclear fallout. It was a big deal. The threat of nuclear war and all that meant was hard for a child to understand, I only understood fear. We had tornado drills and fire drills. I had a little real life knowledge about those. I had in my mind that fallout would be something like falling hot cinders, or falling debris. As an adult, I understand more fully what the threat is about. As an adult, I understand the threat of fallout of many kinds. The nuclear kind being the least.

I'm talking about the residual consequences of an action. The residual consequences of a nuclear accident or explosion is what the news is focused on during a nuclear event, the fallout and threats to life. Will it reach me?

The residual consequences of a fallen world seldom have much focus, especially from the media, but it does reach me. And you. And every human ever to exist. There is fallout from the garden, and it's still falling, and it's still deadly. What can we do to protect ourselves? Absolutely nothing. We need outside intervention. And so, He came. He provides a way.

"This is how much God loved the world: He gave his Son, his one and only Son. And this is why: so that no one need be destroyed; by believing in him, anyone can have a whole and lasting life. God didn't go to all the trouble of sending his Son merely to point an accusing finger, telling the world how bad it was. He came to help, to put the world right again. Anyone who trusts in him is acquitted; Anyone who refuses to trust him has long since been under the death sentence without knowing it. And why? Because of that person's failure to believe in the one-of-a-kind Son of God when introduced to him. "This is the crisis we're in: God-light streamed into the world, but men and women everywhere ran for the darkness. They went for the darkness because they were not really interested in pleasing God. Everyone who makes a practice of doing evil, addicted to denial and illusion, hates Godlight and won't come near it, fearing a painful exposure. But anyone working and living in truth and reality welcomes God-light so the work can be seen for the God-work it is." (John 3:16-21 The Message) "For God loved the world SO much… that He gave His only Son…so that whoever would believe in HIM shall not perish…" (John 3:16NIV)

BRIDGES

We now have a bridge across our ditch. It's not a deep ditch, but sometimes it stands in water. Sometimes it looks a little snaky with all the leaves that gather there. Now I won't have to wade or jump to cross.

God didn't need to build bridges to cross over wet places. He caused the water to part and the bottom to appear, dry, not mushy and muddy. People just walked right thru. And snakes? Well, he put them on their belly! (Gen. 3:14, wonder if they walked or flew before then....).

Joshua 3 & 4 tells an amazing story about the water of a river piling up instead of running downstream. Exodus 14 tells another story of such an incidence. I encourage you to read them for yourself. Check to see if your Bible tells it like mine does. God didn't need a bridge to get across. He just made a way through. After all, He IS God, He IS in charge, He DID create every single thing that is reality to us. It is you and me who need the bridge, a way to get back to Him, back like it was in the beginning in the garden.

I am not like God. You aren't either. No thing we do enables us to cross the gap that is between us and Him. We can't un-do the sinful condition we are in. We can't press thru it, can't swim it, can't stop its force. I couldn't roll back the waves of sin and guilt that engulfed me. I couldn't manage to stop the rush of it, it just kept coming over me. No matter how hard I tried, and believe me I did try....it just kept happening. The more I identified sin, the more sin I saw in myself. I am in good company...my brother Paul had the same issue. "The law...started out as an excellent piece of work. What happened, though, was that sin found a way to pervert the command into a temptation, making a piece of "forbidden fruit" out of it...The very command that was supposed to guide me into life was cleverly used to trip me up....But the law code itself is God's good and common sense, each command sane and holy counsel..... "Does...that mean I can't even trust what is good [that is, the law]? Is good just as dangerous as evil?" No again! Sin simply did what sin is so famous for doing: using the good as a cover to tempt me to do what would finally destroy me...What I don't understand about myself is that I decide one way, but then I act another, doing things I absolutely despise. So, if I can't be trusted to figure out what is best for myself and then do it, it becomes obvious that God's command is necessary. But I need something more! For if I know the law but still can't keep it, and if the power of sin within me keeps sabotaging my best intentions, I obviously need help! I realize that I don't have what it takes. I can will it... but I can't do it. I decide to do good... but I don't really do it. I decide not to do bad, but then I do it anyway. My decisions, such as they are, don't result in actions. Something has gone wrong deep within me and gets the better of me every time. It happens so regularly that it's predictable. The moment I decide to do good, sin is there to trip me up. I truly delight in God's commands, but it's pretty obvious that not all of me joins in that delight. Parts of me covertly rebel, and just when I least expect it, they take charge. I've tried everything and nothing helps. I'm at the end of my rope. Is there no one who can do anything for me? Isn't that the real question?" (misc. Romans 7, The Message)

Praise God, there's been a bridge built to allow us to Passover this horrible problem we humans all have "The answer, thank God, is that Jesus Christ can and does. He acted to set things right in this life of contradictions where I want to serve God with all my heart and mind, but am pulled by the influence of sin to do something totally different." (Romans 7:25 The Message) Won't you choose that path? It's a glorious path!

TOLERATE

Some days I can tolerate more than others, wonder why that is? There are days when things just don't bother me much. Other days, those same things just drive me nuts. I could knock somebody's head off! Occasionally, it might be because I'm over-tired, didn't sleep well, perhaps I'm not well, feel a little sickly. Most often though, and even in those times, it's because I'm not going to The Source of my strength for help for the day. Like the manna that fell in the wilderness (Ex.16), strength falls from heaven daily for me, I just have to pick it up. I have to feed on it. There will never be a day that is impossible to tolerate, because there is One Who is ready and willing to bear the load, provide the way, supply the strength. He has gone to such great length to salvage His creation. That would be ME. And YOU. There is always a way to tolerate any situation or circumstance.

Because He CAN.

And I am His.

Are you?

RETREAT

In days past, I have attended a retreat. Webster says it's an act of withdrawing oneself from a place. On the day of this writing, I am withdrawing from the place of my routine life.

Webster also says it's a state of privacy or seclusion from noise, bustle or company. Privacy? There's supposed to be 3000+ people! I'm not a fan of crowds. I have a bit of attention deficit so it's hard for me to concentrate with so many people to distract me. I have sensitive ears so the noise is bothersome. I get cold usually. Whine whine.

But retreat I have done, in the midst of the throng. "You're my place of quiet retreat; I wait for your Word to renew me." (Ps. 119:114 The Message) "How blessed ....O GOD, ...is the woman you instruct in your Word...providing a circle of quiet within the clamor....Who stood up for me against the wicked? Who took my side against evil workers? If GOD hadn't been there for me, I never would have made it. The minute I said, "I'm slipping, I'm falling," your love, GOD, took hold and held me fast. When I was upset and beside myself, you calmed me down and cheered me up. .....GOD became my hideout, God was my high mountain retreat..." (selected from Ps.94:12-22 The Message) "You will seek me and find me when you seek me with all your heart." (Jer. 29:13) He is my retreat and He can always be found when I seek Him with an undivided heart.........even in the middle of Dallas, Texas with the bustle and noise of 3000 other people.

SHOUTED

How do you feel about being shouted at? I suppose it depends on the message of the shout. A shout-out 'Hi!!' from a friend compared to a shouted 'Get out of my way!' from a stranger? Ever think about God shouting?

"Shout! A full-throated shout! Hold nothing back--a trumpet-blast shout! Tell my people what's wrong with their lives, face my family .... with their sins! They're busy, busy, busy at worship, and love studying all about me. To all appearances, they're a nation of right-living people-- law-abiding, God-honoring. They ask me, 'What's the right thing to do?' and love having me on their side. But..." (Isaiah 58:1-2 The Message)

You drive your employees much too hard. v.3

You bicker and fight v.4

You aren't sharing your food with the hungry, you aren't inviting the homeless poor into your homes. You aren't putting clothes on the shivering ill-clad. You aren't being available to your own families.v.7

Your hands are drenched in blood. Your fingers dripping with guilt. Your lips smeared with lies. Your tongue swollen from muttering obscenities. No one speaks up for the right. No one deals fairly. They trust in illusion. They tell lies. (ch.59:3,4)

You fast, (religious activity), but at the same time you bicker and fight. You fast, (religious activity), but you swing a mean fist. The kind of fasting (religious activity) you do won't get your prayers off the ground. Do you think this is the kind of fast day (religious activity) I'm after: a day to show off humility? To put on a pious long face and parade around solemnly in black? (Isa. 58:4-5)

God shouted thru His prophet and servant Isaiah. And we would all do well to listen as He tells us what is wrong. We would be wise to examine our hearts, our attitudes, our intentions. I've heard His shout, and have been faced with His questions. What is at the core of my religious activity? Is it based on ritual? Or is in based on an intimate relationship? Does my religion have any effect on anyone but me? Does it go beyond my personal growth? Or is it just all about me after all? (...which would in fact be idolatry...the worship of ME.)

The purpose of a shout is to get attention. He got mine. What about you?

SINFUL

An offender. Criminal. Guilty of an offense. Scripture says that there is no one who is not guilty. "Everyone has sinned. No one measures up to God's glory. "(Rom. 3:23 NIrV)

I don't measure up to God. He is perfect. I am not. I no longer try to hide that fact. No more do I try to fake it, pretend, put the mask on. Neither do I wallow in the guilt and shame. Yet I don't wear my sinfulness as a badge. I have learned my enemy's method of operation. He is an accuser. He is a liar. I have also learned my Savior's love and grace. His very coming to this world was a sacrifice, leaving the perfection of His place in that unknown realm we refer to as 'heaven' was surely a sacrifice. Stepping into the womb of a young girl, birthed, potty training, puberty, adolescence, rejection, cruel execution. What sacrifice!

I will never attain right-ness. Never will I be able to perfect my life, my attitudes, my thoughts, or my actions. I wear HIS right-ness. "....I see that the job is too big for me, ... it's something only God can do, and I trust him to do it--I could never do it for myself no matter how hard and long I worked--well, that trusting-him-to-do-it is what gets me set right with God, by God. Sheer gift. (Rom. 4:5 The Message, personalized by me)

You may see me put on a cross. I may wear a Jesus-Girl shirt. But I will not make light of my sinfulness and insult my Savior who suffered so much to save me from the penalty of it. Sinful? Yes. But I don't want it tattooed on my body or stamped on my clothing. Saved? Indeed so! "When I received Christ, I… put away my sinful nature…Not by my own human hands… Christ did it…"(Col. 2:11 personalized by me)

Saved. And at such great cost to Jesus. Let us never make light of that cost, and let us never insult His effort on our behalf. Let us wear His Name. Not our sinfulness.

FRIEND

A companion. An associate. Someone you keep company with, have affection for. Simply someone we are not hostile to? Have you counted them? Do you categorize them? Rate them? Friends for different activities? Friends for fun, friends for sadness, friends when you need help? What kind of friend are you?

'Friend Day' at our congregation challenged me on this issue.

Jesus called the disciples His friends. "I'm no longer calling you servants because servants don't understand what their master is thinking and planning. No, I've named you friends because I've let you in on everything I've heard from the Father."(John 15:15 The Message)

"I chose you and appointed you to go and bear fruit...fruit that will last."(John 15:16) I am one of Jesus' friends. He has shared everything He knows from The Father with me. "I/we have the mind of Christ." (1Cor.2:16) What kind of friend will I be to Him? Will I bear fruit that will last? What kind of friend will I be to all those people I call 'friend'? Will I share with THEM all The Father has made known to ME? Will I let THEM in on everything I'VE heard from Him? What kind of friend am I if I don't share Him? He is enough. Sharing Him does not diminish Him for me. It is only multiplied. "...I will receive many times as much in THIS age, and in the age to come... eternal life."(Luke 18:30TNIV, personalized by me)

Purpose to be a true friend. A friend to Jesus, and to all those that He misses when He looks at His flock. A true friend to all those we so casually refer to as 'friend'.

SHELTER

The weather experts often advise us to take shelter. They issue warnings on days that threaten tornadic activity and tell us to take shelter when we are in the path of danger.

I have a couple closets that come to mind. I've actually been in one of them before, when our youngest son was home. I once herded everyone into the bathroom of the salon during a tornado warning. The kids thought it was fun. The mothers, not so much. My husband has experienced a tornado. actually saw the roof leave the house. Me? I've just seen pictures and heard stories.

I know in my head that preparing shelter is a good idea, and I have the knowledge about where the best suited places of the house or some public place might be. When the threat becomes real, I act on that knowledge and preparation.

All of it makes me think again about the Garden scene. God said don't choose that fruit of knowledge, the knowledge of good AND evil. Adam and Eve already knew good. They had daily fellowship with God. Up close and personal. But choosing to know evil, well, that messed the whole perfect scene up.

I don't have the knowledge of tornados. But I believe they exist. I believe they can be dangerous. So, I choose to act on the information I have. I don't need to wait for the experience of it. I take steps to be protected, and know that I am eternally secure even if one of them blows my life away.

So it is with sin. When God says '...ah, Child of mine, don't do that', I accept that He says it for a reason. I don't need the knowledge/experience of it, I take steps of obedience, steps that go away from it, never toward it. I know His promised protection from it and from its consequences. "Who shall separate me from the love of Christ? Shall trouble or hardship or persecution or famine or nakedness or danger or sword…or flood or tornado? No, in all these things I am more than conqueror through him who loved me. For I am convinced that neither death nor life, neither angels nor demons, neither the present nor the future, nor any powers, neither height nor depth, nor anything else in all creation, will be able to separate me from the love of God that is in Christ Jesus my Lord. (Rom. 38:35-39 personalized by me)

I am eternally secure even if a tornado blows my life away.

HOLY HOLY HOLY

Holy X 3 = YAHWEH. An incredible equation.

"Holy, holy, holy.is The Lord Almighty. The whole earth is full of His glory." (Isaiah 8:3) The Self-Existant, Eternal One. Jehovah, The Lord Almighty. The Holy One of Israel.

The morning of this writing, I finished the study of Isaiah for the Bible Study Fellowship year. It has been a year! I've been stretched. Challenged. Disciplined. Reprimanded. And I've been loved and ministered to by the Holy One of heaven, thru the recorded oracle of the prophet Isaiah. Ole' Isaiah was a regular guy, human to the core, just like me and you. He could not know, as he wrote the words that are now divided into 66 chapters, that this blonde hairdresser would be reading them thousands of years later. He could not know how God's call on his life, and his obedience to that call, would impact me and so many others.

How thankful I am for servants like Isaiah. I purpose to listen for God's call on my life. I purpose to hear and answer. "Then I heard the voice of the Lord saying, "Whom shall I send? And who will go for us?" ...and I said, "Here am I. Send me!" He said, "Go and tell this people...." (Isaiah 6:8-9a)

What might He do with my meager life? What might He want to do thru yours? "Come now, let us reason together," says the LORD. "Though your sins are like scarlet, they shall be as white as snow; though they are red as crimson, they shall be like wool. "(Isaiah 1:18) He invites. Even though He is holy and I am NOT, He invites... "If you are willing and obedient, you will eat the best from the land; but if you resist and rebel, you will be devoured by the sword." For the mouth of the LORD has spoken. "(Isaiah 1:19-20)

He invites, and He offers the best to His willing and obedient ones. We won't be giving ANYthing up that will matter!! We will not be short-changed, or miss out. But, it's our choice."

This is what the Sovereign LORD, the Holy One of Israel, says: "In repentance and rest is your salvation, in quietness and trust is your strength, but you would have none of it. (Isaiah 30:15) Turning back to Him…completely, without reserve, is where the sweet spot is. But will you have none of it? It's your choice. "As for me, I will serve the LORD." (Joshua 20:14 personalized by me)

GETTIN' READY

I spend much less time gettin' ready these days. Once, it took hours. Now, I don't fret over it so much. We get ready for lots of things. Some of it is exciting. Some, we dread. Sometimes we are equipped, sometimes we must scour around to find the right stuff.

Getting ready for a trip. Getting ready for the day. Getting ready for an event. Getting ready for something fun, or something not so much. Children need help getting ready. At least if they are really ready!

On the day of this writing, I helped a bride get ready. She will wake up a wife for the first time in the morning. She has been getting ready for months.

I am being readied to be a bride myself. I'm gettin' ready. I have quit scouring around to find the right stuff to fix myself up. He has taken care of all that. He even sent me a Helper. (...this Helper doesn't do hair, but His help is way better!)

Jesus is coming soon. Better be gettin' ready folks!

PRIEST

I am a priest. Seems strange to even type those words. Stranger to think of myself that way. But, "God chose you to be his people. You are royal priests. You are a holy nation. You are a people who belong to God. All of this is so that you can sing his praises. He brought you out of darkness into his wonderful light." (1 Peter 2:9) In ages past, before Christ, there were rigid requirements about who was permitted to carry out the office of priest. The priest was the intermediary between sinful man and a holy God. Priests were Jews but only Jews from the family line of Levi, with other requirements to be met as well. Much ceremony and ritual was to be done before the intercession could occur. The rituals of that time were teaching tools that reveal to us exactly what it meant for Jesus to bleed, suffer, and die. Payment is made. The wages of sin being death, His death is MY substitute. I am permitted to live. Now I can enter the holy of holies. Now I can enter the Throne Room of The Creator of the universe. With confidence. Boldly! (So, let us boldly approach the throne of grace. Hebrews 4:16)

The Body of Christ has a charge to keep. "...He has given us the task of bringing others back to Him through Christ." (2Cor.5:18) "God has trusted us with the message, that people may be brought back to Him. So, we are Christ's official messengers. It is as if God were making His appeal through us." (2Cor. 5:19-20)

I come before Him reverently because He is God and He is King. (Hebrews 12:28-29)

I come boldly because Jesus is my Friend, and through His Holy Spirit, I have access to The Father. (John 15:15, Eph. 2:14-19)

I come believing because Jesus said "..you will receive whatever you ask for in prayer." (Matt. 21:22). Not a blank check for my every whim, but submitting my will to an all-knowing and Almighty God, just as Jesus did when He prayed "…Your will be done on earth as it is in heaven. (Matt. 6:10) I is not just about me. "He wants everyone to be saved. He wants them to come to know the truth." (1Tim.2:4) Who will I meet on my path today that Jesus misses? Who will I see that may need Him so badly? Lord, open my eyes and ears to be sensitive to others and to You as I carry out the business of my day.

JOINED

Over forty years ago, the preacher said something about 'what God has joined together". Joined. Connected. Fastened together. Yep. That would be me and my man. I can't fathom life without the extension of myself. After that ceremony years ago, we were pronounced to be 'joined in holy matrimony', but that ceremony isn't what did it. The ceremony and following physical events had little to do with it. All of those things could not and would not have joined us together as we are today. But it was the beginning.

To our culture, I became his wife on that day, because of a legal document and ceremony.

To me, I became his wife on that day because of the choice I made to trust his love and commit myself to him.

I have joined few other things in my life.

I joined a sorority, for about a month. (I was young and ignorant.)

I joined a network of pyramid sales, for about 3 months. (I was young and ignorant)

I joined a gym, for a year. (I had a son who wanted to work out…and the contract called for a year or I surely would have quit sooner!)

But God didn't join me to those things. My checkbook joined me to them for the most part. God did join me to my husband, and He did not do it through a legal document or a physical act. Only He can do that, only He can really join, and it's a pity that so many people don't include Him and experience the power and influence of His Holy Spirit in their lives.

God has also joined me to Himself and to His children. There is one body and one Spirit…one Lord, one faith, one baptism; one God and Father of all, who is over all and through all and in all. (Eph. 4:4-6)

If you wear the Name of Jesus the Christ, our Father has joined me to you, together with our Savior, in His One Body. Not by some ceremony, not by some legal document, not by the power of some state, but by the power of the cross.

"His purpose was to create in himself one new humanity… in one body to reconcile both of them to God through the cross."(Eph. 2:15-16)

COMMITMENT

Commitment is not just warm and fuzzy. Feelings are often warm and fuzzy. At least to begin with..But commitment is a far cry from feelings. The Bible teaches that love and commitment should develop together. "Do not arouse or awaken love until it so desires" "Don't stir up love. Don't wake it up until it's ready." (Song of Songs 3:5 NIV and The Message)

We should not just act out of 'feelings'. What we feel is not always true. "A human heart is more dishonest than anything else. It can't be healed. Who can understand it? The LORD says, 'I look deep down inside human hearts. I see what is in people's minds...." (Jeremiah 17:9-10)

So often we discover that truth painfully. Having learned the hard way, we have picked forbidden fruit from our own 'tree of knowledge of good and evil'. We chow down on it and have our eyes opened to the reality of evil. We look back on our mistakes and see that God's way was right, and we were dreadfully wrong. Even though we 'felt' so very sure. And we bear the consequences.

God is Creator. He is The Designer. He is The Engineer. He drew up the plans and laid out the boundaries. Why is it we challenge His design? Why are we so set against listening to Him? He wants so desperately to guide us. We are wise to follow His council. Commitment and love must develop together. We should not arouse intimate relationships before there is a strong enough commitment to sustain the relationship. Warm and fuzzy (...or hot and sweaty), simply won't do it.

STRENGTH

Is it strong muscles? Physical power?

Is it emotional toughness? An ability to resist?

I've never had much physical strength, although I once thought I was pretty tough. The older I get, the more I realize my weakness, and the more I come to understand the Source of any strength whatsoever. And I don't have it.

Jesus said that His grace is all I need. He says that His power is strongest when I am weak. (2Cor. 12:9) What does that mean? To me, it means that I can choose my own 'strength' or I can choose to lay that aside and trust His way. I can choose to stay away from the knowledge that He has forbidden. (.the knowledge of evil.), I can depend on my human tendency to choose and act poorly, or I can choose to follow what He has said. Simply because He said so. (By the way, His way sure doesn't make sense sometimes, and is seldom what I 'want'. .It's the enemy's same Garden of Eden tactic...take a 'look', then question God)

"...the serpent said to the woman, "Did God really say, 'You must not eat from any tree in the garden'?...When the woman saw that the fruit of the tree was good for food and pleasing to the eye, and also desirable for gaining wisdom, she took some and ate it. She also gave some to her husband, who was with her, and he ate it. " (Gen. 3:1,6)

Yes, God did really say....and if she had forgotten or not paid attention,she could have asked HIM for clarification. Instead, she fell for the enemy's twist on what God had said, and the tactic that encouraged her to doubt God's motives. Instead of simply doing what God said simply because He had said it. Instead of trusting that He had a very good reason for His instruction.

You see, God is not mean and nasty. He doesn't say stuff just to take the fun out of life. He has said what He has said for a single purpose. To protect me.

And you To protect us from evil. To protect us from choosing the knowledge of it, from experiencing it. Once that happens, the consequences fall. And strength is not something we gain from it. We are so foolish to believe we are strong enough to dabble in what God has forbidden and come away unharmed. That is another devil's lie.

Only God can repair, restore, redeem and produce good from our wrong choices. Only God can clean up the mess we make and restore purity And He wants to. Will you take your brokenness to Him? Will you just trust what He says? He is always and only ...good.

WORTH

I remember the old hair color commercial where the woman says, "I'm worth it!" .You remember the one...she has bought this certain brand of hair color.. (I guess it is more expensive than some of the others) She has colored her hair at home and it turned out great. (...which is not great for my job security!) Then she declares that she's 'worth it'.

Just what is she worth? And who decides? How do you measure that worth? Is it the price of the hair color? Does she decide what she is worth? Is it measured in simple dollars and cents? (...then why is she not 'worth' a trip to the salon? Just wondering...)

It was a good marketing tactic. The slogan caught on and it is still repeated when we want to justify something. But are we worth anything?

To whom? For what?

And what causes us to be valued? This could be joked about easily, lots of clichés come to mind, but I look seriously at myself and ask, 'What of myself is of value?'

"I consider my life worth nothing to me, if only I may finish the race and complete the task the Lord Jesus has given me—the task of testifying to the gospel of God's grace." (Acts20:24)

That He values me is beyond my comprehension. And value He did...enough to leave heaven, enter the flesh of a human infant, be dismissed as an adult as unimportant, and executed on a trumped-up charge in an illegal court. All of it just to enter humanity, and restore what was horribly wrong.

"Great is the LORD and most worthy of praise; his greatness no one can fathom." (Ps. 145:3)

REJECTED

Well, I was warned that I would be, "....you will be hated." (Matt. 24:9)

"Count yourself blessed every time someone cuts you down or throws you out, every time someone smears or blackens your name...What it means is that the truth is too close for comfort and that that person is uncomfortable." (Luke 6:22 The Message)

Speaking God's truth is confrontational. It shines His Light into dark corners, and none of us like to see what hides in our corners. Yet, we are called to speak His truth and share His Message, His Good News. We are sent. "Go into the world. Go everywhere and announce the Message of God's good news to one and all. (Mark 16:15 The Message)

It is difficult. But rejection cannot stop us. It didn't stop Jesus. "He was despised and rejected by men, a man of sorrows, and familiar with suffering. He was despised, and we esteemed Him not...He took up our infirmities and carried our sorrows. He was pierced for MY transgressions, He was crushed for MY iniquities The punishment that brought ME peace was upon Him, ...and by His wounds I am healed." (Isaiah 53:3-5)

MENTOR

Ever have one? Ever BE a mentor? I was once asked to share how God has worked in my business life through mentoring. My mind began to recall the many the mentors I have had. Some very good ones. Some however, taught me a lot from negative examples. I wonder what others have learned from me, and how? In mentoring others, have I shared and encouraged thru Godly examples fleshed out in my own life, or have others learned from me thru negative examples?

The negatives in my own past experience have made me adamant about some things. There are memories of how I was made to feel, and I want never to make someone else feel anything similar. So, I am not prone to making those mistakes. (I just make other ones!)

Mentoring is making disciples. Jesus said, "Go…make disciples…" (Matt. 28:19)

I have a charge to keep. "…teach them to obey…" (vs. 20) I can do that in the ordinary moments of my day. If no other way than by my own actions.

PERFECT

Wouldn't you love to be perfect? Have a perfect life? What would it take for you personally? Less temper and more patience? Skinnier and prettier? Smarter? Richer? Well-mannered children? Doting spouse? Is it even feasible? Is it possible to attain? I think not. Enough is never enough. People will always be humans who fail. There is only One Who will never fail. Only One Who provides security and sure foundation.

Jesus told this story: "The farm of a certain rich man produced a terrific crop I'll tear down my barns and build bigger ones...and I'll say to myself, Self, you've done well...Take it easy and have the time of your life!' But then... you die, and your barnful of goods--who gets it?' "That's what happens when you fill your barn with Self and not with God."

Jesus continued, "Don't fuss about what's on the table at mealtimes...or if the clothes in your closet are in fashion. There is far more to your inner life than the food you put in your stomach, more to your outer appearance than the clothes you hang on your body." "Has anyone by fussing before the mirror ever gotten taller by so much as an inch? "...People who don't know God and the way he works fuss over these things. Steep yourself in God-reality, God-initiative, God-provisions. You'll find all your everyday human concerns will be met. Get yourselves a bank that can't go bankrupt...The place where your treasure is, is the place you will most want to be, and end up being. (Luke 12 asst. verses from The Message)

Again Jesus speaks..."These words I speak to you are not mere additions to your life, homeowner improvements to your standard of living. They are foundation words, words to build a life on...work the words into your life But if you just use my words in Bible studies and don't work them into your life, you are like a dumb carpenter who built a house but skipped the foundation. When the swollen river came crashing in, it collapsed like a house of cards. It was a total loss." (Luke 6:47- 49 The Message)

Lord Jesus, thank You for chiseling away at me...for the perfecting work of Your Spirit. I continue to be a work in progress.

NIP IT

Barney Fife's advice to Andy was always to "Nip it in the bud. Nip it! Nip it! Nip it!!!" There is much wisdom in that, though Barney was always a bit excitable and tended to over react…. I thought about Barney as I read Song of Songs this morning. (You may know the book as Song of Solomon…and I know, that's hard to imagine Barney and that book of the Bible in the same thought!) "Catch for us the foxes, the little foxes that ruin the vineyards, our vineyards that are in bloom." (Song of Songs 2:15) Little foxes were a problem for vine keepers. They nipped at the tender vines bearing new fruit. Not only did they eat the fruit, they could destroy the vine in the process. They would also dig holes, damaging the roots…. just a major menace. So, the vine keepers wanted to 'nip it in the bud'. They purposed to catch the foxes, even the babies, and do away with them before the problem was even birthed. (…I can just hear the mournful 'awwww….' of all the animal lovers reading this….)

There is much wisdom in this teaching. There is much to be gained from catching the foxes before they dig the holes and tear up the vines…. before they strip away the new fruit being grown on the vine.

Whether it is in our churches, in our businesses, or in our personal relationships, we are wise to do away with little foxes. Little foxes are a problem for all of us. We are wise to agree with Barney Fife and 'Nip it in the bud. Nip it! Nip it! Nip it!!'

BIRTHDAY

We count them. We celebrate. We have cake, give gifts, sing songs. We mark the occasion of time having passed. Every one of the days I gave birth to my children is a day that I count and remember. The day of this writing is the occasion of a friend's birthday. It is also the day her father is lying in a casket awaiting a different occasion tomorrow. I am sad for her, sad for her loss. I am saddened that her birthday will have this shadow cast on it. But I am happy that she knew the love of her father and for the relationship she had with him.

Birth days are exciting, new babies arrive on birth days. Birthdays are fun, we party and feast on family and great food. They are days that we greet new life and recognize the passing of the years.

Funerals are of a different sort, yet for those who belong to Jesus, they too are days we recognize the passing of time in this realm, and greet new life in the next. We will all pass thru the veil from this realm to the next. Unless Jesus comes back first, and even then, "…..a mystery I'll probably never fully understand. We're not all going to die--but we are all going to be changed. You hear a blast to end all blasts from a trumpet, and in the time that you look up and blink your eyes--it's over. On signal from that trumpet from heaven, the dead will be up and out of their graves, beyond the reach of death, never to die again. At the same moment and in the same way, we'll all be changed. In the resurrection scheme of things, this has to happen: everything perishable taken off the shelves and replaced by the imperishable, this mortal replaced by the immortal. (1 Cor. 15:51-53 The Message)

My friend's father will have a funeral. I may have one too. Or maybe He will come before then. Either way, I'm a winner.

REUNION

I attended one with my husband the night before this writing. His classmates of forty years ago gathered, remembering and reuniting. Many weren't really friends 40 years ago. They shared a classroom and teachers, walked down the same hallways, attended the same school functions and sporting events but never really knowing one another. Not really. But as adults, we look back with different perspective. We see what we had in common all along...youth.

Some classmates were absent because of choice, simply choosing not to participate. Others just could not because of circumstance. Others still were absent because they are simply gone on. Whether by accident or illness, or even on purpose.

As young graduates, we leave high school and soon leave teenage years. Then what? Life choices get harder and harder. So it is with life on this earth. Receiving that diploma is only a beginning, and so it is with our life with Christ, receiving Jesus Christ is a beginning. "So then, just as you received Christ Jesus as Lord, continue to live in him, rooted and built up in him, strengthened in the faith as you were taught, and overflowing with thankfulness. See to it that no one takes you captive through hollow and deceptive philosophy, which depends on human tradition and the basic principles of this world rather than on Christ." (Col. 2:6-8)

As I sat looking out over a room full of middle aged people who received a high school diploma on the same night some 40 years ago, I thought about the years since I received Christ. In both cases, mistakes have been made, lessons have been learned, lots of growing up and maturing have taken place, perspectives and priorities have been altered. .I pray we continue to live and continue to be built up in Him. "…. School's out; quit studying the subject and start living it! And let your living spill over into thanksgiving.…" (Col 2:7 The Message)

"Let the peace of Christ keep you in tune with each other...let the Word of Christ—the Message--have the run of the house...Give it plenty of room in your lives...let every detail in your lives--words, actions, whatever--be done in the name of the Master, Jesus, thanking God the Father every step of the way..."(Col. 3:15-17 The Message)

The reunion was great. But there will be a greater reunion. One day....

INOCULATION

The idea is to get just a little bit of it, enough to make you have a few symptoms, but not have the real thing. I was inoculated for small pox when I was a child. I remember the needle, and I remember having a giant scab on my arm. I was inoculated for flu a few years ago. I also remember that needle, and I remember that it made me feel so bad I decided not to do that again. Why be sick on purpose? (That may be unwise. The real flu can be deadly.)

What have you been inoculated for? Have you been inoculated against sin? Or, have you been inoculated against the gospel of Christ? It's not an original thought. It is a concept I heard from an evangelist. I was a little taken back, but the point is very valid. Many people have been inoculated against the gospel of Christ by 'religion'. They have had a small dose, enough to give them a few symptoms, but they don't have the real thing. Are you 'going to church' and getting a tiny little dose? Only to leave the building unchanged? "A sow that is washed goes back to her wallowing in the mud." (2 Peter 2:22) Maybe you leave the building having swept away a little of the dirt in your life. Did you decide to stop some behavior that is sinful? But you have nothing in its place? Do you operate on your own willpower? Jesus warned, "When a corrupting spirit is expelled from someone, it drifts along through the desert looking for an oasis, some unsuspecting soul it can bedevil. When it doesn't find anyone, it says, 'I'll go back to my old haunt.' On return, it finds the person swept and dusted, but vacant. It then runs out and rounds up seven other spirits dirtier than itself and they all move in, whooping it up. That person ends up far worse than if he'd never gotten cleaned up in the first place." (Luke 11:24-26 The Message)

Operating on your own willpower, however strong it is, will fail. Eventually. And permanently.

If you don't have His Presence within you, you have no inoculation against sin, and sin WILL kill you. Eternally.

I had doses of religion for many years. Those small doses kept me from having a full-blown relationship with Christ for a time. Those small doses of religion were used by the enemy to give me a few symptoms but not a heart change. Praise God, I am now inoculated against sin by His power, not my own. Jesus, The Christ, came so I can be healed from the rampant disease of sin, the disease that kills. "For whoever wants to save his life will lose it, but whoever loses his life for me will save it." (Luke 9:24)

Thank You Jesus, I didn't just get a few symptoms and live thru it. I was sick, and died.in order to live! And live eternally...in the Presence of Almighty God.

FACE-TO-FACE

I anticipate a face-to-face encounter.

In this age of technology, there are many people I call friend with whom I have never had a face-to-face meeting. It is a concept I've wrestled with over and over. Do I know these people? On the other hand, do I even know the people I see and touch? How do we come to 'know'? Do we need to see? Is seeing with our eyes the only way to see? (If seeing with eyes is required, then blind people would know absolutely no one!) So, knowing someone has little to do with sight., perhaps even time and space.

Relationships come in many ways, shapes, and forms. As I anticipate this face-to-face meeting with a friend, I think about meeting Jesus face-to-face. I 'know' Jesus. He is my Savior, and my very best friend. But I have never shaken His Hand, never looked into His eyes. I know Him thru the Words of scripture, and through the power of His Spirit. Our relationship is spiritual. It is genuine. It is real. And it's the most treasured relationship I have.

After this coming encounter with a friend, I will know him better. Our relationship will have a new facet, face to face. How I anticipate a face-to-Face meeting with my Best Friend! One day I will meet Him face-to-Face. One day, our relationship will be changed by a face-to-Face encounter. A physical encounter to enhance the spiritual relationship that exists now. "Now I see but a poor reflection as in a mirror; then I shall see face to face. Now I know in part; then I shall know fully, even as I am fully known." (1 Cor. 13:12 NIV personalized by me) "Dear friends, now we are children of God, and what we will be has not yet been made known. But we know that when He appears, we shall be like him, for we shall see Him as He is." (1 John 3:2 NIV)

Whether you know Him or not, you WILL meet Him face-to-Face. And you will bow. "...all created beings in heaven and on earth--even those long ago dead and buried--will bow in worship before this Jesus Christ, and call out in praise that he is the Master of all, to the glorious honor of God the Father. (Philippians 2:10 The Message) Glory!!

GIVING

I have a problem with it sometimes. The hardest thing is not deciding IF, it is deciding what to give and who to give to. I don't consider myself stingy. I do struggle with my flesh and selfishness, yet I don't think I am completely selfish. I know there is fault within me, and I pray "God, see what is in my heart. Know what is there. Put me to the test. Know what I'm thinking. See if there's anything in my life you don't like. Help me live in the way that is always right. (Ps. 139:24 NIrV)

Having spent quite some listening to some challenging messages about who Christians are and how they impact the culture they live in, I drove down a nearby street and was twice approached while at a stop light by people asking for money. The accusing voice came…"so…are you going to give? You have a cross around your neck, may I remind you that Jesus said, "Give to every man who asks you." (Yes, He did say that, in John 6:30 and Rev. 12:10 speaks of the accuser.)

It is a dilemma. I am thankful for the whole of scripture, and thankful for the teaching of Paul, "For even when we were with you, we gave you this rule: "If a man will not work, he shall not eat." We hear that some among you are idle. They are not busy; they are busybodies. Such people we command and urge in the Lord Jesus Christ to settle down and earn the bread they eat." (2Thes. 3:10)

There ARE people who need help. Yet somehow, if a person can stand on a concrete sidewalk, beside lanes of hot asphalt with hundreds of cars going by, in the heat of a scorching Texas day, could they not be doing something besides asking for handouts? Seems to me like they are working awfully hard just to NOT work.

DISAPPOINTED

You can't be disappointed if you don't have expectations. I don't know how you do that. How do you NOT have some sort of expectation? While trying to keep an opened mind, while not setting unrealistic expectations, I just end up having LOW expectations. I suppose it's better to be pleasantly surprised by having low expectations blown away than it is to be sadly disappointed when high expectations are unmet.

I recently set some very low expectations. I expected what I have experienced in the past. What a pleasant surprise to have those expectations unmet! What a joy to find that some same ole things are not the same. The apostle Paul had the dilemma as well. "I do admit that I have fears that when I come you'll disappoint me and I'll disappoint you, and in frustration with each other everything will fall to pieces-... " (2Cor. 12:20 The Message)

I had a face-to-face meeting with a friend I had never met. I admit that I had fears that I would disappoint him, he would disappoint me, and the friendship would fall to pieces. I was tempted to opt out of the meeting. I am so thankful that I did not. I am so thankful that God's people are one, regardless of the sign-on the-front of the building. I am so thankful that my un-met friend now has skin on. I am even thankful that God has shown me my sin in acting out of my own experience and passing judgment on others based solely on those experiences.

LOVE

Is it a feeling? Is it an emotion? Can it be achieved? Or is it a super-natural zap from a little red cupid arrow? What does it mean to love?

I read a line in a fictional story about a real person, Bathsheba. Speaking of the husband her father had chosen for her. "I will show him the respect and obedience he deserves. But love cannot be commanded" (Rivers, Francine 2009-01-10, A Lineage of Grace (p. 316). Tyndale House Publishers. Kindle Edition)

Love can not be commanded? Hummm....tell that to Jesus. "A new command I give you: Love one another. As I have loved you, so you must love one another (John 13:34)

The problem arises from our definition of the word. What do you consider love to BE? Does it accompany physical attraction? Jesus was NOT loved because of his physical attractiveness, regardless of how many pictures of a good looking man you see, scripture is plain, "He had no beauty or majesty to attract us to him, nothing in his appearance that we should desire him. (Isa.53:2) I fear that in our culture, we misuse and overuse the word love. We say it quickly. We use it easily. And we forget we even say it. Something so easily forgotten can not be love.

SHADE

I have a new and deeper appreciation for shade. Never in my lifetime do I remember such intense heat. Maybe it's been this hot and dry before...maybe I'm just old and soft now. I have always loved sitting in the deep shade of the sweet gum tree in my back yard. I prune the limbs each year so that the limbs make an umbrella around where my swing and chairs sit. We have bird feeders and squirrel feeders, a bird bath, invitations to creatures to share our shade.

When the hot sun beats down with intense heat, we look for something to put between it and us. We look for something to make a shadow for us to stand in, away from the direct sunlight. When life beats down with it's own intensity, we again look for relief and escape. Where do you go? "...LORD, you are my God. I will honor you. I will praise your name. You have been perfectly faithful. You have done wonderful things...You have been a place to hide when storms came. You have been a shade from the heat of the sun...." (Isa. 25:1,4)

"I look up to the hills. Where does my help come from? My help comes from the LORD. He is the Maker of heaven and earth. He won't let my foot slip. He who watches over me won't get tired. In fact, he who watches over me won't get tired or go to sleep. The LORD watches over me. The LORD is like a shade tree at my right hand. The sun won't harm me during the day. The moon won't harm me during the night. The LORD will keep me from every kind of harm. He will watch over my life. The LORD will watch over my life no matter where I go, both now and forever." (Ps. 121:2-8 personalized by me)

Think you've been left out? Is the heat on? Can you not find the comfort of shade from the intense circumstances of your life? Maybe this phrase I left out of verse one is the key... A song for those who go up to worship the LORD." Do you only want the shade? Or do you enjoy and value the Maker of it? Do you seek His Face? Or only the blessing of His Hand?

"God is serious business, take him seriously; He's put the earth in place and it's not moving. So, let heaven rejoice, let earth be jubilant, and pass the word among the nations, "GOD reigns!"(1Ch. 16:30,31 The Message) "For great is the LORD and most worthy of praise; He is to be feared above all gods. (1 Ch. 16:25NIV)

COOL

In the heat of summer, I have a new appreciation for cool. I have often thought about what it was like to have lived in The Garden. Tending it would have been pleasant, before the ground was cursed, "...through painful toil you will eat of it all the days of your life. It will produce thorns and thistles for you, and you will eat the plants of the field. By the sweat of your brow you will eat your food until you return to the ground..." (Gen. 3:18,19)

Life in The Garden was perfect in the beginning. Everything was provided and readily available, everything except the fruit of that one tree, the one that brought knowledge of good AND evil. It was the only thing off limits.

Life in The Garden was lived in the company of Creator God Himself. When He came to visit, it was cool. "Then the man and his wife heard the sound of the LORD God as he was walking in the garden in the cool of the day." (Genesis 3:8)

Cool of the day...hummmm... I haven't felt that in quite some time, only this Texas summer heat!! No cool of the night either, for that matter!

God has repeatedly provided protection from the heat of the sun. He provided a shade vine for Jonah, even though Jonah had disobeyed. "...the LORD God sent a vine and made it grow up over Jonah. It gave him more shade for his head. It made him more comfortable. Jonah was very happy he had the vine." (Jonah 4:6)

God provided protection from the sun beating down on a tribe of people traveling in a desert. "God spread a cloud to keep them cool through the day". (Ps. 105:39)

I have a house with air conditioning that keeps me about 20 degrees cooler than the temperature outside. I have plenty of water, enough even to water some of the flowers and plants I enjoy. He provided me a shade in a giant sweet gum tree in my back yard. Even though I too disobey Him at times, I want to walk with Him in the cool of the day. I will to walk with Him in the heat of the mid-day sun. I purpose in my heart to walk with Him, right behind Him, in His steps. Even and especially when it is not easy and not popular. Cool or not cool.

EXHAUSTED

Exhausted… Someone I love is really exhausted tonight. Too many long hot hours, not enough sleep. I pray that he makes it safely back home at the end of the work shift, safely to his bed for a long and thorough time of rest.

I'll likely be exhausted myself in a few hours. Sleep seems to elude me tonight. I slept soundly until 2:00. Tried twice to snuggle down and drift off again. Not happening…

I've considered how exhausted many people have been these last weeks, those who work all day in this unusually hot summer. Exhausted. They must be so very exhausted.

The heat seems to suck all of the energy from a person.

There is satisfaction in being tired from a good day's work. The reward we see in what we have accomplished (and the paycheck we cash!)

I have been really tired a lot of times. But I've never known exhaustion like the spiritual exhaustion I struggled with for years. I worked and worked, yet seemed to get no where. I wanted to quit, but felt obligated to keep on and on…trying, harder and harder.

I did quit eventually. I just said, Lord, I can't do it. I am sorry. But I just can't 'do' all 'do's and I end up 'doing' the 'don't's. So….I give up.

It was the turning point in my life.

And I'm in good company with the dilemma I was in.

"What I don't understand about myself is that I decide one way, but then I act another, doing things I absolutely despise.

So if I can't be trusted to figure out what is best for myself and then do it, it becomes obvious that God's command is necessary.

But I need something more!

For if I know the law but still can't keep it...

and if the power of sin within me keeps sabotaging my best intentions, I obviously need help! I realize that I don't have what it takes.

I can will it, but I can't do it.

I decide to do good, but I don't really do it; I decide not to do bad, but then I do it anyway.

My decisions, such as they are, don't result in actions.

Something has gone wrong deep within me and gets the better of me every time. It happens so regularly that it's predictable. The moment I decide to do good, sin is there to trip me up.

I truly delight in God's commands, but it's pretty obvious that not all of me joins in that delight. Parts of me covertly rebel, and just when I least expect it, they take charge.

I've tried everything and nothing helps. I'm at the end of my rope. Is there no one who can do anything for me? Isn't that the real question?

The answer, thank God, is that Jesus Christ can and does. He acted to set things right in this life of contradictions where I want to serve God with all my heart and mind, but am pulled by the influence of sin to do something totally different."

(The apostle Paul's words, Romans 7:16-25 from The Message)

"Are you tired? Worn out? Burned out on religion? Come to me. Get away with me and you'll recover your life. I'll show you how to take a real rest. Walk with me and work with me--watch how I do it. Learn the unforced rhythms of grace. I won't lay anything heavy or ill-fitting on you. Keep company with me and you'll learn to live freely and lightly." (The words of Jesus, Matt. 11:28-30 from The Message) Hallelujah. I found that peace 'which passeth all understanding' (Phil. 4:7)

Thank You Lord…..

HELL

Hell is a hot topic. (Pun intended.) There seems to be a stir in the Christian community about the reality of hell. There have been books written, some prominent teachers speaking against the reality of hell. I don't know why we are so shocked, most of us have lived our lives like it doesn't exist.

The reality of hell I suppose is important, yet I don't spend a lot of time trying to convince people of it, and even less personal time thinking about it. But, there was a long period of my life that I did, and I considered it simply the less attractive of the two choices.

There was a time that heaven didn't lure me. I didn't really yearn to live there eternally. God was there and He was scary. But the devil was in hell, and he was scarier. Plus, it was hot and painful there.

I don't think about hell much now, and I realize that I don't try to convince folks they need to find 'the way' to stay out of hell. (...and there is only one way.)

I do think about our Creator Father a lot, and I do try to convince folks to come to know Him. Not just as an 'out' for hell, but because of Who He is. He is I AM!

Maybe I need to revisit my thoughts about hell. Maybe people need to be freshly warned about its reality and finality. Jesus spoke of hell many times. "Do not be afraid of those who kill the body but cannot kill the soul. Rather, be afraid of the One who can destroy both soul and body in hell." (Matt. 10:28)

Obviously, it is real, and it is NOT good, and it is NOT where He will be. For me, that is all I need to know, I don't want a closer look, don't really care for more information...just thankful for a way of escape.

Then again, I've already heard many a hell-fire-and-brimstone sermon in my youth. Maybe I would never love my Father as I do, had I not been forced to consider the reality of the fires of hell. "Fear-of-GOD is a school in skilled living-- first you learn humility, then you experience glory." (Proverbs 15:33 The Message) "The fear of the LORD is the beginning of wisdom, and knowledge of the Holy One is understanding." (Prov. 9:10)

Fear kept me from doing many unwise things, and eventually brought about true knowledge of and love for The Holy One. What about you? What do you know about our God? Where do you want to live out eternity? Do you really want to live in His Presence when this realm of life is over? Or do you just not like the other choice? If that be the case, you have chosen, God help you.

There have always been two choices...good and evil. God has always allowed us to choose. "...as for me...I will serve the LORD." (Joshua 24:15 personalized by me)

Both choices are very real. They will one day be final. Eternally.

NECESSITY

What is on your list of necessary things? Vehicle? Computer? Cell phone? What IS necessary really? Certainly not those things. We have to have food. And water. Maybe shelter.

I've been praying for rain for a couple weeks, ending my request with 'in Your time'. I know that God knows how long it has been since raindrops have fallen on my head. (...and on my yard.) Perhaps I was being a bit pious when I added that phrase to my prayer. I did not expect Him to wait this long. I expected a 'yes' to my prayer by now. Since it has not come, I struggle with really submitting to His time. Last night, as I held the water hose in my hand, pouring out water onto parched plants and flowers, I was complaining again to God about my desire for water to fall from the sky. My complaint was answered with "Look how available water is to you!"

No, He hasn't sent rain yet, but He has provided the necessary water for me, and even an abundance to pour out on plants that aren't necessary, flowers aren't the food that goes on my table. (I also have more than the necessary food supply required.) My necessity of water is readily available. But in this relatively small matter, my faith is challenged and stretched. How sad.

I hear Jesus' words in Luke 12,"Connie, consider how the lilies grow. They do not labor or spin. Yet I tell you, not even Solomon in all his splendor was dressed like one of these. If that is how God clothes the grass of the field, which is here today, and tomorrow is thrown into the fire, how much more will he clothe you Connie, O you of little faith!" (personalized by me, FOR me)

"He split the rocks in the desert and gave them water as abundant as the seas; He brought streams out of a rocky crag and made water flow down like rivers. But they continued to sin against Him, rebelling in the desert against the Most High. They willfully put God to the test by demanding the food they craved. They spoke against God saying, "Can God put food on a table in the desert?" (Ps. 78: 15-19NIrV)

Lord forgive me for such mumbling and complaining. I must sound just like your people in the wilderness with Moses. Thank You for the abundance of water and food that are so readily available to me.

REGRET

Remember as a child, while playing some game, you could call for a 'do-over' when something went wrong? Wouldn't it be great if we could 'do-over' those things in our adult lives that we regret?

Reflecting on the first 8 verses of the longest chapter in the Bible, Psalm 119, I have personalized it from The Message paraphrase.

"I am blessed when I stay on course, walking steadily on the road revealed by GOD. I am blessed when I follow His directions, doing my best to find Him. That's right--not going off on my own; but walking straight along the road He set. You, GOD, prescribed the right way to live; now You expect us to live it. Oh, that my steps might be steady, keeping to the course You set; Then I'd never have any regrets in comparing my life with Your counsel. I thank You for speaking straight from Your heart; I learn the pattern of Your righteous ways. I'm going to do what You tell me to do; don't ever walk off and leave me."

There are many things I regret. A number of them are not things I did that I wish I had not, but things I did not do, things I did poorly, effort I did not put forth. Some of the things I regret are the impulses and reactions that were birthed out of my own fear and insecurity, my lack of faith. Living without regret is only possible one way...keeping our steps on the course that is set... walking in 'The Way', comparing our lives to His.

It is just simply fact...God designed. God created. Trying to manipulate what He has engineered and use it in a way He never intended just causes problems and regret.

Each morning, I make an effort to submit my will to His. Again. 'I'm going to do what YOU tell me to do....' I am so encouraged to find the rest of that sentence, 'don't ever walk off and leave me.'

I am comforted even more to remember the very words of my Savior, Jesus the Christ. "…you can be sure that I am always with you, to the very end." (Matt.28:20)

He IS doing it over….

"You have started living a new life. It is being made new so that what you know has the Creator's likeness." (Col 3:10)

Hallelujah.

PURE

Webster says unmixed. Separated from every other thing. What is pure? More importantly, who is pure? Are you?

I tried. And although I don't have some of the stains of impurity that somebody else may have, there are stains. The second section of 8 verses in Psalm 119 address the issue of personal purity. "How can a young person keep his life pure? By living in keeping with Your word. I trust in You with all my heart. Don't let me wander away from Your commands. I have hidden Your word in my heart so that I won't sin against You. LORD, I give praise to You. Teach me Your orders. With my lips, I talk about all of the decisions You have made. Following Your covenant laws gives me joy just as great riches give joy to others. I spend time thinking about Your rules. I consider how You want me to live. I take delight in Your orders. I won't fail to obey Your word." (Psalm 119:9-16NIrV)

Purity is important to God. He calls us to be pure. And at the same time, He knows that since the catastrophe of the garden, it is impossible without His intervention. ONLY by His Word can a young person (OR an old person) have a pure life. Only by knowing WHAT He has said can we act on it and DO what He has said. There is power in the Words uttered from His Mouth, power in the Word that is so readily available to us in written form. But it won't leap off the page by itself. We still have that same liberty of choosing. "Who can say, "I have kept my heart pure; I am clean and without sin"? (Proverbs 20:9) Certainly not me.

Praise God that He also said, "If we confess our sins, He is faithful and just and will forgive us our sins and purify us from all unrighteousness." (1John 1:9) Choose today to spend time thinking about what He has said

TRUTH

There is absolute truth. You might believe a devil's lie, you might be deceived, you may question it, but nothing changes truth. Who gets to define what truth it?. God. Absolutely.

It has been demonstrated to humanity that we are subject to believing lies, prone to try to over-rule truth, making it what we decide it should be. But all those efforts are useless, and thinking we have prevailed in it will eventually be obvious to us. Painfully obvious. We do well to admit our foolishness and rebellion sooner rather than later.

In my study of Psalm 119, in the third section of 8 verses, I am drawn to verse 18. "Open my eyes so that I can see the wonderful truths in your law. "Eve was deceived and believed a lie. I do not want to be like my mother Eve. "Your covenant laws are my delight. They give me wise advice." (verse 24)

Truth is hard sometimes. Truth about myself is often very hard. And very ugly...certainly not delightful. I am thankful to have come to know Jesus well enough that even when He shows me hard ugly things, I hear Him speak with a Voice of love and not condemnation. I know that He is not mean and nasty, I know that what He says IS true, and that He wants only what is good and better for me. But I do not forget that what He says is truth. Whether I like it, or whether I don't. Whether I choose to make my decisions accordingly, or whether I try to re-define it. What He says, IS. Absolutely.

Lord, open my eyes and make me see the wisdom of what you say. Help me to see the folly of ignoring or refusing truth.

WORN OUT

Old and tired....

I say it jokingly almost daily...that I'm old and tired. It becomes more true all the time! Reflecting on verses 25-32 of Psalm 119, I am drawn to verse 28... "My sadness has worn me out. Give me strength as you have promised."

On nights when sleep leaves too soon, I am left to be awake with my thoughts, and my mind is assaulted by those nasty flaming arrows of the Accuser. Liar that he is.

'You should have...'
'You could have...'
'You didn't...'
'You'll never...'
My sadness wears me out.
Father, give me strength as You have promised.

I recognize them sooner that I once did, but the accusations and lies of the enemy still sting. Praise God I do recognize them, and that I have learned that although '. I do live in the world... I don't fight my battles the way the people of the world do. The weapons I fight with are not the weapons the world uses. In fact, it is just the opposite. My weapons have the power of God to destroy the camps of the enemy. I destroy every claim and every reason that keeps people from knowing God. I keep every thought under control in order to make it obey Christ. (2Cor. 10:3-5 NIrV)

"I have chosen to be faithful to you. I put my trust in your laws." (Ps. 119:30NIrV)

"I'll run the course you lay out for me if you'll just show me how" (Psalm 119:32 The Message)

And He will....

"I have put myself under God's mighty hand.... I turn all my worries over to Him. He cares about me.... He always gives me all the grace I need. So, I will only have to suffer for a little while. Then God Himself will build me up again. He will make me strong and steady..." (1Peter 5:6,10NIrV personalized for me, by me)

Hallelujah.

PRIORITIES

It is so easy to get them wrong. Why do we so often put value on something worthless?

Reflecting on the fifth section of Psalm 119, I am drawn to verse 37, "Turn my eyes away from things that are worthless.... keep me alive as You have promised." It is difficult to keep priorities in order. It is easy to be deceived and believe a lie about the worth of some 'thing'. We mistakenly think that in 'things' we secure ourselves somehow...then the enemy comes with accusations, pointing out the mistakes and the foolishness, urging us in some new direction where he tells us that security might be found. The enemy of our souls would have us continue to seek fulfillment and life down those empty paths he points out. Paths that take us in the opposite direction of God and true life.

In the words of this Psalm, David prays for divine perspective and divine restraint. I also pray for those. I pray that my eyes do not look upon worthless things and believe them to have more value than they do. I pray that the habits and manners of my life do not divert or detour me from the life God intends for me.

Father, I pray that in YOUR way, You will give me life, and empower me to see the richness of it. And I thank You for the magnificent wealth of my now.

THEN

Webster says: next in order of time.

Reading that definition, I think of that cliché,' First things first' So often we get last things first.

Reflecting on verses 41-48 of Psalm 119, I am impressed with the order that should be in place in our lives. Knowing and understanding the love of God is paramount. THAT is the first thing, and sadly, I think there are a whole lot of people who don't have a clue about the love of our Creator. God's love, His promises, the salvation He provides, then the 'then'...

"May your unfailing love come to me, LORD, your salvation, according to your promise; then I can answer anyone who taunts me, for I trust in your word. (Psalm 119:41-42)

I am convinced that once we are secure in the love of God, trusting completely that what He says is always and only good and best, our will changes, our 'want-to' changes. It makes absolutely no sense in the world's way of thinking, but the freest freedom we can experience is obedience to God.

Again, I pray with David. I pray that I put first things first. Always... "Let your love, GOD, shape my life with salvation, exactly as you promised; THEN, I'll be able to stand up to mockery because I trusted your Word.... your commandments are what I depend on. I'll guard with my life what you've revealed to me...And I'll stride freely through wide open spaces as I look for your truth and your wisdom; Then I'll tell the world what I find, speak out boldly in public, unembarrassed. I cherish your commandments--oh, how I love them! =-relishing every fragment of your counsel." (Ps. 119:41-48 The Message)

First things first....

THEN......

HORRIFIED

I was warned that I would be. I was…

I made it my business to find out what all the hoopla is about a certain reality show. I don't watch much television programming, especially the craze of reality shows, I already have enough reality to suit me thank- you-very-much. Besides, it should really be called exaggerated reality. Surely people don't really live and act like that…. Or do they?

I am far from perfect. So very far. But God help me to never accept the flaws, help me to continue to be a better person, more like You. Especially help me to never embrace the flaws, never allow me to celebrate the imperfections, allow me no joy in that.

Continuing to reflect on Psalm 119, verse 53 from the next section stood speaks to me in my horrified state…. "Horror hath taken hold upon me because of the wicked that forsake thy law."

What little I saw was offensive to me, but that's not the deal. The deal is that so many people live an absolute Godless life. They revel in it, and have no idea how miserable they really are.

It reminds me of the years I suffered before having surgery to remove diseased female organs. I had absolutely no idea how sick I was, how awful I felt all the time, because it was my normal. I didn't know anything else…ever. When it was removed and I began to get healthier, I was horrified that I suffered so much for so long. (Thank You God for hysterectomies!)

People without God have no idea how sick they are. Tragically, the symptoms of sin sickness lead to an eternal death. People are without God simply because they choose to not know Him. And He is the most amazing, awesome Person…. He knows every thing…has every thing…can do every thing… Why are there so many people who are not the least bit interested?

"….. people have turned away from your law. No matter where I live, I sing about your orders. LORD, during the night I remember who you are. That's why I keep your law. I have really done my best to obey your rules." (Psalm 119:53-56NIrV)

I want always to remember Who You are. Help me that no matter where I am I will remember Your Presence with me. You see and hear every thought, every word, every act. And You want only the best for me. Always and only the very best….

LIFESTYLE

I recall they made a television show about the lifestyles of the 'rich and famous'. I'm not rich and famous, so I don't have a lifestyle portrayed on that show. Our house is fairly small and quite plain. But it is ours. We don't have those fancy cars, but ours are dependable and comfortable. Then again, what is the measuring stick for fancy? Pricetag? Seems in our culture, we measure most everything by the price tag. Nope. I am not famous.

Then again, I am important to the God of the universe, so important that He came down to rescue me.

I am not rich.

Then again, I have never known hunger, never been without clothing, never without a home and safe transportation. Maybe I am rich and famous after all.…

Continuing to reflect on Psalm 119, I am drawn to verse 59. "I have thought about the way I live……"

It is a good thing to honestly reflect on the way we live. Honestly…oh boy, that's the kicker. It is not easy to be honest with ourselves, it is tempting and so easy to rationalize our wrong attitudes and decisions. After all, our own heart will trick us. Scripture warns that it is deceitful. (Jer.17:9) 'Following your heart' isn't such a good idea always!

How do I live? Do I put others needs before my own? Whose rules of engagement do I follow? Do I make up the rules to suit myself, making them up as I go, to benefit me? Who/what determines how I use the money I have? Do I spend my money to bless others or only myself? Do I use my money to manipulate? Do I put my own price tags on? Do I use my money in effort to pay off my other bad behavior?

"…I have decided to follow your covenant laws." (Ps.119:59b)

Lord God help me to let You be the boss today. YOU be the Commander in chief, YOU be the decision maker, and help me to bend my stubborn prideful will to Yours. Your way is always right and best. I have learned that so painfully, and forget it so easily.

BEFORE

Before, I was thinner. Before, I had less wrinkles. Before, I had more years ahead of me. Before today, I was younger, the day of this writing is my birthday.

I come to the section of verses 65-72 in my study of Psalm 119. This passage speaks so much to me personally today, both in encouragement, and in reprimand. Some much too personal to share in an open forum. I pray with David this morning, "LORD, be good to me as you have promised. Increase my knowledge and give me good sense, because I believe in your commands..."

Good sense... Did you notice how that phrase is followed with 'because 'and connected to more of the sentence? Where does good sense come from? Certainly not years, not necessarily!

One of the phrases you may hear me say is 'young and ignorant'. The younger we are, the less life experiences we have, therefore...ignorance. You just can NOT know what you do not know. Each year that passes, I again reflect on how ignorant I am, recognizing again just how little I know and understand. God HAS blessed me with knowledge and understanding, for I know and understand so much more than I did at one time. Yet as I grow older I am faced with the reality of how powerless we really are, how utterly helpless to control any single thing except our OWN choices. And those are difficult...

I believe the wisdom that age brings is this very thing...being wise enough to know how ignorant you really are!

I have many flaws, many wrong thoughts, many wrong motives. I have made many wrong choices. I have caused suffering, and I have suffered. I regret causing pain. While I do not like pain, the suffering I have personally experienced has brought me much good. "Before I went through suffering, I went down the wrong path. But now I obey your word....... It was good for me to suffer. That's what helped me to understand your orders." (vs.67,71) How thankful I am for His forgiveness, and that He doesn't leave me to my own resources.

Father, help me to follow Your way with every part of me.... nothing held back, never in my own effort, but always and only depending on You to orchestrate my life. Help me trust You more completely.

UNDERSTAND

Understand. Do you? Can you? How?

In reflecting on the next section of Psalm 119 I keep coming back to this one phrase from verse 73. "...give me understanding, that I may learn thy commandments." How is it that we come to 'understand'? I can think of only these two ways...logic and experience.

When God issues a command, sometimes I fully understand why. He says, "don't murder'" and I understand that if I murder, I have overstepped and enforced my will over another person, I am choosing FOR them...to die, even if they choose to live. That is wrong. It is not my choice. And wrong on many other levels.

God has said lots of 'do's and 'do not's and a lot of them I understand with the logic that He has created in me. Other things He has said, I have come to understand the same way Eve did. I found out for myself.

Experience is a good teacher. I could list hundreds of lessons I've learned the hard way. From all those hard lessons, I want most to learn and remember one thing...when God says something, there is a very good reason for it. I don't have to understand it with my logic. I don't have to experience it to know for sure. I can just take Him at His Word.

The Message puts that phrase very well. "... breathe Your wisdom over me so I can understand You." He has done that for me time and time again...given me His wisdom. "I can see now, GOD, that your decisions are right." (vs.75)

He is right every single time about every single thing. Logic or no logic. Experience or no experience.

Lord, help me not to choose to experience. Especially those things that Your directions intend for me to avoid. Help me to learn from Eve's mistake and not to make the same ones. I want to simply trust, simply obey. Forgive me for depending on my own logic. It is so flawed.

"May my heart be without blame as I follow your orders. Then I won't be put to shame." (vs.80)

ADDICTION

Addiction is rampant in our culture. Think you are immune?

You don't have to have a drug problem to be an addict. It doesn't have to be alcohol or cigarettes, although those are some common ones. I am addicted to caffeine. I like coffee, tea, cola, chocolate, chocolate, chocolate, and chocolate.

While I don't share the addiction to television, I fear I am addicted to my computer and cell phone. I don't have any addiction to drugs, neither prescription ones or illegal ones. I don't

frequent porn sites, and I am not a gambler. The reason I can say most of that however, is not because of some special thing about myself. I have just stayed clear of those things, choosing instead not to take the chance on having a problem or becoming an addict.

I have seen addiction. I have seen its destruction. I have heard the justifications for them, the excuses, the blame-laying. But addictions aren't anyone else's fault. The circumstances may not be our personal choice, but our response to the situation is. An addiction can be anything. When we desire a thing so much that we will do anything necessary to get it…that is an addiction, and an addiction is idolatry. The addiction has become god.

"Do not run after other gods until your sandals are worn out and your throat is dry. But you said, 'It's no use! I love those gods. I must go after them.'" (Jer. 2:25)

We go after all kinds of things. Compromising all kinds of things. Then all those things end up bringing us harm. The very things we have pursued and sacrificed our character and principles for become the opposite of what we were seeking. Instead of blessing us, they become a curse.

"…. when you are in trouble, you say, "Come and save us!' So where are the gods you made for yourselves? Let them come when you are in trouble!" (Jer. 2:17,18) When the curse comes down on our head, we have no choice but to see the truth. The addictions in our lives bring nothing but trouble and heartache. Praise God that His desire to restore us never changes.

"Return to me. I will heal you." (Jer. 3:22)

LIFE

We have a heartbeat, we breathe, we move around…and we call it life.

We say, 'live it up!' and do all sorts of things thinking that's what we are doing…living it up. Yet the search is never ending. Where does it end? I read Psalm 119 and identify with David's words in verse 82. "My eyes grow tired looking for what you have promised"

I know what that feels like. Searching for that contentment, fulfillment, pleasure, purpose, call it what you like. It is endless. Doing the dos and not doing the don'ts. It is exhausting.

David also has the key in this section of his psalm. "According to Your steadfast love give life to me; then I will keep the testimony of Your mouth" (Ps. 119:88 AMP)

Without being granted spiritual life from our Creator, we have a heartbeat, we breathe, we move around, and we wear ourselves out in efforts to find what He offers to provide. Without the life that in His steadfast love He gives, we will never know how shallow and empty our so-called lives are. And we will never ever be able to line our lives up with a holy God and His Word.

Thank you that You have given life to me. Thank you, Father, for the power of Your Spirit, the power that enables me to follow You. "All your commands are trustworthy." (vs.86) I want to simply believe what You say, and accept the help that you provide to me thru Your Spirit.

IT IS WHAT IT IS

We sometimes say that phrase when there is something we don't really like but we can't change. As I continue to reflect on Psalm 119, I discover this in scripture! "Forever, O LORD, thy word is settled in heaven." (vs. 89) It is what It is.

What God says, IS. His Word is spoken and settled. Not one single act of denial or rebellion changes that fact. The problem is, it's not settled on earth. Jesus prayed for that to come about, and taught His disciples to pray in that way. "Our Father which art in heaven, Hallowed be thy name. Thy kingdom come, thy will be done, on earth, as it is in heaven." (Luke 11:2)

Like Eve, there is still a tree of knowledge that I can choose to eat from. Every moment of every day, I am faced with decisions and choices. I walk around that tree and examine the fruit, often hearing the enemy lies and sometimes falling for his deceptions. Every waking moment it is my place to settle it. My will, or His?

It is settled in heaven. It is spoken to me, here on earth. How will I settle the matter today?

Father, "Your laws continue to this very day "(vs.91) Help me to "never forget your precepts, for by them you have preserved my life" (vs.93) "I've learned that everything has its limits. But your commands are perfect. They are always there when I need them." (vs.96) Your Word...It is what It is, forever. Let it be settled in my heart and manifested in my life. Today and every day.

INSTRUCTIONS

Do you read them first? I admit it, I usually don't. I arrogantly assume I will know how. But I will also confess…most of the time I end up going to the instructions. We have been given instructions. How to live has instructions. How to have relationships, how to conduct business, how to deal with conflict, how to care for our bodies, maintain health, on and on and on goes the list… instructions.

But we never have to read them. Putting together something without using the instructions can be done. Sometimes we can get it put together pretty good. Other times it comes out all wrong. Sometimes it can be corrected. Other times we've damaged it in some way that leaves it warped and beyond repair.

So it is with our lives. We can opt to live it without going by the instructions, and sometimes get by without much damage. But life is not an entertainment center, regardless of how you try to make it one. Living and ignoring the instructions will eventually prove that fact. Eventually, it will be far from entertaining.

As I continue to reflect on Psalm 119, I read these phrases, "Your commands make me wiser" (v.98) "I have more insight." (v.99) "I have more understanding…" (v.100) "I gain understanding from your precepts." (v.104) Following the directions, (obedience), brings about wisdom. Knowledge alone doesn't make us wise, only the application of knowledge (obedience). Reading the directions is useless unless you put the entertainment center together like it says.

Father, help me to "…keep my feet from every evil path so that I might obey your word." (v.101) Help me to remember and to believe, that what You say, You say for very good reasons, always and only for my greater good.

DARK

Walking around in the dark is dangerous. You can veer off where you intend to walk. You never know what is there…could be a hole, something to trip over, a snake in the grass. It is wise to use a light. When you have light, you dispel darkness… you can see.

Scripture uses the concept of light/darkness often. As I continue to reflect on Psalm 119, I come to one of my favorite verses. "Thy word is a lamp unto my feet, and a light unto my path." (v. 105)

God's Word, what He has said, is the light that reveals the dangers we encounter. When we use His Light, we are able to see those things and escape harm. We can see where we need to walk, avoid falling into a pit, tripping up, falling and getting hurt. We can avoid the snake lying ready to strike… and he is there.

Are you able to see? I confess with the psalm writer. "I keep putting my life in danger." And I purpose that "I won't forget to obey your law." (v.109)

What God says, He has very good reason for. There is a snake…

METAL

What kind of metal are you made of? When I was younger, I remember older people talking about someone's character and use that phrase. "We'll see what kind of metal he/she is made of" they would say. When the fire gets hot and the testing comes, you do indeed find out what kind of metal you are made of.

I don't know a lot about metal working. I know that a new iron skillet is awful when it's new, it needs to be heated and oiled, 'seasoned' before it is useful for cooking. I know that silver has to be heated so that the 'dross' comes to the surface and is removed, leaving the silver pure and beautiful.

As I continue my reading of Psalm 119, I come to this:"All the wicked of the earth you discard like dross; therefore I love your statutes. My flesh trembles in fear of you; I stand in awe of your laws." (v. 119,120) Dross is discarded.

I reflect back on my life and I can see times of heated testing, and can be thankful for those very painful times. Now, but certainly not then. Refining is not pleasant. But it is necessary.

My God is holy and perfect. Every thing and every one else is just simply… not. We fall so far short of perfection, and we are so incapable of fixing that problem. I too find myself in awe of His law, of His perfection. I too tremble when I see my imperfect sinful self, compared to His holiness. "Sustain me according to your promise, and I will live; do not let my hopes be dashed. Uphold me, and I will be delivered." (v. 16,17)

He is the only hope I have. His upholding me is my only chance of deliverance. "You are my refuge and my shield; I have put my hope in your word." (v. 114)

STORM

Webster calls it a rushing violent wind. A storm is defined as a violent assault on a fortified place.

At the time of this writing, I sit and watch a hurricane headed toward the east coast of the United States, threatening New York City, I wonder why we convince ourselves that we are fortified against a breeze, much less a storm. It's a lie.

"You would have no power over me if it were not given to you from above." (the words of Jesus as recorded in John 19:11) We have no power that is not granted to us by The Hand that controls the nature He created.

I fully understand there is a science of air flow, pressures, cold and hot atmospheres...all of these things contribute to how these storms form and move. But that does not change the fact that it is God's science, He is The Scientist!

"For He spoke and stirred up a tempest that lifted high the waves. They mounted up to the heavens and went down to the depths; in their peril, their courage melted away. They reeled and staggered like drunken men; they were at their wits' end. Then they cried out to the LORD in their trouble...." (Psalm 107:25-28) Then...THEN they cried out to Him. Isn't that always the way it is with us?

Did He send this hurricane I see on the television radar images? Good question. I know one thing without question. He can stop or control it. He speaks and it is. Period. Will He? Obviously not. It is happening.

What will the response be? It is during times of threat beyond our capacity to control that we historically turn to Him. My prayer is for safety, especially for those I love. But I also pray that some person who has never really turned to Him, never felt a real need for Him, would seek Him in a new, more real, more honest, and more complete way than ever before. "You will seek me and find me when you seek me with all your heart."(Jeremiah 29:13) I pray that this storm will be used by God to prepare people for a new beginning, with HIM at the center. When He is center, the eye of any storm has no power to threaten us, can never take away the calm and peace of a heart inhabited by His Spirit.

Hallelujah.

DO SOMETHING

Ever be in some life situation where you feel like somebody just needs to DO something? Waiting is not one of my virtues, I don't do it easily and certainly don't do it well. Waiting while a hurricane named Irene crept up the east coast toward where our kids live was not an easy wait. But wait we did, and I couldn't do a single thing. Even though my mind was screaming "Do something!!", I could not. Doing something is not always the right thing. Sometimes waiting IS the thing to 'do'. There have been times that I answered that screaming from within to 'do something' only to wish I HAD just waited. The 'something' that I did…well, it was the wrong thing.

I complain to God quite often about his in-action. I want him to 'DO something!!' I want Him to do something about so many things. I want Him to fix what I messed up. I want Him to intervene in wrong behavior. I want Him to stop corruption. I want Him to withhold blessings from people I consider not worthy. I want Him to punish those I judge guilty. I want Him to make my life easier. And as I sit this morning reflecting on Psalm 119 again, and I type out those words, I am so thankful that He isn't at my command. I'd just mess some more stuff up and make my life far from easier. He is God. And I am not.

"Make sure that everything goes well with me…Help me to understand what is right…. LORD, it's time for you to act. People are breaking your law…I love your commands…I consider all of your rules to be right. So, I hate every path that sinners take…" (Psalm 119:22-28)

I identify with the Psalmist… 'me, me, me.'. Over and over again, I go to Him to ask that everything go right with me. Usually after I have failed at taking care of it myself. I pray the hardest when it is a matter I am powerless to 'do something' about.

I too consider His rules to be right. He is the Creator. He engineered, designed, and produced all that is reality to me. Even my own self.

I too detest the path of sin. I know it from choosing it. I learned from experience that He commands for very good reasons. And I too say to Him, "Lord, 'do something!!'…people are breaking Your law !!" And I find myself so thankful that He waits for HIS time and only then does He 'do something'.

I can be assured that it will be the best time and the best thing.

ENTRANCE

You can't get 'in' without one.

As I continue to reflect on Psalm 119, this verse draws me. "The entrance of Your Words gives light; it gives understanding to the simple." (v. 130)

The truth here is profound. You don't have to be a rocket scientist. All you must be is sincere. He fills in any deficiency. I've heard people say they can't understand the Bible, so they don't read it. I've said it myself. I didn't understand it because it didn't say anything I wanted to hear. I didn't understand it because it clashed with my rationale. I didn't understand it because it was not logical. One thing I have learned, and I know that I know this...His Holy Spirit is capable and willing, even eager to teach. He teaches us where we are.... super intelligent or simple. We don't become scholars overnight, we become and remain students of His as long as there is a today.

Another thing I have learned, and I know that I know, is that God is not bound by my human logic. Or yours. But when His Words enter our discussions and into our thoughts, when we truly consider what He has said, light bulbs will come on. The problem with light is that the brighter it shines, the more dust and cobwebs you can see. And when it is God's Light shining, we see where we don't measure up, we miss being perfect and holy by a zillion miles, and we have a very real enemy poised to pounce and accuse.

Let the Holy Spirit of God give you light. He provides understanding to a heart that is undivided in its motive. Read His Word, and as you do, never forget that every word is overflowing with love for YOU. Every word is meant for your greater good. Every word...even to the point that "The Word became flesh and dwelt among us..."

He stepped out of glory for you, into a dying body of flesh, even to the point of a horrible death He loved you...Let His Word give you light. You may be surprised just how dark it is where you are.

TRY

Over and over. Again, and again. I get tired of trying. Don't you? It is so tempting to just throw down the towel and say," forget it".. Sometimes, I just don't want to care anymore…just wish I could NOT care. But I have prayed so many times for God to use me. I have asked Him to help me submit myself to Him, that He could do His work thru me, ministering to others.

As I continue to reflect on Psalm 119 I read, "'My zeal wears me out, for my enemies ignore your words" (v. 139)

My zeal. There lies the problem…it is not about me. I know this. I have had to re-take this course over and over, again and again. I am not the one who gets a single thing accomplished in another person's life. Ever. He asks me to follow. Not navigate or drive!

"Anyone who intends to come with me has to let me lead. You're not in the driver's seat; I am. Don't run from suffering; embrace it. Follow me and I'll show you how. Self-help is no help at all. Self-sacrifice is the way, my way, to saving yourself, your true self. What good would it do to get everything you want and lose you, the real you? What could you ever trade your soul for? "If any of you are embarrassed over me and the way I'm leading you when you get around your fickle and unfocused friends, know that you'll be an even greater embarrassment to the Son of Man when he arrives in all the splendor of God, his Father, with an army of the holy angels. (The words of Jesus, Mark 8:34-38 from The Message)

Lord Jesus, forgive me as I again get out of the driver's seat.

INSOMNIA

Webster says it is a "prolonged and usually abnormal inability to obtain adequate sleep". Seems like my inability to obtain adequate sleep has become pretty normal. I remember being chastised for sleeping too much. "Still asleep at noon on Saturday!!" my folks complained loudly. "You are sleeping your life away!"

I sometimes can't sleep past midnight now, much less sleep until noon! So, I get up and continue to reflect on the next section of Psalm 119 and just look what I find.

"Lord, I call out to You with all my heart. Answer me, and I will obey Your orders. I call out to You. Save me, and I will keep Your covenant laws. I get up before the sun rises. I cry out for help. I've put my hope in Your Word. My eyes stay open all night long. I spend my time thinking about Your promises. Listen to me, because You love me. Lord, keep me alive as You have promised. Those who think up evil plans are near. They have wandered far away from Your law. But Lord, You are near. All Your commands are true. Long ago I learned from Your covenant laws that You made them to last forever." (Psalm 119:145-152)

It brings a smile to my heart that He is so sweet, in His perfect timing He speaks. On time. Every time.

On sleepless nights, my brain bounces back and forth with all the concerns of my life. I discuss it with Him, complain to Him, whine to Him…and every single time, if I will just go to His Word…every single time, if I will just shush my spirit and listen…

He speaks.
He is near.

All His words are true and eternal. I must just keep my hope in that Word and focus on His promises, they do indeed last forever.

AFFLLICTED

Webster says: affected with continued or often repeated pain, either of body or mind.

My parents and grandparents called people afflicted when today we say handicapped or special needs.

On the night of this writing, as I am afflicted with sleeplessness, I got up to continue my reflecting on Psalm 119. I find verse 153...." Look on my affliction, and deliver me."

I am so thankful God continues to love, continues to care, and continues to listen. Aren't you? He could stop. The word in the original language is 'oniy'. It is defined as a state of oppression or extreme discomfort, physically, mentally, or spiritually. Depression. Misery.

It made me think of the song on Hee-Haw from years ago, "Gloom, despair, and agony on me, Deep dark depression, excessive misery, If it weren't for bad luck, I'd have no luck at all, Gloom, despair, and agony on me...."

Those hillbilly characters were afflicted. (...and maybe a little lazy.)

When the afflicted cry out to God for deliverance, God hears, and answers. He cares. "Lord, You have deep concern for me. Keep me alive as You have promised. (v.156)

How well do the afflicted listen for His answer, how well do they follow His instructions as He provides deliverance? When affliction comes, we can't sit around with a jug and a gang of buddies, wallowing in self pity. When affliction comes, it is more important than ever to kneel at The Throne of grace and mercy. It is the ONLY place to find help, true deliverance, and recovery. The only way to remove the deep darkness...

Excessive misery and all.

SHALOM

Shalom is a Hebrew word. Most people know it means peace, but what is peace?

Is peace simply absence of conflict or war? What steals peace away, what prevents it from being the norm for us? People search for it, try all sorts of methods to gain it, trying to chase away the inner conflict and be complete somehow. .ANY how, any way at all. The problem is that we cannot stand alone against daily pressures of life for very long. We run into the unfriendly, the unhealthy, the incomplete, the discontent…and it takes our peace. Oh, we may convince ourselves that we do in fact have peace, that we do not CARE about the unfriendly, unhealthy, incomplete, and discontent. And maybe you don't. But IF you don't, your peace is diminished whether you admit it or not. You are less than you were created to be if you become calloused to the unfriendly, unhealthy, incomplete.

Knowing the love of God, and living in relationship with HIM, is the single way to true peace. He is the single answer. The enemy will give you some attractive alternatives, fashion some good counterfeits for you, and present some misleading choices that will give you a short lived sort of peace that will blow up in your face eventually.

As I continue to reflect on Psalm 119, I read the section of verses 161-168 and find great comfort for my lack of peace this hour..(He's so good, He sends the right Word every time) "Great peace have they who love Your law, and nothing can make them stumble." (Ps.119: 165)

My peace is not in a perfect life, because I don't have one.

My peace is not because there is no conflict, there is plenty.

My peace is not because I have no aches and pains, no unfriendly people to deal with, or situations that make me wish for a different one. I have plenty situations that I'd just as soon not have to deal with. My hands and feet are old, tired, and about worn out. My life does not always unfold as I expected. But my peace does not depend on any of those things. I have peace because I have a God Who will always act toward the welfare of His children. I serve a God Who defines what it is to be complete. And He loves me.

I am in covenant relationship with Him. As for me, I'll just take up the cross and follow. (Mt. 16:24) I will know His peace even in a raging storm. "But if serving the LORD seems undesirable to you, then choose for yourselves this day whom you will serve, whether the gods your forefathers served beyond the River, or the gods of the Amorites, in whose land you are living. But as for me and my household, we will serve the LORD." (Joshua 24:15)

I do not comprehend why so many refuse Him, why they refuse to accept the peace and security that is found in living by His design and standard.

But I can't want it bad enough for you…you get to pick.

SUPPLICATION

Webster says it is an earnest request. I don't use the word in conversation, I don't hear anyone else use it really. It is one of those Bible words, a word connected to prayer, directed toward God.

As I complete my reflecting on Psalm 119, I am challenged about my prayer life. "Let my supplication come before Thee…" (verse 170) "…Give my request your personal attention." (v. 170 from The Message)

I regularly present my prayer list to God, and I often find myself giving Him suggestions about how He should fill my needs, or to be truthful, my wants. Selfish, short-sighted, self-centered wants. While it is certainly true that God is interested in my every need and desire, He sees far beyond my moment, and knows far better than I how to answer and how to fulfill my requests. He has an uncanny way of bringing about what I ask for, but in ways I don't expect and never see coming. In this last section of the psalm, I am reminded… He is God. I am not.

"…. give me wisdom according to Your Word" (v. 169)
"…. deliver me according to Your Word." (v. 170)
"…. You have taught me Your Precepts." (v. 171)
"…. all Your Commandments are righteousness." (v. 172)
"…. I have chosen Your Precepts." (v. 173)
"…. Your Law is my delight." (v. 174)
"…. let Your judgments help me." (v. 175)

This book we call The Bible is unique. It is only paper and ink, maybe a leather cover, but the message it communicates is incredible. The more I read and study it, the more I realize how bottomless its teaching is. His Word, what He has said…IS. Period.

The epitome of "it is what it is". God's Word IS. It is the source of wisdom, deliverance, right-ness. And I for one need all that. Desperately.

"I have gone astray like a lost sheep; seek Your servant; for I do not forget Your Commandments." (v. 176)

How thankful I am that He does come looking for me, calling me back close to Him. If you hear Him, whether it is a shout or a whisper…listen for Him. And go to Him. Run to Him. He is so good.

FOLLOW

Follow? Or would you rather lead, be in front, choose the direction? I admit it. I like to lead. I like to pick the way to go. And I also admit that if I'm not leading, I am prone to tell you how to get there too. "Be careful to follow every command I am giving you today, so that you may live and increase and may enter and possess the land the LORD promised on oath to your ancestors." (Deut. 8:1)

I fully realize that these words were spoken to a nation of people concerning a literal, geographical piece of property...land. But I believe every word of scripture has a message for every person of every time. Today, I hear Him saying once again, "...follow Me Connie. Listen and remember what I have said so you can have a fuller and fuller life. Follow Me, don't get ahead of Me. You will never be able to get there on your own...please, listen to Me, I know what I'm talking about."

Sigh....

Sometimes He just doesn't go fast enough. Sometimes He picks a road with too many curves and bumps. And I complain and whine.

"Remember how the LORD your God led you all the way in the desert these forty years, to humble you and to test you in order to know what was in your heart, whether or not you would keep His commands." (verse 2)

So, I'll make another round in the wilderness, learning and re-learning. I want the "so that" of verse 1.

So, I purpose in my heart once again to follow. Even though it seems to me He is going waaaaay too slow....

Printed in the United States
By Bookmasters